THE WHALES,
THEY GIVE THEMSELVES

Oral Biography Series

Edited by William Schneider

B ooks in the Oral Biography Series focus on individuals whose life experiences and personal accomplishments provide an intimate view of the events, personalities, and influences that have shaped Alaska history. Each book is created through a collaborative process between the narrator, an editor, and often other community members, who record the oral history, then transcribe and edit it in written form. The result is a historical record that combines the unique art of storytelling with literary technique and supporting visual and archival materials.

VOLUME ONE
The Life I've Been Living
Moses Cruikshank
Recorded and compiled by William Schneider

VOLUME TWO
Kusiq: An Eskimo Life History from the Arctic Coast of Alaska
Waldo Bodfish, Sr.
Recorded, compiled, and edited by William Schneider in collaboration with
Leona Kisautaq Okakok and James Mumiġana Nageak

VOLUME THREE
With a Camera in My Hands: William O. Field, Pioneer Glaciologist
William O. Field
Recorded and edited by C Suzanne Brown

VOLUME FOUR
The Whales, They Give Themselves: Conversations with Harry Brower, Sr.
Recorded and edited by Karen Brewster

THE WHALES,
THEY GIVE THEMSELVES

Conversations with Harry Brower, Sr.

Edited by Karen Brewster

University of Alaska Press
Fairbanks

© 2004 University of Alaska Press

P.O. Box 756240-UAF
Fairbanks, AK 99775-6240
toll free in U.S.: 888.252.6657
phone: 907.474.5831
fypress@uaf.edu
www.uaf.edu/uapress

Printed in the United States of America.
This publication was printed on paper that meets the minimum
requirements for ANSI/NISO z39.48-1992 (Permanence of Paper).

Paperback ISBN: 1-889963-66-6
Cloth ISBN: 1-889963-65-8

Library of Congress Cataloging-in-Publication Data

Brower, Harry, 1924-
  The whales, they give themselves : conversations with Harry Brower,
Sr. / edited by Karen Brewster.
      p. cm. -- (Oral biography series ; v. 4)
  Includes bibliographical references and index.
  ISBN 1-889963-65-8 (hardcover : alk. paper) -- ISBN 1-889963-66-6
(pbk. : alk. paper)
  1. Brower, Harry, 1924- 2. Inupiat--Alaska--Barrow--Biography. 3.
Whaling masters--Alaska--Barrow--Biography. 4.
Inupiat--Fishing--Alaska--Barrow. 5. Whaling--Alaska--Barrow--History.
6. Barrow (Alaska)--Social life and customs. I. Brewster, Karen. II.
Title. III. Oral biography series ; no. 4.
E99.E7B763 2004
979.8004'9712--dc22
                              2003026340

Cover design by Lisa Tremaine.
Text design by Pattie Rechtman.
Cover photo: Harry Brower, Sr. in sealskin parka, *Nalukataq*, Barrow, Alaska, 1986.
    Courtesy Trish Brower McFarlin.
Back cover photo: © Bill Hess.

Contents

Preface   *vii*
Acknowledgments   *xv*
Map of Northern Alaska   *xvi*

PART ONE: INTRODUCTION

1. Visiting   3
2. A Place Called Utqiaġvik   15

PART TWO: CONVERSATIONS

3. "We Had Fun Anyway"   45
4. "I Walked That All Over"   73
5. "No Rest For the Wicked"   95
6. "I Never Get Scared of Nothing"   103
7. "A World of Possibilities"   123
8. "He Gave Himself"   131

Epilogue: Through Other Eyes   *165*
Appendix: Outside Looking In   *191*
Endnotes   *203*
References   *217*
Index   *227*

Preface

A friend of Harry Brower once said, "His house was like a train station, there were always people coming and going." Harry Brower, Sr. was a whaler, community leader, architect of the Arctic Slope Regional Corporation boundaries, and a facilitator and key link for the Alaska Eskimo Whaling Commission and scientists. As this life history reveals, he had a unique ability to communicate in a variety of contexts, surely making strategic decisions about how he said things. Race did not matter to Harry. When I asked him how he felt about a photograph of a Cat Train building marked "Eskimos Only", that I had recently seen, he said, "Well, that's their problem. They just do whatever they want to do. I don't let it bother me." This outlook, combined with his own self-confidence, enabled him to work with everyone. His positive attitude and the talent to get along with all kinds of people were keys to his success in new environments.

Some of Harry's stories were standard; he told them to everyone, though not necessarily in the same detail. Others were not. Craig George, a biologist with the North Slope Borough Department of Wildlife Management, visited Harry frequently to talk to him about bowhead whale behavior, navigation, and population distribution. Craig said, "I'd heard some of those same stories, some I hadn't. And some had more detail than I remembered hearing. I worked with Harry on whale stuff. He didn't talk about his self-history as much with me."[1] Clearly, Harry took a different approach to conversations with me, a non-Native woman, than he did in conversations with his grandson, biologists, politicians, neighbors, and any of the diverse people Harry interacted with throughout his life. I do wonder how my conversations with Harry might have been different if I had been a man, if I was Iñupiaq,[2] or if I had had more experience with whaling, hunting, and trapping. I might have been able to ask more detailed questions about how to take a whale, how to read sea ice, or how to navigate on the flat, seemingly featureless tundra. These were the things he talked about with his sons, who he felt needed to know this, and who had grown up listening to his stories and lessons. But Harry did share with me some aspects of his life that he kept hidden from other outsiders, such as the hardship of raising a large family with little money, how he felt when his father died, and

(Opposite) Harry Brower during Sigma Xi award ceremony, Fairbanks, 1988. Photo by Bill Hess.

conflicts he had with his older brother. There are also parts of his life that he talked about because I specifically asked. For instance, because of my interest in backpacking in wild country, I pursued Harry's stories about walking across and mapping northern Alaska in more detail than someone else who might not have been as excited by the subject.

The timing of my relationship with Harry Brower was right for both of us. I was new to Barrow and eager to learn about Iñupiaq culture. He was getting older and his declining health meant he could no longer go out traveling and hunting as he had in his younger days. He now had time to spend sitting around the house in the evening telling stories, hours that otherwise would have been spent cleaning fox skins, feeding a dog team, preparing whaling gear, or caring for his family. Harry also was at a point in his life where he recognized the pressing need to pass on what he knew. He came to trust me and realize that I was serious with my questions. He shared his life with me amidst the ebb and flow of friendly conversation, not as formalized interviews with set questions. He enjoyed the company and the attention my visits provided: his children were grown with families and busy lives of their own, and his grandchildren were either too young, too busy, or seemed not to be interested. I was able to devote my full attention to Harry; I could spend many hours at a time with him, and heard his stories with a fresh ear. My visits with Harry also helped him to pass time and keep from getting too lonely. "Your visits really kept him going," his brother-in-law Sam Hopson told me after Harry died. They did the same for me.

My relationship with Harry was unique. I was not a scientist looking for answers about specific biological or environmental questions. Nor was I a family member who had lived these stories or heard them over and over again. In a way, I was in-between the two. I was an outsider raised within the Western, scientific paradigm, who wanted to learn about another culture, and had some insider privileges not available to most outsiders. I became a surrogate family member of sorts—Harry gave me an Iñupiaq name, Aaka, meaning mother or grandmother, and I joined his whaling crew. Harry always made me feel welcome, which helped ease many a cross-cultural tension in other parts of my life. Although I know I will always be an outsider, my friendship with Harry and his family, and joining in activities like skin sewing, cooking, and Eskimo dancing, have made me feel part of the community. Although I was only a few years younger than Harry's youngest children, I often viewed him as the grandfather I never had. This "in-betweenness" is reflected in how Harry related to me and influenced my eventual choices for how to present his stories. Thus it is important that I include excerpts of our conversations to offer the reader a glimpse of how Harry and I interacted and why he chose to tell particular stories.

While this life history is predominantely about Harry Brower, Sr., it is also the story of our friendship, our cooperation on this project, and my personal journey toward cross-cultural understanding and community acceptance. In this way, Harry's and my stories are intertwined like strands of braided thread. Like Jean Briggs' classic book *Never In Anger* (1970), my work with Harry is both ethnography and journal.

The challenge of oral history is how to give perspective to someone else's experiences. In the past, written oral histories were solely a narrator's words and stories. There was no sign of an interviewer, or any explanation of the setting under which the stories were collected. Anthropologists, oral historians, and folklorists have begun to recognize the critical role the interviewer plays in the collection of oral history, and the way the narrator and the interviewer together shape the interview.[3] It has long been accepted that readers need to know a narrator's background to understand his or her words and stories—the meanings behind what the narrator says and why he or she says it.[4] But the importance of knowing something about the interviewers, their backgrounds, and the perspective they bring to the interview has been less appreciated. Whether an interviewer is male or female, part of the culture or an outsider, a relative or a non-relative all affect which stories get shared and how they are told. The stories in a life history are not told to just anyone, but to someone specific at a particular time.

My choice of presentation style is based upon extensive reading of other life histories. Margaret Blackman presents the life histories of Florence Edenshaw Davidson and Sadie Brower Neakok in an uninterrupted format, with personal, historical, and cultural information separated into introductory chapters.[5] While she succeeds in including crucial information about herself and contextual information about Davidson and Neakok, I felt this left the women's stories in isolation. Ruth Behar's life history of a poor Mexican woman, *Translated Woman: Crossing the Border with Esperanza's Story* (1994), proved a useful model of a more integrative style. Behar appears throughout the book as another character in the story. We learn her personal history and her motivations and thereby better understand the questions she asks and the relationship she develops with Esperanza. As she says, "We ask for revelations from others, but we reveal little or nothing of ourselves; we make others vulnerable, but we ourselves remain invulnerable."[6] It is important that the oral historian be present but not dominate the story, and this is perhaps the most difficult balance to strike. I felt that Behar's presence was too strong and so detracted from the overall story.

In response to these other styles of life histories, I present background information about myself and Barrow in introductory chapters, but also weave my presence into Harry Brower's narrative to more closely represent the way the interviews really happened. I have arranged Harry's stories in chronological and topical order so the stories take on the shape of his life, rather than that of our conversations. Harry did not talk about his life in order. We simply engaged in a normal conversation; we did not do structured oral history interviews where I ran down a list of prepared questions. Harry told bits and pieces of his life as they occurred to him, as he was reminded of them by something else we had been talking about, or as they came up in response to my questions. A current event might jog his memory—when a whale had just been landed he reminisced about whale hunts from his younger days. Sometimes we talked about the same part of his life across a number of sessions, little pieces coming out as he told the same story again or provided more detail.

Even within stories, Harry did not always move in a straight line. He wandered off on tangents, skipped details, or doubled back to an earlier time to give the background needed to understand the story. This could all become quite confusing. I have left Harry's stories as intact as possible, but have included historical and ethnographic background where necessary to clarify meaning and to set Harry's life and stories in the context of the world and culture from which he came. I turned to his family members when I needed clarification.

In transcribing the tapes of our conversations, I tried to replicate Harry's speaking style, pace, and emphasis as much as possible but deleted false starts, repetitions, and long pauses to keep the stories flowing. The shorter sentence structure and fragmentary style replicates and reflects the way Harry spoke. I do not know if Harry spoke this way when he was a younger man without health problems, but this is how he talked when I knew him. I removed or incorporated my questions and comments into the narrative so that Harry's stories progressed uninterrupted. I made minor corrections to his English grammar, and standardized his verb choice for the sake of consistency and readability. I did maintain aspects of his word choice that, although nonstandard, reflect his personal style, such as his description of a mother polar bear "with a little cubs on it." In this way, I hope the reader is able to hear Harry, as I do when I read these stories.

Harry's life history has importance beyond the context of our friendship and our conversations. Dr. Tom Albert, Chief Scientist for the North Slope Borough, said, "Harry was so humble. He'd never blow his own horn, let alone even pick it up."[7] Yet Harry demonstrates one man's successful transition into the rapidly changing modern world. While Harry may have had an advantage over other members of his generation because of his mixed heritage, he had a way of dealing with the pressures of a changing lifestyle that serves as a good example for everyone.

Harry's narrative complements what we already know about Iñupiaq ways of being and the variety of ways people choose to express themselves within Iñupiaq culture. Harry's life was unique in terms of what he did with his mixed heritage, but it is not the only life story of a North Slope elder to be written. *Kusiq: An Eskimo Life History from the Arctic Coast of Alaska* (1991)[8] and *Sadie Brower Neakok: An Iñupiaq Woman* (1989)[9] are the stories of elders whose lives followed paths distinct from Harry's, as well as from those around them.

Waldo Bodfish, twenty years older than Harry, grew up when pre-contact Iñupiaq traditions were more prevalent. He lived in and around the village of Wainwright, and his stories focus more on reindeer herding and other inland activities than on his whaling experiences. Harry's life centered around whaling and other coastal hunting. Although Waldo and Harry both had white fathers, Waldo's father spent little time in the Arctic and had little influence on his life. Harry's father was already getting old by the time Harry was born, but was still a powerful figure in Harry's life and in Barrow. Charles Brower designated himself "the northernmost American," and was the storekeeper, postmaster, magistrate, and welcoming committee for outsiders visiting Barrow between 1900 and 1945.

Sadie Neakok and Harry were siblings, but their lives were very different. Sadie was eight years older and was sent away from Barrow for a formal education. She was the last child in the family sent out to school and even completed two years at the University of Alaska, Fairbanks. As Sadie said, "Harry grew up mostly under a subsistence way of life. He went to school and went with Mom. Mom was the hunter in the family."[10]

In adulthood, their lives continued in opposite directions. As a teacher and Barrow's first magistrate, Sadie led a public life, while Harry's was a private life away from the limelight of politics. Their stories complement each other and provide a fuller view of life in Barrow from the 1920s to the 1990s. Sadie's life tells us about the educational, social, and judicial institutions that shaped Barrow's history. Harry's work with military, scientific, and oil exploration groups shows us some of the less well known aspects of this same period. It is important to remember that the life and experiences of these two Brower children were not typical for Barrow Iñupiat of their generation. People from less well-off families or of non-mixed heritage normally had less access to money, had fewer opportunities to meet "outsiders," and were more directly dependent upon a subsistence lifestyle.

༄

I can pass on Harry's stories with relative ease, but the telling of stories is more than just words. It is an experience shared between the teller and the listener. In the case of Harry and me, it was a gift given to a friend. Though I can never recreate or fully explain to the reader this act of sharing, I have tried to offer a sense of it by including myself in the narrative, by setting the scenes of my visits, and by explaining what Harry talked about. The biggest challenge was to provide explanation and background without detracting from Harry's own telling. I am writing for two audiences: the Iñupiaq community who knew and loved Harry; and the distant audience of readers who want to learn about Iñupiaq life and can learn from Harry's experience. My hope is that people will gain a sense of who Harry Brower, Sr. was, and also will appreciate the story of how I got to know him and how he chose to share his stories with me. I have attempted to keep Harry the focus of this work.

The way Harry chose to talk about his life shows who he was, what his priorities were, and how he viewed the world around him; but it also hints at how he was shaped by his culture and how Iñupiaq, cultural, and personal emphasis on whaling makes sense given that modern Iñupiat identify themselves by their whaling traditions. Harry Brower's narrative provides an intimate look at one man's life amidst the people and events in North Slope history. As such, it contributes to the unfolding story of life on Alaska's North Slope in the twentieth century.

Style Note

In the two introductory chapters, I describe my relationship with Harry Brower and offer historical context for readers unfamiliar with Iñupiaq history and culture. The chapters in the section Conversations include conversations between me and Harry, and include some additional commentary and context. I describe the scene when Harry told me the story, show which of my questions may have prompted him to tell a particular episode, or include necessary explanations.

Harry's words, set in a different font, have been transcribed from tape recordings, so there are occasions where the sentence structure and word usage may be different from what is normally expected in written English. Clarification of Harry's words or meanings appears in brackets, and detailed explanations or related points are included as footnotes.

Iñupiaq words are written in italics, and upon first use are accompanied by their English equivalent in parentheses. Some Iñupiaq equivalents for English words are also provided.

Note on the Illustrations

All photos from the Archives, University of Alaska Fairbanks are located in the Alaska and Polar Regions Department of Rasmuson Library, at the University of Alaska Fairbanks.

To my parents

Renate and Stuart Brewster

Acknowledgments

None of this would have been possible without the generosity of Harry Brower, Sr. who shared pieces of his life with me. For that I am eternally grateful.

I also wish to thank his children: Eunice, Eugene, Ronald, Charlie, Price, Harry, Jr., Dorothy, Teresa, and Vera for their support of this project, their patience in waiting for it to get finished, their assistance with answering my questions, and for their friendship.

I also thank the people of Barrow for teaching me about Iñupiaq culture, showing me the joys of living in the Arctic, and making Barrow home.

Thanks also go to William Schneider for his undying enthusiasm and for pushing me to finish this project; to Dave Norton for his appreciation of and commitment to good indexing; and to my editors for helping to make my thoughts sound better on paper and getting me through the complicated publishing process.

And finally, my deepest appreciation goes to my family and friends for their constant encouragement and support, and for accepting my love of Alaska.

(Opposite) Whalebone arch and umiaq *at Barrow. Photo by Karen Brewster.*

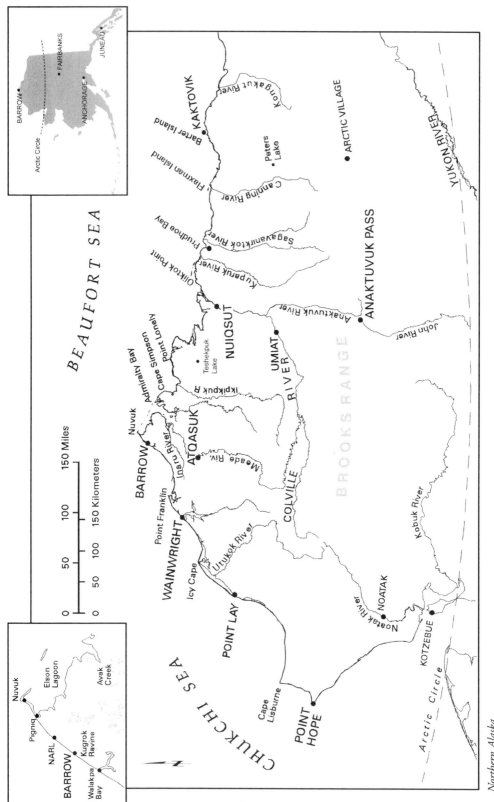

BEAUFORT SEA

CHUKCHI SEA

BROOKS RANGE

KAKTOVIK
Barter Island
Flaxman Island
Peters Lake
ARCTIC VILLAGE
Kongakut River
Canning River
Sagavanirktok River
Prudhoe Bay
Oliktok Point
Kuparuk River
Anaktuvuk River
ANAKTUVUK PASS
John River
YUKON RIVER

NUIQSUT
UMIAT
COLVILLE RIVER
Teshekpuk Lake
Ikpikpuk R.
Point Lonely
Cape Simpson
Admiralty Bay
Nuvuk
ATQASUK
Meade Riv.
Inaru River
BARROW
Point Franklin
WAINWRIGHT
Icy Cape
Utukok River
POINT LAY
Cape Lisburne
POINT HOPE
Noatak River
NOATAK
Kobuk River
KOTZEBUE
Arctic Circle

150 Miles
150 Kilometers
0   50   100   150
0   50   100   150

Nuvuk
Elson Lagoon
Pigniq
NARL
BARROW
Kugrok Ravine
Avak Creek
Walakpa Bay

BARROW
FAIRBANKS
JUNEAU
ANCHORAGE
Arctic Circle

Northern Alaska.

PART ONE

Introduction

Visiting

Approaching the large, gray house with red trim, I walked past snowmachines (snowmobiles) waiting to be driven across the tundra or out onto the ice to whale camp, and slipped around a beige Subaru station wagon in its usual spot alongside the front door. I stepped into the *qanitchaq*—the small, enclosed entry designed to keep the cold, wind, and snow from entering the house—and the pungent aroma of yellow seal oil immediately hit me. The *qanitchaq* was full of the bounty of a successful hunter: frozen and dried fish; plastic shopping bags overflowing with chunks of frozen caribou and whale meat; containers of pickled *maktak* (the black skin and top layer of pink blubber from the bowhead whale) and preserved meats; a saw; a pickaxe; a shovel; old rusty fox traps; and a pair of Carhartt coveralls stained black with animal blood and whale oil from years of butchering.

A handwritten sign on the door to the house read, "No Smoking." Another, "Please take off your boots."

I knocked on the inside door as I opened it and called, "Hello!"

"Come in!" Harry answered from way inside the house, his Iñupiaq accent barely noticeable. He was expecting me—it was seven o'clock in the evening, my usual visiting time.

"Hi!" I said joyfully as I took off my boots at the door and entered the main room.

༃

Harry Kraft Brower, Sr. was born on October 18, 1924 in Barrow, Alaska, the northernmost community in the United States.[1] He was the youngest son of well-known whaler and trader Charles Dewitt Brower, one of Barrow's earliest and most powerful white residents, and Asiaŋŋataq, who is remembered for her sewing skills and her generosity toward the poor families of Barrow. Harry was given the Iñupiaq name Kupaaq, after his grandmother. He and his eight siblings grew up speaking Iñupiaq with their mother and English with their father. They ate frozen raw meat dipped in seal oil with their mother at lunch time and were served pot roast, boiled potatoes, and canned vegetables at the dinner table with their father. Every day, summer or winter, they had to do their household chores before they could go out and play, and then they had to be home again by 8 P.M.

(Opposite) Harry Brower and Karen Brewster in 1991.

Harry Brower's house, Barrow, Alaska. Photo by Karen Brewster.

Harry's mother and her brothers taught him how to hunt and showed him what it meant to be Iñupiaq. He accompanied his mother when she distributed food to the elderly and the needy. He followed his uncle, Taalak, on extensive trips inland to check his trapline, and joined his other uncle, Ahsoak, for whaling and seal hunting.

Their father's fame outside Barrow as "The King of the Arctic" made the Brower home and trading post a focal point for Arctic visitors, explorers, teachers, and missionaries. This exposed the children to a wide variety of people and ideas.

Harry Brower's two-story house and collection of shed-like outbuildings were a little more than a block from the beach and stood across the street from the Bobby Fischer Softball Field and the old post office and three blocks from the town center—comprising the bank, video store, borough and corporation buildings, courthouse, hospital and Presbyterian church. The lot was kept neat and tidy; no old, rusty snowmachines, no dismantled car engines, no trash. The skeleton-like frames of two *umiat* (skin boats) were stored in front of a shed he called "the garage." A bright pink plastic float used for whaling lay atop another shed. Harry's eighteen-foot aluminum boat topped with a home-built plywood cabin sat on a trailer in front of the house.

The main room of Harry's house was a combination dining room, family room, and workshop. It was dominated by a long wooden table, big enough to seat twelve. Harry's family (the seven of his nine children who lived in Barrow and their kids) gathered at this table every day for lunch to eat *maktak*,[2] seal oil, caribou or goose soup, strips of dried *ugruk* (bearded seal) meat, and a variety of frozen meats or fish. It was the favorite family gathering place.

The garage and shed complex behind Harry Brower's house. Photo by Karen Brewster.

When I came in, Harry would customarily be sitting in his orange plastic kitchen chair at the old desk in the corner that he used as his carving and baleen boat-making work area. Red and gray toolboxes filled with screwdrivers, hammers, files, pliers, and hacksaws for cutting ivory lined the shelves on the wall behind him. The desktop was covered with whale baleen and ivory projects in various stages of completion and the small dental tools he used for carving ivory. He was hunched over a small cardboard box full of baleen shavings, edging a piece of baleen for one of his boats. He was well known for his exquisitely crafted model baleen boats.

"Hi there! Come in, come in." When Harry got excited he spoke so quickly that the words got pushed together into one long syllable, as if he forgot to take a breath in between.

As he looked up, his deep-set eyes and round face matched those in the poster-size black and white photo of Charles Brower that hung on the wall behind him. Harry was only five feet, five inches tall, but he had great strength and stamina. His hands were thick and wide; he had short gray hair that spiked out in a crew cut. Outdoors he always wore the same brown wool watch cap and blue denim work parka with wolverine ruff. A pale complexion was the only hint to his mixed heritage. He had oval eyes that lit up like a Fourth of July sparkler when he was happy, a large nose that dominated his small face, and a sneaky grin that stretched from ear to ear when he let out his characteristic fun-filled laugh.

Harry had a quick sense of humor, and was always ready with a tease or a funny story. He would laugh so hard sometimes that he would interrupt his own storytelling, as when he told me about a trick he played on his grandson, Gregory. They were in the car at Piġniq (Shooting Station) where eider ducks fly over in the late summer. A large flock appeared on the horizon, but Harry did not have a gun. He pulled out the wooden cane he always carried in the back the car and aimed it just like a shotgun. "Bang, bang, bang," Harry called out as he imitated the kick of a gun being fired. All of a sudden a few ducks fell to the ground nearby.

Harry described the scene to me: "Gregory had the biggest eyes you've ever seen and he said, 'Wow, how'd you do that, Papa?'"

"Magic!" Harry replied.

Harry giggled while telling me the story and remembering what had really happened. Someone nearby had fired a gun at the same flock and had hit several ducks that fell by Harry and Gregory. "What a good joke that was!" Harry laughed.

꒳

Harry spoke in short phrases with a slow, regular, and sometimes laborious cadence, pausing often to rest or take a deep breath because of his congested lungs. He elongated words by holding the sound in his throat longer or by lengthening the vowels, saying "aall" or "weell" when he used them at the beginning of a sentence. He emphasized his point at the end of sentences by raising his voice, pausing briefly, then punching the last phrase with a harder and upbeat tone. He often mumbled and could be hard to understand, especially when his Iñupiaq accent was strong. "Winter" became "winder." "Sent" and "send" were nearly indistinguishable. "Craig" sounded like "Greg," "Barry" like "Perry." He also shortened words and dropped endings: "just watchin' her;" "I told 'em." Yet the patient listener, or reader, who sticks with Harry to the end of his story, who works hard to hear both his words and their meaning, is rewarded.

When he began to tell stories Harry became lively and animated. He sat up in his chair. He gestured with his hands and frequently tapped the table. He offered subtle details, paused for emphasis, and would make a joke out of things. He imitated voices of different characters. His voice turned deep and gravelly when he was repeating what Vincent Nageak said when he taught Harry how to trap foxes: "Weell. OK. I'll show you. But I'm only gonna do it just once."

I describe Harry's voice at length because he made his world, past and present, come alive through his stories. This is one of the things that drew me to Harry and made his oral history particularly valuable. He had the ability to retell pieces of his own life in an interesting, informative, entertaining, and reflective style.

꒳

I took off my big down parka, laid it on the small velvety couch under the window, and sat down near the end of the big table. Hot air blasted from the "Warm Morning" heater behind me. While Harry went to the kitchen for tea and cookies, I set up the tape recorder and looked around the room at the assortment of mementos from the more than forty years spent in this house with his late wife, Annie. Even though Annie had died six years earlier, her old sewing machine cabinet full of pins, bobbins, thread, and fabric scraps was still there under one of the windows. Above were shelves of knickknacks—salt and pepper shaker sets Annie had collected, ceramic animal figurines from Rose brand tea boxes that Harry collected, and souvenirs from vacations in Hawai'i and the Lower 48. The walls were covered with family photos of all sizes and from all generations. In addition to the photo of Harry's father, there were old black and white prints of his uncles Taalak, Ahsoak, and Ugiaġnaq; a faded color print of Harry and Annie holding a newborn grandchild; family portraits of children and grandchildren at various ages; and large color photos of whales, whaling, and whale hunting camp. A framed certificate hung prominently over Harry's workbench. It was the award he received in 1988 from the Sigma Xi Scientific Research Society for his contribution to arctic science.

For over thirty years, Harry assisted researchers from around the world by sharing what he knew about arctic animals and their environment. This career began when, as a boy, he helped his father collect bird and egg specimens for the Smithsonian Institution, the American Museum of Natural History, and the Denver Museum of Natural History. However, his knowledge of the Arctic and its animals really stemmed from his Iñupiaq training as a hunter and a whaler. Harry started hunting when he was a young boy and by the age of fifteen knew enough about whaling to help run one of his father's whaling crews.[3] Close observation, understanding of animal behavior, and knowledge of the natural world were essential to Harry's success as a hunter, trapper and whaling captain, and were also the skills that made him an excellent scientific collaborator. He was respected and known for his generosity and willingness to help others within both the Iñupiaq and scientific communities.

During the late 1970s, when the International Whaling Commission (IWC) wanted to abolish Native subsistence whaling, Harry persuaded hesitant Barrow whaling captains to support research on bowhead whales. He reasoned that politicians were more likely to believe scientific data about the bowhead population than what Eskimos said about the animals, but also used his traditional knowledge of whales to influence the research questions the scientists pursued. For example, he mentioned that whales sometimes swim under the ice or along the far side of the open leads where scientists did not see them. Eventually, scientific research confirmed that this was true, and that there were more whales than the IWC previously believed. After a long political battle, Alaska Native subsistence whalers were allowed to continue whaling, although limits were set for their annual harvest. Harry was always proud of his active role in this victory. Harry also used his knowledge of the land and experience with early mapping surveys of northern Alaska to help define and delineate Iñupiaq territory during the Alaska Native land claims efforts of the 1960s and 1970s.

While his reputation for these accomplishments often preceded him, I first got to know Harry in the comfort of his own home, amidst his family and his daily routine. I met Harry in 1989; he was sixty-five and health problems kept him close to home. Of course, he still put out a fish net and hunted ducks from his car in the summer, jigged for tomcod in the fall when the sea ice was just forming, and sometimes even set a fox trap near the road or tried to hunt a caribou from his Subaru. He also carved ivory bracelets, necklaces, and figures, and made miniature baleen boats. "There's no rest for the wicked," he would say. As I got to know him better over the next three years, I discovered a talkative, hospitable, and modest man. He patiently answered my many questions and willingly shared his life with me. It was only after many evening chats that I discovered Harry's role in Barrow's social and political history. I enjoyed his stories, was intrigued by what he had done and what he knew, and thought it was worth sharing.

Harry represented a generation of people who successfully navigated through great change; his life was so unlike my own. He grew up in the 1920s and 1930s learning to hunt and live off the land; I was raised in the upper-middle class suburban sprawl of the San Francisco Bay Area during the 1970s. He learned to handle hardship and to overcome it through his own ingenuity. He learned to depend upon himself. I took dance and art classes, went to museums and musical performances, and took summer vacations with my family in the eastern United States, Hawai'i, and Europe. I never knew hardship or shortage. Nobody in my family hunted, nobody lived off the land, nobody even went camping.

Harry's knowledge came from the natural world and the people around him. I learned from books and classrooms. As was expected in my family, after high school I went to college. His classroom education extended only through the fifth grade.[4] His wisdom came from a lifetime of direct experience in the Arctic, where even the slightest mistake can mean the difference between life and death. Success was not judged by letters on a report card, but by survival and by putting food on the table.

Although Harry had traveled around the United States, visited children and grandchildren in Montana and California, and cruised the Arctic Ocean by icebreaker, Barrow and the surrounding country were home. "I walked that all over," he would proudly say, referring to how he hiked from the Canadian border to Point Hope when mapping for the U.S. Navy. This was where he was most comfortable, where he felt he belonged, where his family was. He gained his strength and identity from this place. His eldest son, Eugene, said, "My dad was most happy when he was out hunting."[5]

I first came to Alaska in the summer of 1986 when I was twenty-two and in my last year at the University of California Santa Cruz. I attended the Inuit Circumpolar Conference in Kotzebue and spent one month conducting research on Native subsistence issues for a bachelor's degree thesis in environmental policy and sociology. I fell in love with the wildness of Alaska, and moved to Anchorage in the summer of 1988. I spent the next year doing odd jobs, and first went to Barrow in January 1989. My friends thought I was crazy. One of the coldest winters in recent memory had a firm grip on Alaska—it had been twenty-five degrees below zero in Anchorage every day for two weeks and communities along the upper Yukon River in interior Alaska reported record temperatures of seventy to eighty below. Being a native of California, where at forty degrees *above* zero people put on down jackets, I never expected to survive such cold. It was minus forty when I arrived in Barrow.

In January 1989, the North Slope Borough Planning Department brought eleven of us from Anchorage to help complete the Barrow census. I spent two weeks in this community of 3,000 people on the edge of the Arctic Ocean, wandering from house to house in my designated section of town, attempting to complete the remaining census booklets. The sun had just reappeared above the horizon for the first time since November, but there were still only a few hours of dusky daylight in the middle of the day. Seeing Barrow mostly in the dark gave me a poor perspective of what then seemed like a little ramshackle town. Constantly turned around and confused by the flat, windswept landscape, the snowy tundra and the frozen ocean looked the same to my uneducated eye. It was an odd introduction to the community that I later was to call home.

I did not actually meet Harry that January. His house was on my list, but he refused to do the census. I barely got through his front door when his daughter stopped me. He sternly yelled from the back room, "I'm not interested! I did that survey already." I got the message and left. At the time I had no idea who he was, or that I would eventually come to be close friends with him. I got to know Harry later that same year when, at the age of twenty-five, I moved to Barrow permanently to help conduct a local subsistence study. I kept track of the hunting and fishing activities of one hundred households. Harry's house was one of them. After a few visits to document his subsistence harvests, I realized how much he knew about animals, hunting, and whaling. Even though his own harvest activity was low now that he was older and stayed around town more, he was always willing to visit with me and tell me about what was happening with hunting and fishing.

"They went out whaling today," he told me in October when Barrow's whaling quota had been met and I wasn't expecting any more whaling that year.

Another village transferred one of their unused whale strikes to Barrow. When the sea ice was thickening and people began to ice-fish, he told me: "They're catching tomcods." He also kept me informed of who was catching what: "Joe got a polar bear yesterday." He knew this information was important to me and would help improve my monthly reports about the community's overall subsistence activities. But it was more than that—he also knew that I needed to know these things if I was ever going to understand anything about the Iñupiaq hunting lifestyle and the activities that shaped his life.

When the subsistence study was over, I continued to visit Harry's house to find out what was going on. If I ran into him at the store or post office I stopped to chat. I was drawn to him. At first, I stopped at Harry's once a month to get the latest hunting news, then every two weeks, then once a week. Over time our friendship developed and we shared more of our lives with each other. I listened to stories about hunting whales and killing polar bears, about raising polar bear cubs, about how to trap foxes, and about his time spent walking across the northern foothills of the Brooks Range.

ᠵᡃ

I realize now, many years later, that I had been searching for someone to teach me about traditional Iñupiaq culture. I had read about how the Iñupiat hunted whales, seals, and polar bears out on the ocean ice; how they traveled in the winter by dogsled; how they lived in semi-underground houses heated with seal oil lamps. I had seen museum exhibits of their harpoon points, lances, tools, and clothing. I was impressed by their adaptations and by their creativity and flexibility. There were other Iñupiaq elders who also might have taught me, but Harry and I were immediately comfortable with each other, and I quickly became an eager student.

One day I had asked Harry if I could tape-record him. Slightly embarrassed by the attention, he refused and changed the subject. In June 1990, I switched jobs and became the oral historian for the North Slope Borough Iñupiat History, Language, and Culture Commission. This work increased my awareness of the knowledge of elders that was not being passed along. I wanted to document Harry's life, knowledge, and unique experiences, though I had never done an oral history interview before. By the fall of 1991, his health had worsened. When I asked again about tape recording, Harry agreed.[6] He knew that this might be his last chance to tell these stories as he remembered them, and he believed in the importance of sharing and teaching the young how to hunt, navigate, and survive in the Arctic. He wanted to be sure the future hunters and whalers of the North Slope learned the same lessons he had about "living the right way" and knowing what it meant to be Iñupiaq.

For the next five months—until he grew too ill to continue—I visited Harry two or three evenings a week and recorded conversations whenever we were alone. Initially, I was a little embarrassed about asking questions, and did not want people to think I was prying. I was also concerned that the background noise of a full house would obscure the recording. Later, however, my reasons changed—I realized that Harry and I talked differently when other people were there. His children knew him so well that he skipped over details when telling them things, when I brought other visitors who did not know Harry or much about Iñupiaq culture, he told sanitized, well-rehearsed stories. I was less self-conscious when Harry and I were alone, and felt freer to ask him to repeat things or describe something in more detail.

Finding time for tape recording was not as easy as one might expect. Harry's house was rarely empty, even though his nine children lived independently. Sons or daughters might stop by and join us for a cup of hot tea and candy, or grandchildren might be brought over to play. And, Gregory, Harry's ten-year-old adopted grandson, lived with him.

Harry and Gregory were inseparable. Harry showed him how to trap foxes, how to shoot ducks, and how to hunt caribou. Gregory helped Harry check fish nets set in Elson Lagoon, a few miles north of town. Harry loved Gregory deeply and spoiled him with attention, devotion, and with things Gregory wanted. Yet once Harry started getting sick, who was taking care of whom became increasingly unclear. Concerned about his "Papa's" health, Gregory once said, "I wonder why we couldn't live across the street from the Fire Department? 'Cause if he got sick alls they had to do is just back up the ambulance and then come in."

Gregory periodically joined our taping sessions. He mostly listened, but once in a while he asked a question—"What's amber?" when Harry told about finding amber on the mapping survey, or "What was that building before it was Videobank?" pointing to an old photo of Barrow when the three of us looked through albums. Sometimes, he would emulate his Papa and tell his own story.

"Last night, when Jim was working on putting running water in, you know. I looked in the pipe and I saw these eyes start to glow. Saw eyes start to glow green," Gregory explained after Harry had mentioned an old story about the little people called *Immiñ̃naurat*.

"You saw a mouse!" Harry replied with a laugh.

"So, do you think that was an *Immiñ̃nauraq*?" I asked Gregory.

"Yeah," he answered softly.

Harry's youngest daughter, Vera, her husband, and their two children also lived with Harry from time to time. It was an active household, just the way Harry liked it—he was happiest when surrounded by the sounds of his many grandchildren playing in the house. When it was just him and Gregory, he would lament, "It's too quiet around here. Nobody ever comes around."

Eventually, I visited Harry almost every night, even if it was just a quick hello to see how he was feeling, or to find out how his day had been. "What happened? You get lost?!" he joked when I had not come around for a few days. As our friendship deepened, I baked cookies, muffins, or pie for him and Gregory. He made me an ivory bracelet and an *ulu*, a woman's curved knife. And I helped when his crew landed a whale.

ॐ

Names are important to the Iñupiat. Every child is given an English name and at least one, if not more, Iñupiaq names. Children are named after relatives or recently deceased people as a way of passing on both their name and some of their personality traits. A name is given either when the child displays qualities of their namesake (*atiq*) or in hopes that the child will become like that person. The Iñupiaq name connects a person to their past, to their relatives, to their culture. I often heard other people call Harry by his Iñupiaq name, Kupaaq, but I called him Harry. It was not until I had reached a certain level of familiarity that I felt comfortable in calling him Kupaaq. Once I began to see how he personified the traditional *umialik*'s (whaling captain or leader) generosity, helpfulness, and compassion, I realized that the name Kupaaq better represented who he had become for me. I rarely called him Harry again. Both of his names appear interchangeably in this book, depending upon the context.

Harry and I agreed that the tape recordings were made for writing his life history and for younger generations to learn from. Unfortunately, he passed away before we were able to finish. For the first few years after his death I could not bear to listen to the tapes. Finally, in 1995 I was able to return to this project. Instead of hardship, I found joy. It was comforting to hear his voice. It was like visiting him again.

ॐ

Every evening our recording sessions ended the same way.

"Well," I said hesitantly, having waited for a break in his stories. "It's already ten o'clock. It's late. I should go home. I've made you talk a long time."

With a hint of disappointment, Harry said, "Yeah. OK."

I packed up the tape recorder, cleared the teapot, cups, and crumbs from the table, and bundled up again for the cold walk home.

"Good night. Thanks! See ya," I said as I left.

"Good night. Don't get lost!" Harry replied, reminding me that I should not stay away too long.

I strolled home through the darkness along the footworn path that wove around the half-dozen buildings that stood between Harry's house and mine. As I carefully stepped among the jagged snowdrifts I gazed upward, hoping to catch a glimpse of the northern lights. This was one of the few places in the middle of town where the glare of the streetlights did not block out the aurora's eerie white and green bands of light.

Harry Brower with his adopted grandson, Gregory, in 1988. Photo courtesy Bill Hess.

I trudged through the snow and cold, back to my empty apartment. I stopped just before turning between the abandoned warehouse and my building. Kupaaq once admitted that he watched me from the small window of his freezer room to make sure I made it home safely. The opening between buildings was just wide and straight enough so he could see me clearly all the way to this point. As I rounded the corner, I turned, waved, and under my breath said, "Good night."

A Place Called Utqiaġvik

Barrow Today

At the northernmost spot in Alaska—what the tourist industry calls "the top of the world"—the narrow gravel spit of Nuvuk, or Point Barrow, juts out into the Beaufort Sea.[1] It is like a finger pointing the way to the end of the earth, the last bit of terra firma refusing to give in to the sea's dominance. Here the north-south current of the Chukchi Sea intersects with the east-west movement of the Beaufort Sea, creating leads of open water in the sea ice just offshore. Marine mammals are attracted into these leads to feed on the sea life made possible by rich nutrients. The ancestors of the modern Iñupiat took advantage of this good hunting and settled here.

The only visible remnants of the once-flourishing village at Nuvuk are the sunken outlines of an old house, bones and strips of baleen eroding out of the bluff face, and a nearby cemetery.[2] Every year gnawing waves of the stormy ocean pick away at the gravel bluff, sloughing off another few feet and exposing another layer of history.

The community of Ukpiaġvik, as it was originally spelled, which means "the place to hunt snowy owls," about ten miles down the coast from Nuvuk, is now the modern town of Barrow.[3] About 4,600 people live in this mostly Iñupiaq community squeezed between the gravel beach and the flat, treeless tundra peppered with lakes.[4] In the summer's twenty-four-hour daylight, the tundra's low-growing plants look like a lush green carpet when seen from the air. In the winter, the landscape is shrouded with snow whipped into hard, rippled snowdrifts by an ever-present wind. Its uniform whiteness mixed with the pale violet dusk of the short midwinter days makes ice-bound lakes, the sea ice, and the land indistinguishable to an untrained eye.

The only way in or out of Barrow is by airplane, although cars, school buses, heavy equipment, gasoline, modular house units, and building supplies come by barge in the summer. Large public buildings—three schools, a senior center, administrative office buildings, a cultural center, the courthouse, and two grocery stores—dominate the skyline. There are two gravel baseball fields, the high school has an indoor swimming pool, and there is a covered outdoor ice rink. A bus system winds a circuitous route past almost every house. The shelves at the Alaska Commercial Company store—called Stuaqpak, the "big

(Opposite) Aerial view of Barrow, Alaska, 2003. Photo by Kalen Texiera.

store"—are stocked with everything from fresh South American strawberries and frozen reindeer stew meat to Asian coconut milk and rice noodles. At this one-stop shopping mart, you can also rent videos; have film developed; and buy furniture, hardware, clothing, Native arts and crafts, and souvenirs.

Parked in front of almost every house in Barrow is at least one snowmachine, a four-wheeler for tundra and beach travel, and a car or truck. The four-wheel drive Ford Explorer has replaced the Chevy Suburban as the vehicle of choice. People cruise the thirty miles of gravel roads that lead nowhere just for entertainment. It does not seem to matter that gas costs over $3.00 a gallon.

Millions of dollars flowed into Barrow and the other seven North Slope villages after oil was discovered at Prudhoe Bay in 1968.[5] Before drilling could commence, the state of Alaska was forced to settle Native land claims. In 1971, the United States Congress passed the Alaska Native Claims Settlement Act (ANCSA), which provided money and land rights to Alaska Natives through a regional and village corporate system. The Iñupiat formed the Arctic Slope Regional Corporation (ASRC). In 1972, Eben Hopson, Sr. had the inspiration to incorporate the North Slope Borough as an Iñupiaq government based upon Prudhoe Bay as a tax base. Throughout its thirty years of operation, the North Slope Borough has made large, expensive capital projects a priority. The borough is committed to providing its residents with the standard features of modern life and jobs. People are now accustomed to and have come to expect this from the borough.

As the largest village, Barrow became the financial and political hub of the region. There was money to finance big construction projects. Housing improved as running water and flush toilets were introduced.

Grassy bumps—the remains of semi-subterranean sod houses inhabited by Barrow's original Iñupiaq inhabitants—lie across the street from Arctic Pizza in the old section of town. Many of the older homes here have been upgraded with new siding, remodeled interiors, and running water, while others remain rundown and still use a "honey bucket" for a toilet—a bucket with a seat and lid, lined with a plastic bag. The bucket is standard issue across rural Alaska, where the permafrost (permanently frozen ground) and remoteness have made construction of sewer systems prohibitively expensive. The North Slope Borough offers free daily honey bucket pickup and disposal service.

In the newer part of town called "Browerville," which lies across the lagoon to the northeast, pre-fabricated three- and four-bedroom homes and multi-unit apartment buildings constructed by the North Slope Borough in the early 1980s are the norm. In the newest part of town, even farther to the northeast, large, two-story, metal-roofed, super-insulated, brightly colored modern homes have popped up like dandelions after a spring rain. Now that they can afford it, people are ensuring that their new homes have all the amenities of Lower 48 living: they are fully equipped with running water and flush toilets, and have lots of windows despite Barrow's extremely cold three months of near total darkness. They have decks for barbecues, although the average summer temperature hovers below fifty degrees Fahrenheit. Some even have saunas, steambaths, and jacuzzies, though water costs six to eighteen cents a gallon.

These new homes get running water and toilets in one of two ways. Some have indoor water holding tanks with insulated sewage tanks attached to the outside of the house. The water is pumped in from a truck by private businessman "Joe the Waterman," who even in winter wears just a tee shirt. A North Slope Borough sewage truck pumps out the waste for free. Other homes are on the "Utilidor," Barrow's underground water and sewer system. The pipes are buried eight to fourteen feet into the permafrost surrounded by inches of special insulation to keep the liquids from freezing. Closer to the main sewer and water treatment plant, the pipes run through heated tunnels. The newest parts of Barrow are just now getting connected.

In the last ten years, Barrow's population and economy have expanded. The state's booming oil economy meant money flooded the borough's coffers. Outsiders moved north, attracted by high-paying jobs and seemingly endless entrepreneurial opportunities in a previously under-serviced area. Barrow now has eight restaurants serving everything from pizza and sushi to burgers and fries, a fast food and deli counter in Stuaqpak, and just like in the rest of the country, folks can grab an espresso on their way to work.

Although Barrow doesn't really have a downtown, the bank, police department and jail, the Arctic Slope Regional Corporation headquarters, the school district offices, courthouse, North Slope Borough administration building, historic Presbyterian church, and the hospital are centrally located, all within a couple of blocks of each other.

Across the lagoon is Utuqqanaaġvik, Barrow's senior center. Hot lunches are served every weekday; employees clean the residents' apartments and do their laundry, a van service drops off and picks up elders wherever they want to go. Donations of *maktak*, fish, seal, duck, and polar bear meat for the elders sit on the porch in boxes.

To the casual observer, Barrow has a stark, unforgiving aspect. There are no trees, green lawns, or sidewalks. The streets, driveways, and most yards are gravel. The town is smothered by dust in the summer and mud puddles prevail when it rains. All winter everything is frozen and cloaked by a white blanket of snow and hoarfrost—frozen dew that covers all surfaces with a thick, furry white coating. Most buildings are weathered. Old snowmachines, trucks, and rusted equipment lie in front yards surrounded by stretched animal skins, pieces of black meat, and yellow fish hanging out to dry.

But Barrow is a subtle landscape that takes time to appreciate. In the spring, the low angle of the sun reflects a magical pink glow across the frozen landscape and abstract shapes of the rumpled sea ice. The only break in the quiet is the

Looking south from the old village site in Barrow. Photo by Karen Brewster.

roar of a distant snowmachine or the flap, flap, flap of a flock of eider ducks flying along the breaks in the ice to their summer breeding grounds east of Barrow. In the summer, the green tundra is alive with birds, small mammals, mosquitoes, and flowers. You can find small nests of shorebird eggs camouflaged in the grass if you look carefully enough. The short tundra plants put on a brilliant show of reds and yellows in the fall, just like their taller counterparts in lower latitudes. In August, gray whales swim south and feed and spout just off the beach. A young polar bear might wander into town on an October evening, attracted by the smell of a recently butchered bowhead whale carcass or looking for an easy meal at the town dump. The meat and skins in people's yards are the products of a hunting-based diet and economy. Old vehicles are kept as resources to be mined for parts when another machine breaks down. Recycling is more economical than paying the high local prices or expensive shipping rates for ordering new pieces, and can be a necessity.

Barrow embodies a unique contrast between old and new, Native and non-Native. People walk their dogs, play softball, or watch videos, while an eighty-three-year-old Iñupiaq seamstress hand-sews exquisite dance boots and teaches her craft to those with the interest and fortitude to try. There is the young Iñupiaq woman who cuts up the bearded seal (*ugruk*) her husband just brought home, divides shares and stores them away, cares for her children, sews the family's parkas, and works a nine-to-five office job. There is the man who mushed dogs to the North Pole and now just keeps a team for fun, and the scientist who has devoted nearly twenty years of his life to studying bowhead whales and learning about Iñupiaq whaling. There is the gourmet chef who collects hot sauces and spends his evenings and weekends at the high school woodshop creating knife handles and boxes out of rare woods. There are loners who fled the fast-paced world of big cities, or something worse, and are grateful for the isolation.

Despite modern amenities, western bureaucratic institutions, and the younger generation's lack of knowledge of the Iñupiaq language, Iñupiaq culture and identity remain strong. Eskimo dances, with their deep, rhythmic drumbeat and high-pitched singing are well attended and more children are joining the organized dance groups.[6] Iñupiaq conversations are still heard in the store, the post office, at work, or at hunting or whaling camp. A man will miss a day of work to go out seal hunting or take a month off for whaling. Women hand-sew *ugruk* skins together into the coverings for the skin boats used in spring whaling. Women still wear the hooded shirt-dresses (*atikłuk*) made of calico fabric and styled after the traditional parka. People walk down the street braced against the cold in beautiful hand-made *maklaks* and parkas with intricate trimming, and wolf or wolverine ruffs—the women in brightly colored and highly patterned cotton or velveteen and the men in dark canvas or corduroy.

Historic gravesite on the tundra. Photo by Karen Brewster.

The gravel streets of modern Barrow are busy with traffic and criss-cross what used to be sod houses and grassy tundra. Familiar remnants remind passers-by of the ancient ties the Iñupiat have to this place. Fragments of stone blades and ivory harpoon points erode from ancient houses onto the beach in front of town.[7] Frost heaves push old graves to the surface, returning the ancestors to the present. Thirty-foot, double-ended wooden dories, introduced by Yankee whalers and now outdated, lie behind houses.[8]

The Presbyterian Church and manse, as well as the Brower whaling station, warehouse, store, and residence, are historic buildings. The current Presbyterian minister lives in the manse, and Wednesday night and Sunday services, funerals, and weddings are held in the church. The former whaling station is a restaurant and tourist attraction with a pair of whale jawbones arched over an *umiaq* next to the building.

Shiny gray ringed seal skins stretched inside circular frames soak up the spring and summer sun. Once dry, the skins will be used for boots, hats, or mittens. Strips of black *ugruk* meat dry on racks, finally becoming jerky in the constant daylight and warmer temperatures of the two-month summer.

Traditional practices and values still influence the modern Iñupiaq way of life, although they have changed to meet current needs. Whaling continues to dominate life in the twenty-first century. While modern Iñupiat whalers use explosive weaponry and motorized equipment, they still believe that whales give themselves to deserving hunters. Young boys are trained to be whalers, men take great pride in being whaling captains. The yearly cycle of hunting revolves around whaling.

Bearded seal meat drying on rack to make paniqtaq *(dried meat). Photo by Karen Brewster.*

Hunting and Whaling: The Land and the Sea Provide

For the Iñupiat, hunting is not recreation; it is a way of life.[9] Harvesting wild food from the sea, sky, and land links generations of Iñupiat in one long seasonal cycle, and provides nutritional, spiritual, and cultural sustenance: "Every time I go out—go somewhere down south, you know—and I have to eat some of your food, I'm not really satisfied in my stomach. I have to eat caribou or *muktuk* (*sic*), whatever we have—the Native foods. That makes you feel good, makes you strong."[10]

For generations, Iñupiat men have hunted the bowhead whale (*Balaena mysticetus*), or *aġviq* in Iñupiaq. The first non-Native people to visit the Iñupiat observed widespread community-based whaling, wrote down what they observed, and collected whaling-related artifacts.[11] They saw Iñupiat living in large winter communities located at coastal hunting spots, where large areas of open water, called leads (*uiñiq*), developed in the ice near protruding points of land.[12] They described an Iñupiaq society based upon whaling crew membership and the leadership of *umialgich*.[13] They observed group whale hunts and the important place whales had within Iñupiaq cosmology.

Whaling remains a dominant force in the lives of modern Iñupiat in northern Alaska. Whaling is the culmination of the year's hunting activities. People talk about whaling, they have pictures of people whaling on their walls, and they survey the ice all winter wondering how it will affect the whale hunt in the spring. Young people are encouraged to whale by doing chores at whale camp, by listening to and watching older crew members, by helping to butcher, and by cooking and serving at the feasts. During the spring and fall whaling seasons, most other activity in town ceases while groups of men pursue the bowhead in small boats. All ears are attuned for word coming back to town of a whale being caught. Cheers of excitement and calls of congratulations ring over VHF radios when the good news is heard.

Modern Iñupiaq whalers believe, as they say their ancestors did, that whales must be treated with respect, and that the whale gives itself to a hunter who is deserving of the gift. Some captains say that the whale itself chooses the worthy captain, that the whale gives itself. Others explain the whale as a gift from God.

The oral and historical record shows that in earlier times whaling was imbued with strict behavioral taboos to please the whale, encourage it to give itself, and to ensure success of the hunt.[14] For example, whalers secluded themselves for contemplation and instruction just before whaling. They put on new clothes and *maklaks* before heading out for the hunt. They did not have dog teams or tents on the ice, nor did they cook food, all for fear of offending the whales. Shamans sang special songs to attract whales, to control wounded whales, to ensure a boat's safe passage back to the shorefast ice, and to create favorable winds that would open the leads. The *umialik*'s wife and the families of crewmembers also adhered to prescribed behavior, such as greeting the landed whale with a cup of water, so he would feel well-treated and encourage other whales to come back the following year; not using a knife, for fear it could cause the lines towing a whale to break; not sewing out of concern that the whale would get tangled in the lines; and being quiet and not speaking ill of others, so as not to frighten the whales away.[15]

Correct behavior nowadays includes cleaning, preparing, and organizing the whaling gear before the hunt; cleaning out the underground ice cellar and

Men butchering a whale in the 1920s. Presbytery of the Yukon Collection, Box 2, Album 1, Archives, University of Alaska Fairbanks.

lining it with a layer of fresh snow; being a kind, generous person who treats others with respect; being quiet when camped on the ice so as not to scare the whales; keeping a clean whaling camp and wearing clean, white cloth parka covers so as not to offend the whales; paddling the skinboat without splashing and making noise; and sharing the wealth of a successful harvest.

Whaling captains were men of wealth and power in the community when non-Natives first came to northern Alaska. An *umialik* was a skilled hunter who owned a boat, earned loyalty from the crewmembers he supported, divided the spoils of the hunt among the participants, and shared his harvest with the rest of the community at public feasts. An *umialik* was a respected leader and good provider who gained his status and skills through years of hard work, patience, and observation. The position was usually passed along family lines; young boys were trained by their fathers, uncles, and grandfathers.[16]

The same is true of whaling captains today. They are respected leaders. Many of the men in political and business leadership roles in the community are also whaling captains. They provide for the community at feasts like *Nalukataq*. They give away *maktak* and meat, and prepare their whaling gear before the new season begins. They stress behaving quietly, unselfishly, and respectfully during whaling. They still speak of whales giving themselves, of acting properly so as to be worthy of the gift, and of getting a whale for the whole community, not just for themselves.

While becoming a whaling captain today may depend less on inheritance than it used to—with enough money, new whaling gear can be purchased and younger men are starting crews—a similar level of responsibility and sharing continues. Harry Brower's life shows just how much whaling captains continue to be respected and admired by the Iñupiat. Many have now come to be recognized by outsiders as well. Whaling captains are consulted as community experts during scientific investigations, environmental impact studies on development, and during oil industry and government regulation and decision making.[17]

Today, Iñupiat hunters drive snowmachines, trucks and powerboats, and they hunt with shotguns, rifles, and explosive darting guns, but they continue to sense a connection between humans and animals. Iñupiat believe in behaving respectfully towards animals, and not offending them, because animals give themselves only to deserving hunters. For example, a man is not supposed to brag, or say with certainty that he will be successful when he goes hunting. Instead, he says, "I'm just going out to take a look around out there." Hunters also cut the heads off land animals right away as their ancestors did, "To let the spirit out," one hunter explained.

The seasonal cycle of hunting—commonly referred to as subsistence by policymakers and others—directs the choices of everyday life for people like Harry Brower, Sr. Men leave their jobs for the afternoon in July if the sun is shining, the water is calm, and the ice has broken up enough so boats can

A successful whaling crew returning from camp with their umiaq *and dog teams in the 1920s. Presbytery of the Yukon Collection, Box 2, Album 3, Archives, University of Alaska Fairbanks.*

navigate through the floating chunks. These are ideal conditions for summer seal hunting. Women do not come to the office the morning after such a day, because they were up all night butchering bearded seals their husbands brought in at midnight. Families take their children out of school for a week in May, so they can all go goose hunting while the temperatures are still below freezing, the snow has not yet melted, and the geese are passing through. And many offices empty when a whale is caught. Most men are already out whaling, others rush to go help butcher, and women drop everything to prepare food for the feast.

The Iñupiaq seasonal round of subsistence begins in early May with whaling.[18] Whalers also shoot eider ducks flying low along the open leads of water. A pot of fresh duck soup is a much-relished treat, both at whale camp and in town. From mid-May to mid-June families travel inland by snowmachine to hunt geese that are en route to their summer breeding grounds.

In June, men check their aluminum and fiberglass boats for holes, make sure the outboard motors are in tip-top shape, and wait for the sea ice to break

Barrow women butchering seals. Photo by Karen Brewster.

up in early to mid-July. Once the ice is out far enough that boats can pass through, the men hunt ringed seals and bearded seals among the floes and along the edge of the pack ice. Female relatives butcher the seals, divide the meat and internal organs, and clean and stretch the skins for clothing, boot soles, and skin boat covers. Walrus also are hunted on the ice floes in July and August, although their presence is more variable. Sometimes the herds do not get to Barrow, the northern limit of their range. Sometimes the walrus are too far into the pack ice for the men to reach them. The men usually cut up the walrus on the ice. They fill their boats with chunks of dark red meat, which is surrounded by a few inches of dense fat under wrinkled skin.

Every day in late July and early August when the wind is not blowing, men, women, teenagers, and boys shoot ducks at Piġniq (about five miles north of Barrow, also known as Shooting Station). Huge flocks cross over this spit on their way south for the winter. During the summer, people also fish and hunt caribou, both near town and at inland camping sites. People hunt caribou any time of year when a herd is nearby or the family's food supply is low. Late summer and fall caribou are preferred, because this is when they are the fattest and have the thickest coats.

Going inland by boat or chartered airplane to camp is an increasingly popular family event and an excellent way to obtain fish and caribou. A few families still spend the entire summer on the rivers, as their more seasonally nomadic ancestors did, but most stay just for a few days or weeks. Some have built permanent plywood cabins at their camping spots, others set up and take down a canvas wall tent each trip. Broad whitefish, humpback whitefish, arctic char, lake trout, grayling, burbot/ling cod, least cisco, and Bering cisco accumulate in nets set in the rivers and lakes. Fathers teach their sons how to pursue caribou from boats on the river. Hordes of mosquitoes swarm every warm-blooded creature—human, caribou, dog. Strips of black caribou meat and halved whitefish dry on racks. Women and girls collect berries and greens. Children swim in the river to cool off (inland temperatures can get into the 70s or 80s in the summer).

By the middle of September, men in boats begin to cruise the open ocean in pursuit of bowhead whales returning south from their summer in the Canadian Arctic. The timing of fall whaling depends upon when whales are spotted, the ice movement, and the timing of freeze-up. The number of whales caught also depends upon how many are left over from the year's quota begun in the spring. In October or November, after lakes and rivers have frozen and there is sufficient snow cover, families head inland by snowmachine to their camps to fish and hunt caribou again. Fish nets are strung along a series of holes chopped through the ice. The nets are pulled out through the last hole once or twice a day, and whitefish and cisco are plucked from their entangled web before they harden in the subfreezing temperatures.

During the dark months from November to January, hunting activity subsides. A young hunter might go out in search of caribou or perhaps hunt seals at the ice edge. Someone else might catch a polar bear. And men haul sledloads of freshwater ice blocks or multi-year sea ice into town to melt for drinking water.[19]

The sun returns to Barrow by the end of January, but February tends to be the coldest month. Typically, temperatures hover around twenty-five degrees below zero Fahrenheit. Nevertheless, a handful of men take advantage of the long days to go by snowmachine to the Brooks Range foothills to hunt wolves, wolverines, and foxes. The furs become hats, mittens, and the ruffs and trim for parkas. In earlier times, a trapline would be set from December to April, but few, if any, Barrow people still put out traps.

Historical Perspective

Aipaani, since time immemorial, is how the Iñupiat describe their ancient ties to their land and culture. Archaeologists try to pin an exact date on Iñupiat arrival in North America, but continue to debate cultural development in northern Alaska.[20] Regardless of when they arrived, the Iñupiat have long been, and continue to be, creative and flexible residents of the North. Survival with limited resources requires quick thinking, patience, observation, accumulated knowledge, and ingenuity. For instance, the men watched whales time and time again to understand their swimming, breathing, and diving habits in order to become better hunters.

For centuries, the Iñupiat built their winter homes partially underground and insulated them with blocks of tundra. They hunted seals from the ice in the winter, pursued whales in the open lead system in the spring, and hunted caribou and waterfowl and fished inland in the summer and fall. They traded

A traditional semi-subterranean sod house with a whalebone entrance. Presbytery of the Yukon Collection, Box 2, Album 3, Archives, University of Alaska Fairbanks.

coastal, inland, and European products along trade networks extending as far east as Canada and as far south as Kotzebue.[21] The early Iñupiat kept food frozen by storing it in cellars dug into permafrost. They stayed warm by eating a high fat and predominantly meat diet and by wearing skin clothing perfectly designed for their active lifestyles in the cold—fur parkas that ventilated during strenuous activity, deep hoods trimmed with fur ruffs to keep the face warm, and multi-layered fur pants, boots, and mittens. They traveled long distances by foot or dogteam, and navigated an often featureless landscape of tundra and ice using detailed knowledge of the behavior of wind, snowdrifts, currents, and ice.

Based upon generations of experience and observations in the Arctic, the Iñupiat developed specialized hunting techniques. They used toggling harpoon heads that did not break off when the struck animal dove in ice-choked water. They channeled caribou down valleys to lakes where men waited in kayaks to spear the animals as they tried to swim across. They flung strings of braided sinew weighted with pieces of bone or ivory into flocks of ducks to entangle their wings and legs and knock the birds from the sky. They depended upon special songs, amulets, and behavioral taboos to help them capture their largest prey, the bowhead whale.

Euroamericans first arrived at Utqiaġvik in 1826. British explorers William Smyth and Thomas Elson, members of an expedition led by Captain Frederick W. Beechey, arrived by small boat from Icy Cape over a hundred miles to the south.[22] Smyth and Elson received a hostile reception from the Iñupiat and did not spend time ashore.[23] They named the new place "Barrow" after Sir John Barrow, a member of the British Admiralty who was never there, but was a strong motivator behind Britain's Arctic and Northwest Passage explorations.

Contact between Iñupiat and non-Natives was sporadic until the 1850s when many British and American ships searched for their missing compatriot, Sir John Franklin, who was lost while trying to find the Northwest Passage.[24] As part of this search effort, the British ship *Plover* was frozen in the ice by Point Barrow from 1852–1854 and its crew were the first outsiders to spend the winter there.[25]

In 1854, due to dwindling whale populations in the North Pacific, commercial whaling vessels first searched for the oil-rich, slow-moving bowhead whale north of the Bering Strait. In 1884, Edward Perry "Ned" Herendeen, backed by the Pacific Steam Whaling Company of San Francisco, established the first shore-based commercial whaling operation in Barrow. By launching small wooden boats into the open leads in April and May, his aim was to get a jumpstart on the whaling season. His competitors had to wait for the ice to break up before they could travel north from their winter ports in Seattle and San Francisco.[26] Herendeen's method did not prove as successful as he had anticipated. During his first years, he did not land any whales.

Charles Dewitt Brower, another commercial whaler, arrived in Barrow in 1886 to work with Herendeen. He had worked for the Pacific Steam Whaling Company in 1884 trying to develop coal fields at Cape Lisburne, and he whaled with the Iñupiat at Point Hope. This knowledge helped Brower turn Herendeen's operation around, and eventually the new shore-based technique took off. In 1893 Brower and a partner, Tom Gordon, started their own whaling operation and trading post. Brower was the first non-Native whaler to send crews of non-Natives and Iñupiat out onto the shorefast ice in the springtime to pursue whales from small open boats, just as the Iñupiat did. After a few years without catching any whales, in 1889 Brower's group landed three and by 1894 they had landed ten in one season.[27] Brower's methods proved more successful than hunting from large whaling ships in the open ocean of summer and made the shore-based whale fishery at Barrow commercially viable.[28] The Iñupiat continued their own whaling throughout the period of commercial whaling and the introduction of Western goods and technology. The Iñupiat who Charles Brower hired to work on his whaling crews were mostly inland people who migrated to the coast or were locals ostracized from Native whaling because they had broken taboos on proper ways to hunt whales.[29]

Brower's Cape Smythe Whaling and Trading Company was driven by profit. Every spring they put out multiple whaling crews to try to land as many whales as possible. The meat from these whales was distributed among the villagers. The more whales they caught, the more baleen, or "whalebone," they harvested, and the more money they made selling it. Before vulcanized rubber, there was a great demand for baleen because of its flexibility and strength. It was used for corset stays, hoop skirts, buggy whips, parasol ribs, mattress stuffing and parts of chairs.[30] Every summer, Brower sent the bundles of cleaned baleen

Interior of a northern trading post, circa 1925. Eva Alvey Richards Collection, acc. no. 78-14-270, Archives, University of Alaska Fairbanks.

via steamship to Liebes Company in San Francisco for sale and distribution in the Lower 48. Brower became one of the most successful and best-known commercial whalers in the Arctic. Being one of the wealthiest and one of the few English speakers in Barrow at the time, he also was a community leader, postmaster, magistrate, and coroner.

The commercial whaling industry ended by 1914 due to over-hunting and a declining market for baleen and whale oil, which were being replaced by plastics and petroleum products. By this time, the economy of northern Alaska was dependent upon access to outside goods.

People exchanged furs for Western goods at trading posts across northern Alaska as early as the 1890s, but after the collapse of the whaling market, trapping became more lucrative. People began to return to the countryside to pursue fur trapping. Prices peaked around the mid-1920s, but people continued to sell arctic and red fox furs into the 1960s. Money that Harry Brower earned from fox sales in the 1950s helped him finance construction of his house, and even in the 1970s, he supplemented his hunting and his wage employment with fox trapping.

Once commercial whaling was no longer economically viable, Charles Brower's Cape Smythe Whaling and Trading Company shifted its focus to fur buying and trading. He accepted fox skins in exchange for Western goods such as sugar, flour, tea, coffee, tobacco, dried fruit, canned milk, and pilot bread, which the Iñupiat had become accustomed to having.[31] He supported a number of trappers in the field, giving them supplies for the trapline in exchange for the guarantee that they would bring their furs only to him. He supported traders and trading posts spread across northern Alaska from Wainwright to Cape

Halkett to Kaktovik. When Harry Brower came of age, his world comprised this trade-based economy and his father's store. He remembered the store shelves stocked with flour, canned goods, and candy.

Reindeer herding was another economic activity around Barrow and across northwestern Alaska that expanded in the early 1900s.[32] Presbyterian minister Sheldon Jackson introduced reindeer to Alaska from Lapland in 1892 to provide what he considered a more stable meat supply to the Native population. He believed the people were suffering hardship and shortages from their subsistence-based lives.[33] In 1898, the Jarvis Expedition brought two hundred deer north from the Seward Peninsula after seven whaling ships were crushed by moving ice before they could head south in September and the whaling crews were stuck in Barrow for the winter.[34] Brower and the local Iñupiat provided locally hunted caribou to the shipwrecked men, so the reindeer proved unnecessary as meat for the stranded sailors.[35]

These reindeer became the nucleus for a northern herd, which peaked at 30,000 animals in 1935. In the 1930s, reindeer herding was important for the Brower family. Tommy, Harry's oldest brother, ran the family's herd at Alaqtaq, seventy miles east of Barrow. Brower's diary indicates that he obtained reindeer in 1904 from the United States Bureau of Education as payment for taking care of the herds when they first arrived in Barrow. He was later informed that he could not keep the deer, because no money had been appropriated to take care of reindeer at Barrow. He ignored this:

> I allready [sic] had mine and had a bill of sale for them. Spriggs wanted me to return the deer, but I would not. I was the first white man to get hold of reindeer in Alaska. For a long time no white or half breed was allowed to even go as an apprentice on the deer. Today my boys own about a thousand, and if there had been good luck with them would have twice as many.[36]

In addition to Brower's reindeer herd, individual Iñupiat owned and cared for reindeer that they either earned through apprenticeship or purchased. The Barrow herd was managed by the schoolteachers as representatives of the United States government. By the 1920s, herds were consolidated under single corporate management. Individuals received shares based on the number of reindeer they had owned in the previous Barrow herd. A single Iñupiat manager was now in charge of the company herd.[37]

Reindeer herding on the North Slope was short lived; most of the herds were gone by 1952. Herding eventually failed because the reindeer ran off with the wild caribou, wolf predation increased, and more lucrative job opportunities enticed herders back to town. Furthermore, moving around the countryside with the herd for long periods of time was incompatible with whaling and the need for families to be close to a school and hospital.[38]

With fewer than fifty non-Natives in the entire northern region of Alaska in the early 1900s—a few traders, a couple of missionaries, some teachers, doctors, and nurses—traveling seventy-five miles by dog team in blowing snow and freezing weather to visit a friend in another village was not unusual. With his father as the center of this web, Harry Brower became accustomed to a steady stream of non-Natives and travelers around the house and store.

ॐ

By the 1920s and 1930s there was more and more mixing of Iñupiaq and non-Native materials, attitudes, and norms.[39] The newcomers shifted the focus of Barrow life. They taught the children to speak English. They emphasized Christianity and cleanliness. They brought silverware, china, and fine clothes with them from home. They had parties and social gatherings that included only non-Natives; they ate cake and other fancy foods; they played cards, darts or pool; and they listened to music on phonographs. This active social circle kept non-Natives entertained during the long, dark winters. While inter-marriage between Iñupiat women and non-Native men occurred, there was little socializing between the groups.[40] Those non-Natives who had not married into the community hired Iñupiat to sew, cook, clean, provide childcare, and to be guides when they went hunting or traveled to other villages by dog team. Some lifelong friendships were formed.

Life in Barrow was also becoming less of a hardship than when the commercial whalers arrived. There were wood-frame homes heated with coal and driftwood. There were luxuries from the Lower 48, such as fresh fruit, eggs, Christmas presents, and candy—although by midwinter the fresh goods delivered in the summer were all used up. While the community at large was beginning to feel the effect of this cultural mixing, the Brower household that Harry grew up in had long been a melting pot of its own.

Guests were welcomed and well provided for at the Brower home. Any explorer, trader, missionary, doctor, or scientist who passed through the Arctic from 1900 to 1945 was sure to stop at the Browers.' The famous Arctic explorer Vilhjalmur Stefansson was a frequent visitor and close friend.[41] Roald Amundsen, the first man to fly over the North Pole, and Knud Rasmussen who traveled by dogsled from Greenland to Alaska in 1924, both stopped at Charles Brower's home.[42] In 1935, Will Rogers and Wiley Post were on their way to meet Brower when their plane crashed twelve miles southwest of Barrow.

The influx of non-Natives after the turn of the century brought many changes to the Iñupiat: Western goods and services, medical care, religion, and education were introduced, but alcohol and illnesses such as influenza, measles, tuberculosis, and various sexually transmitted diseases were soon established as well.

Barrow in the 1920s. Left to right: hospital, manse, church. Presbytery of the Yukon Collection, Box 2, Album 1, Archives, University of Alaska Fairbanks.

A Period of Change

In the early days, the few Western-educated people in Barrow fulfilled multiple duties. L. M. Stevenson arrived in Barrow in 1890 as the community's first Presbyterian missionary and also taught school. Classes were held at Brower's whaling station until the first school and mission house were built in 1894. H. Richmond Marsh arrived in Barrow in 1896 to replace Stevenson and, since he was a former medical student, he also accepted the task of ministering to the community's medical needs. Marsh is remembered by the Iñupiat because he translated hymns and preached in Iñupiaq.

There have been many ministers heading the Utqiaġvik Presbyterian Church, but a handful stand out because of the key roles they played and because they are fondly remembered by the Iñupiat of today. Dr. Henry W. Greist and his wife, Mollie, who lived in Barrow from 1921 to 1936, are two of the best known.[43] He was both the minister and the doctor and she was the head nurse at the hospital. They were active in the community and developed close friendships with many Iñupiat families. Besides serving Barrow, Dr. Greist also frequently traveled to Wainwright by dog team with an Iñupiaq guide to provide medical and spiritual services and went to Nuvuk at Point Barrow every Sunday to perform church services there. Mrs. Greist established the Mothers Club in 1921 to teach Iñupiat women what she considered to be better and more sanitary methods of housekeeping and childcare.[44] As familiar fixtures around the Brower household, the Greists were a significant Christian influence on Harry during his formative years.

Reverend Fred Klerekoper, the Presbyterian minister from 1937 to 1942, was another missionary who spent time at the Brower household. He is especially remembered for traveling by dogsled with Iñupiaq Reverend Roy Ahmaogak to Demarcation Point on the Canadian border in order to conduct a census of families living east of Barrow and to serve their medical and spiritual needs.[45] Reverend Bill Wartes, who served in Barrow from 1950 to 1958, was the first minister to fly the Presbyterian Church's airplane (Arctic Messenger) to the outlying communities of Wainwright, Kaktovik (Barter Island), and Anaktuvuk Pass. Reverend Wartes also designed and oversaw construction of the church building in Barrow that is still being used today. The Wartes family is fondly remembered in Barrow for how well they all integrated into the Iñupiat lifestyle (pers. comm., M. Wartes, 2009). Reverend John Chambers (1958–1965) continued to fly the Arctic Messenger around the North Slope and increased regular mission service to the outlying communities.[46]

The Utqiaġvik Presbyterian Church is not the only church in Barrow today, but it is the oldest. The Assembly of God, Catholic, Baptist, Mormon, and Baha'i churches all have strong congregations. The Iñupiat have taken a creative approach to Christianity and church is fundamental to their spiritual and social world. Some Iñupiat were ordained, and many more are deacons and active members of their various congregations. In 1934, Percy Ipalook was the first Iñupiaq to be ordained into the Presbyterian ministry. He was followed by Roy Ahmaogak in 1946, who, with linguist Donald Webster, translated the New Testament of the Bible into Iñupiaq. Published in 1966, this translation is still used and was the first concerted effort to write down the previously oral Iñupiaq

Utqiaġvik Presbyterian Church, Barrow, 1990s. Photo by Karen Brewster.

language into a standard form. Reverend Samuel Simmonds was ordained in 1961, was the Presbyterian minister in Wainwright from 1972 to 1988, and served as associate pastor in Barrow for many years.

By the 1920s, when Harry Brower was a boy, Western education was also a strong social force in Barrow. The first school was built in 1894, when the federal government took over education from the Presbyterian Church. The presence of a school attracted families living out on the land to move into town. Barrow's population began to grow. Teachers were recruited from the Home Board of Missions of the Presbyterian Church until the 1930s when the Bureau of Indian Affairs became responsible for Native education. Teachers added to the small cadre of non-Natives already living in Barrow, and brought with them more and more of the outside world's commodities, attitudes, value systems, and language. Children learned English and about the world away from Barrow. This created an ever-widening gap between them and their parents' generation with its tradition-based lifestyle.

As with the church, many of the teachers stayed for years, contributed to the community, and formed close friendships. Others did not. But there were also Iñupiat who became teachers and worked at the school, like Annie Kullaluk and Flossie Connery in the early 1900s, Fred Ipalook who taught from 1934 to 1969 despite only having finished the eighth grade, and baleen basket makers Marvin Peter and Qiŋaqtaq who taught arts and crafts in the 1930s and 1940s.

Harry Brower recalled how he liked Marvin and Qiŋaqtaq's classes because they were allowed to speak Iñupiaq there. School administrators required English-only education, because they believed in integrating Iñupiat children into a non-Native world. Teachers punished children for speaking Iñupiaq by slapping a ruler across their open palms, or making them stand in a corner facing the wall. Elder Rex Ahvakana used to tell a story about being suspended, because as student body president he was supposed to keep his fellow students from speaking Iñupiaq on the playground, and one day he did not.

During Harry Brower's boyhood, only the primary grades were available in Barrow. Many students, like Harry, did not even get that far, because family responsibilities, such as hunting, trapping, or caring for younger siblings, took priority. Those who wanted a higher level of education had to leave and attend school in places like Oregon, Kansas, or southeastern Alaska. This was a hardship on both the students and their families. The young people got homesick. They missed their Native foods and customs. Teenagers were gone during a vital stage in their cultural training. Many even forgot how to speak Iñupiaq.

In 1975, the Iñupiat established the North Slope Borough School District to oversee the future of their children's education. The following year, the state legislature required each village in rural Alaska to have a high school.[47] Finally, Iñupiat children could stay home. In 1990, Patsy Nusunginya Aamodt became the North Slope Borough School District's first and still only Iñupiaq superintendent.

Today each of the seven North Slope villages has a large, modern, state-of-the-art school. They have advanced computer facilities and video-conferencing for interactive delivery of classes. Ipalook Elementary in Barrow has an indoor jungle-gym playground, so the children can still exercise when it is twenty-five degrees below zero outside. The District's Bilingual Department has developed an Iñupiaq immersion curriculum for preschool through second grade to teach the children Iñupiaq. The staff and parents hope students will retain more of their Native language than previous generations who went through the Western educational system.

Effects of Disease and Alcohol

From 1851 to 1902, influenza and measles killed large numbers of Iñupiat,[48] and population decline across the North Slope from these epidemics resulted in demographic shifts and cultural change.[49] By the turn of the century, inland groups were moving to coastal towns like Barrow for job opportunities, to be close to medical care and the church, to have their children attend school, and for the reliable supply of food and trade items. Caribou, the major food source for the inland groups, were hard to find because of over-hunting and a natural low point in the caribou population cycle. Families were starving to death. On the coast, these inlanders were exposed to the new diseases. Many died and others carried the diseases inland when they returned home to trade or visit.

Disease spread into the far reaches of northern Alaska and reduced the entire region's population. The remaining small bands turned again to Barrow for conveniences, jobs, and medicine. Disease had left Barrow without able-bodied men and women to hunt, whale, and care for the children, elderly, and infirm, which made it easier for these newcomers to find a niche and become incorporated into the community. Barrow slowly grew into the region's hub.

Population decline from disease continued into the 1920s, when Presbyterian mission doctors arrived with better medical care and began to save lives. Barrow's first hospital was built in 1920 by the Board of Home Missions of the Presbyterian Church. In 1936, the church turned the hospital and medical care over to the Alaska Native Service, a division of the United States government. Under Public Health Service management, the hospital enjoyed more doctors and nurses than it had in the early days; however, services were still limited by Barrow's remote location and poor facilities.

Whalers and traders of the 1800s brought alcohol as well as disease to the Iñupiat. They traded liquor for baleen, ivory, and furs. The sailors taught the Iñupiat how to brew their own alcohol from sugar, flour, molasses, water, and raisins.[50] The introduction of alcohol disrupted people's lives. Over the course of the next hundred years it contributed to tragic stories of abuse, neglect, and death.

Just as in any community, the use of alcohol in Barrow covers a broad spectrum—not all Iñupiat have had drinking problems or have suffered under its painful shadow. It is important to recognize this world in which Harry Brower lived—a world with alcohol abuse, poverty, and violence; as well as joy, family togetherness, and hard work—and to understand the complex role of alcohol in shaping the community.

The Iñupiat are now emphasizing sobriety. There is a local Alcoholics Anonymous group, a substance-abuse treatment center, counseling groups, peer support to stay sober, and public education campaigns. In 1996, Barrow voted to become a "dry" community, making the possession and sale of alcohol illegal. The other seven villages on the North Slope were already dry. In October 1997,

Barrow voted to change its dry status to "damp," once again allowing importation
and possession, but not the sale, of alcohol.

The Modern World Arrives in Barrow

The first airplane landed in Barrow in the spring of 1926, flown from Fairbanks
by Carl Ben Eielson and scientist George Hubert Wilkins. They went on to
explore the Arctic and North Pole skies from 1927 to 1929, using Barrow
as their base of operations.[51] In 1931, Charles and Anne Morrow Lindbergh
stopped in Barrow on their historic over-the-pole flight from New York City
to the Orient.[52] The 1935 airplane crash that killed humorist Will Rogers and
pilot Wiley Post was the culminating event that introduced Barrow to the rest
of the world.

The dam of obscurity had been broken, and from this point forward there
was an increasing influx of outsiders and new technology into Barrow. This
brought new opportunities for wage employment.

In 1943, a coal mining operation was started near Meade River (Atqasuk)
about sixty miles south of Barrow. Not only did this provide jobs for the
Iñupiat, but offered a more reliable fuel source than the seal oil lamps,
driftwood, and oil-soaked sod that people had been using.[53] The hospital,
church, and school already used coal, delivered by ship every summer in 100-
pound sacks, along with the annual shipment of groceries and supplies. The
doctors, missionaries, and teachers did not share their limited supply with the
Iñupiat. They were afraid to run out in the middle of winter, since they did
not have other options to heat their homes and public facilities. The Iñupiat
did not have the financial means to pay for coal shipments of their own. But
Charles Brower did. He purchased his own coal supply from the Lower 48
to burn in his whaling station, store, and home. The local coal mine, which
operated until about 1960, finally gave people the opportunity to purchase coal
at a reasonable price.[54]

In 1944, the United States Navy began exploring for oil in the Naval
Petroleum Reserve Number 4 (NPR4) which encompassed 35,000 square
miles from the Arctic Ocean to the foothills of the Brooks Range and bordered
Barrow.[55] During WWII, the United States' demand for fuel increased and the
government saw the need to develop domestic oil holdings for fear of being cut
off by war. U.S. Navy Seabees landed barges at Barrow and built a large camp
of Quonset huts and a runway on the gravel spit four miles north of town. The
camp served as the base of operations for the nine-year PET4 oil exploration
program.[56] The camp and exploration program provided some minimal
employment for local residents. At first, the navy did not want to hire Iñupiat
because of their high rate of tuberculosis.[57] When it became obvious that the
navy needed Iñupiat expertise in arctic survival, they began to hire locally, but

only after individuals passed medical exams.[58] Eventually, Iñupiat joined field parties making topographic maps, surveying the geology, and drilling test wells. Harry Brower was one of these early navy employees to map the North Slope. The jobs and outside influences introduced by the navy pushed Barrow head-on into the modern world.

In 1947, the Arctic Research Laboratory (ARL) was added to the navy camp's operations and began to hire more and more Iñupiat. Iñupiat worked at the camp and the lab as laborers, equipment operators, carpenters, mechanics, field guides, housekeepers, kitchen helpers, and secretaries.[59] Harry Brower started at ARL as a carpenter, and later became a field assistant, guide, and scientific consultant.

In 1953, the oil program was shut down and the camp was used for the construction of the Distant Early Warning (DEW–line) radar stations. This network of sites established across the Alaskan and Canadian Arctic during the tension-wrought days of the Cold War was designed to protect against Soviet missile attacks. Buildings were constructed in Barrow and dragged to their final locations around the north Alaska coastline, some as far as Cape Lisburne and Barter Island. Harry Brower and other Iñupiat helped build these pre-fabricated shacks on skids, called wannigans, and worked on the Cat trains—Caterpillar tractors hauling giant sleds—to move them to their remote sites. The lab, renamed the Naval Arctic Research Laboratory (NARL) in 1967, continued to use a small number of Quonset huts for offices, labs, and living quarters.

After the DEW–line operations ceased, NARL took over most of the navy's Barrow complex. This facility was a major player in arctic scientific research and in the lives of the Iñupiat of Barrow until its closure in 1980.[60] Individuals like Harry worked hard behind the scenes and were invaluable to NARL's scientific accomplishments. NARL provided a unique opportunity for scientists and Native people to work closely together and learn from each other.[61] Not only did NARL benefit Barrow by providing employment and a great influx of money and goods into the community, but the exposure to scientific research led to a continued interest in and appreciation for science.[62] Barrow's village corporation, Ukpeagvik Iñupiat Corporation (UIC), took over the facility in 1984, and has continued to promote and support arctic science at NARL. It also now contains a hotel, a restaurant, offices, laboratory space, a community college, and residential units.[63]

Natural gas was discovered near Barrow in 1949 during the navy's oil exploration efforts. This offered hope for an alternative and cheaper fuel source than coal and stove oil. The gas did not become available to private homes until 1964,[64] when Alaska's Senator Bartlett got Congress to approve the navy's sale of natural gas from the Naval Petroleum Reserve near Barrow, arguing that lack of access to the gas placed undue hardship upon the Native population.[65]

Throughout the years of government exploration and construction activities, many Iñupiat worked as guides and laborers. They also worked at the Federal Aviation Administration, the United States Weather Bureau, the post office, the school, and the hospital. This wage employment and its subsequent income led to the establishment of new services in Barrow—a bank, movie theater, coffee shop, and stores. Cash was also generated through the sale of local arts and crafts, such as woven baleen baskets, caribou-skin masks, dolls, and ivory carvings.[66]

The Iñupiat developed greater political experience as they became enmeshed in issues outside the boundaries of their own region. In 1961, Barrow Iñupiat joined together to oppose United States Fish and Wildlife Service seasonal restrictions on duck hunting by organizing what is now known as the "Duck In."[67] Most of Barrow's hunters appeared at the federal game warden's office with dead ducks in hand to be arrested for hunting violations. They were protesting the arrest of two Iñupiat subsistence hunters charged with hunting out of season. The Iñupiat continued to fight for subsistence rights, land claims, and political power in the 1960s and 1970s. The "Duck In" was a turning point for the community's effort to gain control over management of their own subsistence hunting and fishing, activities the Iñupiat believed they had the right to pursue and considered essential for their cultural and political self-determination. From these beginnings, subsistence has become an increasingly hot political issue throughout Alaska. The political savvy the Iñupiat developed in these first years benefited them later when they faced the political powerhouses of the state and federal governments in the land claims and whale quota conflicts.

In the mid-1960s, the Iñupiat began to push for control of land they believed generations of use gave them the right to have. The State of Alaska considered this land to be within its jurisdiction. The Iñupiat formed the Arctic Slope Native Association in 1966 to fight for and resolve these land claims. In 1968, oil was discovered at Prudhoe Bay, but before it could be developed the state was required to settle all outstanding Native land claims, including those of the Iñupiat. This led to a lengthy struggle involving Alaska's Natives, politicians, developers, and environmentalists. Much of the conflict was resolved when the United States Congress passed the Alaska Native Claims Settlement Act (ANCSA) in 1971 giving Alaska Natives control of $962.5 million and forty-four million acres of land. Native regional and village corporations were established to administer these resources.[68]

Arctic Slope Regional Corporation (ASRC) and UIC, Barrow's regional and village corporations, like any for-profit company, do business, make investments, and provide jobs and dividends to the shareholders of the North Slope. ASRC and UIC are two of the most prosperous Native corporations in Alaska. Local decision-makers setting up these corporations came to Harry Brower for advice on where to set the boundaries for their region, and he advised them based on his knowledge of Iñupiaq history and his experience mapping the North Slope.

In 1972, under the leadership of Eben Hopson, Sr., the North Slope Borough (NSB) was incorporated as a home-rule government. The borough encompasses 90,000 square miles between the Brooks Range and the Arctic Ocean, an area larger than Kansas. There are eight villages and nearly 7,500 residents within its boundaries, but no roads connect the communities.[69] With the Prudhoe Bay oil fields as a tax base and a $200 million annual budget, the North Slope Borough provides health, planning, education, housing, search and rescue, and municipal services to all its residents. The NSB is the largest employer on the North Slope today and greatly improved the standard of living and the lives of people in northern Alaska.[70]

The political prowess of the Iñupiat was put to the test in 1977. The International Whaling Commission (IWC), the political body responsible for oversight of the world's whale populations, was concerned about low bowhead population estimates and increased hunting pressure, and so concluded that the population was too small to withstand hunting. The Iñupiat were prohibited from whaling. They hired lawyers to fight on their behalf.[71] The North Slope Borough created a rigorous scientific program and the Department of Wildlife Management to count and study the whales. The Iñupiat aimed to prove to the IWC that the bowhead whale population was not in danger. Harry helped scientists measure the whales harvested and told them what he knew about whales, whale behavior, and whaling. Dr. Tom Albert, hired by the North Slope Borough to direct their whale research program, listened to Harry and designed the scientific research to answer many questions that arose from their discussions.[72] Harry rarely spoke of how much time he devoted to teaching scientists about bowhead whales, and how important this issue was to him. "They needed help and I helped them," Harry once explained to his son Eugene.[73]

The Iñupiat eventually won their right to hunt whales, but they had to abide by a quota system and a set of new hunting rules. For instance, to minimize loss of wounded animals, a float is attached when first striking a whale, before any explosive shots are fired. In the old days before these rules, a whale could be shot with a shoulder gun, then harpooned afterwards, or it could be killed with the shoulder gun alone.[74] The Alaska Eskimo Whaling Commission (AEWC) was established to self-manage and oversee this system.[75] In 1979, Barrow crews were only allowed a quota of two whales, but with years of persistence, they have gotten the quota increased. In 1998, Barrow's forty-seven crews were allowed to kill twenty-two whales.[76]

With the help of scientific evidence, the Iñupiat showed that there were more bowhead whales than the IWC thought and demonstrated how culturally important and nutritionally valuable whaling was to their lives.[77] Because of this effort and continued vigilance by Iñupiat and scientists, subsistence whaling continues today. Whaling gathers the people together in cooperation and celebration; it unifies and invigorates the community. It symbolizes what it means to be a modern Iñupiaq. Whaling made life worth living for *umialik* Harry Brower, Sr.

PART TWO

Conversations

3

"We Had Fun Anyway"

B orn in 1924, Harry Brower grew up during a period of increasing outside influences in Barrow. Living in a home of mixed white and Iñupiaq parentage and surrounded by relative wealth provided him opportunities and experiences different from those of his peers: he ate white people's food every day, and he learned to speak English before he attended school. He met explorers and adventurers who came to visit his famous father, and he had easy access to Western material goods, supplies, and food because of his father's trading post. His parents' leadership in the community placed Harry and his siblings in the center of much of the social and political activity of the village. Harry's family background and early home life were key influences on his personal development.

Charles Brower was born in New York City on March 6, 1863.[1] At age fourteen he signed on to a life at sea and never returned to live on the East Coast. In 1884, he joined the Pacific Steam Whaling Company out of San Francisco and went to Corwin Bluffs, east of Cape Lisburne, near Point Hope, Alaska, to develop coal fields to fuel the company's steamships.[2] In 1888, he married a Point Hope woman, Taktuk.[3] This union and the amount of time he spent hunting and traveling with the Iñupiat helped him become one of the first non-Native whalers to realize the potential of Iñupiaq methods of shore-based whaling for the commercial whaling industry.

After Taktuk died from measles in 1902,[4] Brower hired a young woman named Asiaŋŋataq to care for his four children: Bill, James, Flora, and Elizabeth. A few years later, Brower and Asiaŋŋataq married and had ten children of their own: Tommy (1904–1991), David (1907–1985), Jennie (1909–?) Robert (1912–1984), Maria (b. 1914), Sadie (1916–2004), Kate (1919–2003), Arnold (b. 1922), Harry (1924–1992) and Mary (1929–2003). Brower sent the children from his first marriage to the Lower 48 and they never returned to Barrow. When Asiaŋŋataq married Brower, she already had a daughter, Dora. In 1929, Dora and her husband Tony Edwardsen both died of illness, leaving behind two small children, Charlie and Eddie Edwardsen, whom Charles Brower and Asiaŋŋataq took into their home and raised alongside their own children.

(Opposite) Harry Brower and his younger sister, Mary, circa 1938. Father Bernard Hubbard Collection, acc. no. PB-38-78, Santa Clara University Archives.

Harry Brower and his brothers and sisters, circa 1960. Back, left to right: Sadie Neakok, Mary Adams, David Brower, Harry Brower, Robert Brower. Front, left to right: Kate Sakeagak, Thomas Brower, Arnold Brower, Maria Ahgeak. Courtesy Eugene Brower.

Charles Brower, called "Saali" by the Iñupiat, was a charismatic man who could draw a crowd with tales of his arctic adventures. He was a member of the New York City–based Explorers Club and was a popular speaker whenever he traveled; his self-proclaimed titles "King of the Arctic" and "the North-ernmost American" made him well known outside the Arctic. Brower also left a permanent legacy in modern Barrow—many of his children have been important players in various aspects of the community's history. Harry became a hunter, whaler, and scientific consultant. Sadie was the magistrate, Tommy headed up the reindeer herding business, David ran the Cape Smythe Whaling and Trading Company store, and Arnold served as president of Ukpeagvik Iñupiat Corporation. The family remains prominent in both local politics and whaling.

Asiaŋŋataq was well known in her own right. She arrived in Barrow as a baby in the 1870s. Her mother, Kupaaq, was from Shishmaref, a coastal village near Nome. Her father, Aluiqsi, was originally from King Island, an island in the Bering Strait just off the coast from Nome. Hearing of better hunting around the Barrow area, Asiaŋŋataq's parents and their three sons started migrating north. Over the course of several years, they traveled and camped, their movements guided by the seasons and the hunting. They walked through the mountain passes of the Brooks Range; they floated down the Colville River to the Arctic Ocean. After a summer trade fair at Niġliq at the mouth of the

Charles Brower's Cape Smythe Whaling and Trading Post where Harry grew up. Floyd Akin Collection, acc. no. 78-133-78, Archives, University of Alaska Fairbanks.

Colville River they headed west to Barrow.[5] Asiaŋŋataq was born at a camp en route, and her mother died just after childbirth. Asiaŋŋataq's older brother, Roy Ugiaġnaq, carried her the rest of the way and raised her.[6]

Asiaŋŋataq kept her family clothed in warm parkas and mukluks (*kamiit* in Iñupiaq), and she hunted ducks and caribou to help feed them. She taught her daughters how to sew, how to process animals, and how to raise a family. With the help of her brothers she taught her sons Iñupiaq hunting, whaling, and survival skills. She taught all of her children the important Iñupiat values of sharing, generosity, humility, caring for others, respect, and hard work. Asiaŋŋataq shared food and supplies from her own household and from her husband's store with the poor and elderly. Sadie Neakok called her mother "Barrow's first welfare worker."[7] She took her children with her on her regular visits around Barrow where they ate Iñupiaq food, listened to Iñupiaq stories, and witnessed their mother's kind-heartedness.

The Browers lived in a large white wood-frame house on the bluff, a few hundred yards away from the store. The only other buildings nearby were the store's warehouses and a smattering of homes belonging to Brower's employees. The traditional sod houses and newer frame houses of the Iñupiat were concentrated a mile farther south on the other side of a lagoon. A small creek draining the lagoon to the ocean separated the two sections of town.

Charles Brower's household had comforts of the Lower 48 and was in keeping with his East Coast tastes; he had the financial means to keep it that way—he even had a pool table and an extensive library. Many Iñupiat homes at the time had few basic necessities, let alone such luxuries as found in the Brower home. For instance, Brower heated his house and store with coal, and served Western foods like canned goods, eggs, and fresh fruit. In the mid-1990s, Iñupiat elder Rex Ahvakana recalled that he learned to eat bananas and oranges at the Brower house. He watched the Brower kids and learned that he was supposed to peel these strange fruits first before biting into them. This material difference alone was enough to set the Brower children apart from their Iñupiat neighbors.

Charles Brower ran a tight ship when it came to raising his family. The children were required to do chores and were punished with a whip if their father felt it was necessary. They sat at the large dining room table with their father every evening and ate white people's food prepared by Brower's cook, Fred Hopson.[8]

Charles Brower emphasized education. He tried sending his daughters, Jennie and Sadie, to school in San Francisco, but Sadie soon grew too homesick for Barrow and did not complete her education.[9] The older sons, Tom, David, and Robert also spent some time in the Lower 48, but all returned to Barrow without finishing high school.[10] Harry attended school in Barrow through the fifth grade, but the quality of his education is questionable.[11]

Harry was drawn to the tundra and the ocean rather than to books. He followed his uncles when they went whaling, caribou hunting, seal hunting, and trapping. He followed his older brothers, Tommy and Robert, when they herded reindeer at Half Moon Three (the name of the family's house and herd headquarters at Alaqtaq). By the time he was a teenager, he was whaling and hunting on his own or with his brothers and brothers-in-law. Harry was on his way to becoming an accomplished whaler and hunter.

ॐ

On his own, Harry did not talk much about his childhood. Was it not important to him? Did he think that nobody would find it interesting? Or was it too personal to share with someone he did not know well? He was used to telling stories to strangers about his whaling and hunting adventures, or sharing what he knew about animals. He had told these stories so many times it was as if they were rehearsed. This was not the case with memories and experiences from the less public parts of his life.

I had read the life history of Harry's sister, Sadie Neakok, and Charles Brower's book *Fifty Years Below Zero*, so I had a sense of Barrow's history and of life in the Brower family.[12] Sadie's stories provide a glimpse into the household and what it was like growing up both white and Iñupiaq. But not everyone sees and experiences things the same way. I wondered what it was like for Harry, who was a boy and eight years younger than Sadie.

So I began to ask questions: "What was it like living in a household with that many people? Did you all get along?" "How did your father raise you?" "What was life like when you were a kid?" Sometimes, Harry would tell me a story from his early days without prompting, as for example when his memory was sparked by seeing his grandson act just as he had when he was a boy. Over the course of many conversations, Harry told me stories about the Brower household and about life in general during his youth.

There were fourteen of us from Dad's wives.[13] There were nine of us from my mom.[14] My dad didn't spoil any of us. He was mean. He would always have a whip hanging around by the door. He would put you across his leg. That's it. Spank you with it in the butts. But I found out that if I took my aunt along with me when I went home, then once she walked in, my father wouldn't even look at her. And I could walk in, go upstairs, get in bed, and I'd be safe. My mom, she didn't say nothing about the spankings. But my aunt, that's the mean lady. She was my uncle Ahsoak's wife. My dad was afraid of her. Once she walked in with me, he would just look at her and say to just bring him his cards. She would never say nothing, but would sit right beside him until I goes up to bed. Just my aunt does that to me.

But my father he raised all of us the same. We had to be home at eight o'clock every evening when we were boys. That's the worst part of it. Even in the summertime. He would just use the whip if we were late. He never got mad at us the rest of the time, just once we were late that's all.

We wanted to play outdoors, too. All these other kids started playing out all summer. And even in nice weather, here we had to be home. We had to be home at the same time all year around. It was his own way.

༄

Harry often mentioned how he had to eat white people's food, and as with any child, there were things he did not like. You can hear the pain in his voice as he describes having to eat sauerkraut, still one of his least favorite foods as an adult.

No matter if it takes us about two hours to finish the plate, we had to finish up all of what he gave us. But in those early days, they had some of these sauerkrauts and everything that we never grew up with. All the time Dad gave us those sauerkrauts he'd sit at the end of the table until all of the plates were empty. He never said nothing on that. Once he start giving it to us, he'd give us all the same amount and then we'd have to sit there until he finished serving to the last plate. We'd just wait for the last plate he put in there and then we'd have to start eating at the same time. And then that sauerkraut would always hit me! Sometimes it took me a long time to swallow sauerkraut. At supper time, that's the hardest part. He gave us this just at supper time.

We ate Iñupiaq food, too. My dad ate some frozen meat, frozen whale, frozen fish, but he didn't take too much of that seal oil, though. He could take a little at a time. We kids ate it every day, but at lunch. He had his lunch at the store. We had to bring him the lunch down to the store, so he wouldn't have to come home and then go back down to the store again. Supper time, that's the time he came home. Mom would be there, too. Sometimes she'd be eating on the floor with her friends and we'd be with Dad at the table. Well, he didn't mind. He just liked his old friends to enjoy their meal on the floor, too.

He called two of these old ladies his sweethearts, so when they came over he had to give them Masterpiece chewing tobacco. That's the kind they liked. They would get frozen food, whatever they wanted, and they would just sit on the floor and eat, and we'd be eating on the table. That's what made it better, I think, for him. We couldn't go on the floor at supper time, but Mom could enjoy herself with her friends.

Charles D. Brower, circa 1938. Father Bernard Hubbard Collection, acc. no. WRT-38-18, Santa Clara University Archives.

But, most of all, on Sundays we had a house full of old, old people who'd come up. On Sunday the biggest part was for us to do all the dishes. It was just a big room full of meat on the floor. There would be a great big people all around on the floor with all the feast and all kinds of frozen meat around them, and these old timers would be laughing and talking and telling stories all in Iñupiaq. But my dad, he could understand them, anyway. That's the way he enjoyed his friends.

Sometimes Dad and his other white friends would have a drink. A few bottles. That old man Fred Hopson...we used to have fun with him when he'd get drunk...he kept maybe six or seven cigars in his pocket. He smoked nothing but cigars. We'd pull all his old cigars out, and then break 'em up. He didn't know nothing about it. Even though he came up to it [realized what happened], he never asked us who got the cigars. You sure can break them up!

But Fred Hopson, he was a good cook though. Boy, he cooked all that meal for all these guys at Christmas time. And then we'd go to the big store, that big Cape Smythe store, and they had all these tables all over. And we'd be eating down there. All these people from the Barrow side of town goes over there at Christmas time and have a great big supper. We'd have fun. All of us kids like Barrow Morgan, Beverly Morgan [the children of Beverly and Sergeant Stanley Morgan, the Signal Corps radio operator], David Greist [the son of minister and physician Henry Greist and his wife, Mollie]. And then all these others like Charmaigne and Cleo Morris [the children of Oliver Morris, a trader at Cape Halkett].[15] When they were around here, Morris and his wife and three kids lived at what's now my sister, Sadie Neakok's, house. That was their grocery store.

And all that time we used to have fun. When these old folks started playing pool all us kids we'd just go in the other room and start fighting and playing with all the toys. Fight a little bit over one toy. But we had fun anyway in those early days.

Dad had other white friends over, too. They had some parties, but we never joined them, because we don't fool around with those adults. They played by themselves over there. We were always home. We had to be home, that's all. They played pool 'til eleven o'clock or ten o'clock. And the losers had to take a snack around. They divided into two parts; they had partners. And they had a little game board up that they marked every game they won on. And then these guys that lost, before the next pool game was over, they had to bring in some snacks from the loser's wives. And then, if these other guys lost they had to do the same. But, they always have lots of leftovers, cake, pies.

By the time when they were ready to go home we had to harness up some dogs and take 'em home. If my father was out on the other side of town, the Barrow side,

Asiaŋŋataq, circa 1938. Father Bernard Hubbard Collection, acc. no. PB-28-118, Santa Clara University Archives.

Harry's older brothers, David, left, and Robert sitting around the stove at their father's store, circa 1930. Presbytery of the Yukon Collection, Box 2, Album 3, Archives, University of Alaska Fairbanks.

and we were on the Browerville side, we had to go get him with the dog team. He was too old to drive his own team, so we had to—me and Arnold, and Charlie Edwardsen once in awhile. Three of us just wanted to get out. It was a good excuse to go with a dog team. We had to go pick him up at a certain time. He could walk up to the store from the house, but not from where our house was up to the Barrow side. It was too far.

That was nice though. I think it was nice. Then it seemed like nobody scolded you.

౨

Coming from a small family, I wondered about living in a household with so many children. Was it possible for everyone to get along? I struggled with how to ask the question without sounding like I wanted to air the family's dirty laundry. I just wanted to know more about that part of Harry's life. Finally, after I knew that Harry trusted me I asked how he got along with his brothers and sisters.

My brother Arnold's next to me, about a year and a half or a couple years older. We played card tricks and everything, wrestling, fighting. We used to fight a lot just for the fun of it to see who's the strongest all the time. Sometimes I won. Sometimes he won. And then, my mother told us one time, she said, "You fellas have to go get some fish for a midnight snack." There were a whole bunch of people over there at her house that she wanted to feed. We were fighting, so we sat on the floor to do a hand-pull.16 You pull with your fingers to see who's gonna be pulled down and let go first. The loser was supposed to go get some fish from the little shack that was about twenty yards away from the house. He was going to have to go outside.

We sat on the floor and then we started it. Our uncle was watching us. He kept an eye on us. He put a eye on me, so while Arnold was trying to fix his finger to get ready, I pulled him up. I won. And, Arnold he says I cheated.

He said, "You cheat me!"

And my uncle said to Arnold, "Uh, oh. Well, he already pulled you. Time for you to go get some fish!" And after Arnold got some fish, then we started all over again.

My brother Tommy and his whole family never used to stay up here [at Barrow]. Most of the time they stayed at Half Moon Three.17 In summertime when they went out to get some groceries, that's the time they'd come up here. Sometimes in springtime Tommy would come up here for whaling, but he'd always go back. Tommy was already married when I was a boy. Mattie, his oldest daughter, and I are the same age.

Tommy and Robert were at the Half Moon Three most of the time when I was young. But when I got bigger then nobody could stop me. I had my own five dogs. I would go up there to Half Moon Three with my five dogs. I was about eleven or twelve. But when I'm ready, nobody could stop me when I wanted to see my cousin, Mattie. If I wanted to see Mattie, that's it, I had to go. I just asked my dad.

I said, "Dad, where's your keys? For the store. For all the warehouses."

And he said, "They're down there in my pocket." I picked them up, he looked at me for a while and said, "Where you going?"

"I'm going up to Half Moon Three to go see Mattie."

"OK. But be sure to take enough food along," he said. That's all he always said.

Then I would go to the warehouses and pick up what I needed. Sometimes I'd get ourselves cigarettes! A little bit of those cigarettes to take up there, for us to have a cigarette once in a while. Then, I'd go up there.

And when I was about nineteen, Mattie wanted to come for Christmas from Half Moon Three, but they didn't want to bring her here. I told my father if nobody wanted to bring Mattie here I'd go up there and get her.

He said, "Don't get lost."

I said, "I won't. I got a leader that never gets lost." I took off early in the morning, about seven, with five dogs. I didn't like to make a camp between here and there so that then I could make it up there in one day. I was up there about eleven o'clock.

Then we had everything ready and the next day we started heading back to Barrow again. And we made it just before midnight. My dad was just playing cards at the end of the table when we walked in.

Surprised, he said, "You came back already?" I said, "Yes, we're here!"

And, that was nice having Christmas with Mattie at home. My father was really happy. After New Year's was all over then I had to take her back.

ॐ

Charles Brower's four children from his union with Taktuk lived with his family in West Orange, New Jersey. His sister Jennie and her husband, Fred, eventually bought a ranch and moved to southern California. The Brower children went with them.[18] In his diary, Charles Brower mentions a visit to California in the summer of 1920: "I liked the ranch. My sister had bought some land several years before, and I had planned to buy some more. Jim now seemed contented and wanted to stay on the land, while Bill, my second son, was also here, having just finished some of his high school work."[19] Sadie Neakok also remembers visiting this farm with her father and seeing fruit trees for the first time.[20] By the time Kupaaq was a teenager, Aunt Jennie was quite elderly. He never met her.

My aunt Jennie, she wanted me to go down there to take care of her ranch while she was still living. She said she'd show me how, that she needed somebody to run the big ranch. But, my mother said no, so that's it. I was seventeen. Just the right age! Looking for trouble. It would've been fun. I would've seen that great big ranch anyway.

She got no kids, so when she died these other guys that stayed down there took the whole works. They divided it up.

I never met her, but I was the only one that she had in her will. See, I was supposed to go down there and my mother told me not to go and then maybe that's why she was gonna include me on her will, but I don't know. My name was in there, but not the others in my family. And all my brothers said, "How did you get the will?"
I said, "I don't know. The attorney sent it to me."

She left me only just a little money. If I'd gone out there I might have the whole big ranch to myself. I might have been a cowboy! I already got the hat. I wear it in summertime. When the cops are running around and I'm traveling around with my hat on they really look at me from their car. Me with that cowboy hat on!

༆

Iñupiaq children are given a lot of freedom beginning at an early age. They are encouraged to watch, listen, and try new things. They are allowed to make mistakes.[21] In Kupaaq's time, children were allowed to wander and explore where they wished, as long as it was safe. Kupaaq may have gone along whaling or shot his first seal when he was just seven or eight. They were also expected to contribute: to hunt, chop wood, collect water, feed the dog team, and care for younger siblings.

Along the way through our discussions, Kupaaq told me a few special memories of his boyhood world—visiting neighbors, the joy of a simple Christmas gift, going to school, unloading sacks of coal, raising polar bear cubs as pets, the fun he and his cousin had playing on the beach together, and collecting scientific specimens for his father. Considered together these vignettes paint a picture of the look, the feel, and the attitudes of this phase of Kupaaq's life.

We used to go in and out of Harry Riley's house anyway when we were young boys. He was a tannik [white person]. I guess he worked for my father. They used to have their own house right close to our house. His wife used to make all these popcorn balls and all that. She always teased me a lot, though, because I was named after her husband. That's why they wouldn't scold me. So, back and forth, back and forth, I went. It was not too far from our house, about fifteen or twenty yards, maybe. We had fun anyway.

At Christmas time when you had a Christmas present of one ball, you were lucky! Any kind of ball, a small one or a big one, it didn't matter. Got it from the church. I don't know it must be from the Red Cross or something, or whoever sent some things from down in the states. The church gave to everybody; the whole family had their presents over there. That was a noisy place. After the feast they started giving all the presents out. Once you had yours, you could help pass 'em out yourself, as long as you didn't break 'em.

Before they started adding anything on to the church, it was getting too small for everyone to gather in. So, they started doing that gift exchange at home because they didn't have enough room at the church. There was no Assembly of God Church yet, just the one [Presbyterian] church. With all that food that they brought in the church, and all those people coming in, there would be just a little space left. They had these two balconies up on the ends, but not enough room yet! At Christmas and Thanksgiving they took all the chairs out to try to make a bigger room. They'd sit on the floor.

We didn't have a school bus from Browerville to Barrow side. We used to run across in the morning. We'd go home for lunch, come back before one o'clock, go to school, and then at four o'clock we'd start running home again. And then, we made it home, played out a little bit before six, before supper time when we had to come inside. We'd have supper, do the dishes, do some work around the house, and if we finished the dishes before eight o'clock, we'd go out a little bit more. But, we had to be home by eight o'clock every evening. Winter or summertime, it didn't matter. Those were hard days when all these kids started playing out there all summer and here we were at home at eight o'clock, even when it was nice weather.

And then, when I started going with my uncle I had a chance to play outdoors all I want! Came home at eleven o'clock, ten o'clock and wouldn't get scolded. I stayed with my uncle Taalak. And sometimes I spent a summer with my other uncle

Ahsoak. Like when they were out camping down south along the coast. And they were looking, trying to collect some *ugruk* and seals to put away for the year. I'd be out there with them and they'd never say no to me. If I were to be out with my aunt my dad wouldn't say anything. If he said no, the aunt wouldn't be happy. She was good to me. She never scolded me.

After school we just played outdoors, even in this cold weather, with no moon and dark. We'd just go out there and have fun! We played any kind of game, like hide-and-seek. We got no TV, radio, nothing. Most of all we played, fighting around. We just fight. Girls and boys, it made no difference. Like Mildred Leavitt, Uiññiq, she and I used to fight going home for lunch. We lived at Browerville and we'd go home fighting and fighting. And then, we'd go back to school the same way. And when the bell rang we had to run and run! We were just fighting for fun, that's all. We didn't hurt nobody. It was just to see who was the strongest of all.

That old, first school we went to got a big tower on it, with the crow's nest way up high. We'd just climb up and then look out, look everything all over. There was nothing in there. The tower has these guy wires that went way up to the top there. We'd slide down those wires, and then we'd jump just before we hit that great big end of the cable. We landed on the ground. We'd do it winter or summer, it makes no difference. We were dumb guys like that, trying to hurt everybody. It was fun, but you had to be careful at the end of it on the bottom, so you don't hit the big end that was in the ground. And then they had these swings and a great big slide outside by the school. And, those two swings, I'd usually have fun with 'em. I don't know if they brought it all up on the ships or they built it here. It was all framed up with the wood.

And there was a windmill by the school that was for electricity. That was how it was when we were in school. But, when old Joe Sikvayugak was a regular janitor, old man Joe, he had to get that school warmed up before nine o'clock. I don't know what time he went there to get the stoves going. Sometimes he had to take some blubber along with him and put some coal in there. And when that stove started burning he'd put that blubber on top of the coal and get it going real hot. It was one of those cast iron stoves. And when that stove got real hot, red, that whole school house would get warmed up. It was a three rooms in it. But, he got all those stoves going.

The coal came through the ship from states in a sack with hundred pounds. When the ships came in we had to unload sacks of coals. Lots of sacks of coal for the hospital, manse, and then to the school.[22] That was just used for the government buildings those days. My father had his own coal that he bought from down states, too. Hundred sacks. In our house we used wood—driftwood—most of the time. In summertime they'd get lots of driftwood by boat from these barrier islands [along the north edge of Elson Lagoon]. We chopped it. In fall-time you had to cut all of 'em. Every day after school was over we came home and used that great big saw. All of us boys helped. We cut them up and stacked them up. Every Saturday we had to bring in a whole bunch of wood and put it right by the entrance to the store, so we can have all that wood ready for the stove.

We also had a coal bin. Each month we were trying to save some of those woods so in between we used coal. And on every end of the month, we had to fill those hundred pounds. Pulled it back from over in the warehouses to the house on a little sled. And dumped them all up in that coal bin. We got no choice. We had to do all the work. We were the only ones that did all the work anyway. We were trying to get strong.[23]

I had some polar bear cubs when we were living up there at Browerville. They were two little cubs that my brother Robert brought home when they shot the mother. They didn't know that she had cubs. He had them inside his pocket, tied a string around it so he wouldn't drop them. He kept them warm in there. And after he got them home, I had to feed those little cubs with a baby bottle, with evaporated milk. Carnation. And I raised them. I had 'em for three years. I played with them. That's how come the polar bears don't like to eat me.

When you're walking around in the tundra in summertime with the cubs, you could take a nap with each of them facing the opposite way next to you, right in front of you, right close to your body. The head of one of 'em goes this way, another head the other way. They watched the both directions. And when I woke up, when I started moving, they looked at me. If I sat down they sat; if I stood up, they stood up. Then, we'd start walking again. I was about eleven. They didn't go to school with me. I left them home. They stayed inside the house. My dad let them in the house, because he liked them, but they had their own place to sleep in. One time I had a little mouse, and I put it inside the house to see how the cubs would play with it. Those two polar bear cubs they played with that little mouse, but never killed it. They were gentle playing with it. So, I had to take the mouse out and let him go.

After three years, they started to grow too big. They took them down to San Francisco to the zoo on a ship. I had to take them to the ship. It wasn't sad for me, but it was sad for the polar bears. The polar bears didn't want to be in a cage. They had a cage ready on the ship for them. There were two doors on it, one on the close end and one on the far end that I could go out through. Once the cubs followed me in there they locked the first door and they opened the other door. I went out through it and they closed the door after me. A lot of noise they made. And that was the end of those two cubs. I missed them a lot.

꒔

Laughing nearly to tears, Kupaaq told me about playing on the beach one time with his cousin Mark Ahsoak, Sr. and finding a porpoise in the waves. In their eyes, it looked like a small whale.

Me and Mark were running around on the beach with no stockings. The water was rough. And then, there was something when the big water waves came up. We saw something splashing. So, we ran and ran and ran and finally after we got to the same spot where it was and that water went up again we saw it right there. We went over to it and tried to get hold of it, grabbed for the tail. And I throw that whale to the beach, on top of the gravel where there was no water. And Mark helped get it up there. And we laughed. We got a whale! It was about three feet long.

We were just about eight or nine, something like that. And we carried the "whale" home on our backs. We took it down to my father and we put it on the bench. We said, "Hey, Dad we got a whale right here!" He said, "What?" "We carried a whale home."

Well, it was fun anyway. But, my father had to save all the bones to make a skeleton to send out. He just cleaned the meat off, put salt on it, and sent it out. And there were some little bugs that cleaned up these bones better someplace down at a university.

꒔

Charles Brower had scientific collecting permits that allowed him to gather birds and eggs from the tundra every summer for museums in the Lower 48 seeking them for scientific study and permanent viewing in their collections. Brower sent his natural history and anthropological collections to the Denver Museum of Natural History, the California Academy of Sciences, the American Museum of Natural History in New York, and the Smithsonian Institution in Washington, D.C. Harry and other young men walked the country around Barrow gathering eggs from camouflaged nests nestled in the tundra grasses and tussocks, and taking birds of all sizes and species, like phalaropes, dowitchers, sandpipers, eider ducks, and loons. Harry honed his observation and navigation skills and expanded his understanding of the subtle details of his environment. He also learned how to prepare and preserve birds and eggs for scientific purposes.

My father used to get lots of permits for collecting eggs and all kinds of birds. But we were the ones that did all the work. We hunted them. That was the only time we could stay out after eight P.M., when we had some permits to look for all those eggs and birds. When you saw some bird that you'd never found before, then you had to keep an eye on it until you found the eggs. Sometimes you'd be out in the field for two days just watching that bird. And then you'd come home with all these birds that you'd collected. And then the next day you had to skin all the birds and blow the eggs. You'd put a little hole in the end [of the eggs], and there was a little metal thing that you used to blow it out, to blow all the insides out.

Boy, fresh eggs tasted good. We'd make egg sandwiches out of those fresh eggs from phalaropes, snowbirds [snow buntings], and little birds of all kinds. And you'd get some of those aaqhaalliqs [old squaw ducks], spectacled eiders, king eiders, jaegers, loons, and ukpiks [snowy owls].[24] You can find all kinds of birds. When you had lots of loon eggs that was nice. They're not like these geese [white fronted geese]. But, brants [black brant geese], their eggs are good.

They don't even look for eggs nowadays here. But at Point Hope they still go. They go for those green eggs [murre eggs on the cliffs of Cape Thompson].[25] They sent me a whole bunch of 'em one time that were already cooked. The shells were green, and they got these little spots all over. Each egg got its own color. Some of 'em are light, some of 'em are dark, some of 'em are brownish color. They're from kittiwakes. And down there on those cliffs they've got those puffins, the horned puffins whatever they call 'em, all kinds of auklets—they are the little ones—and murres. Once murres get mad, they can fight. They're saying, "Hey, you're taking my girlfriend from me!" and fight over that bird. If you pick them up while they're still fighting and put 'em inside your boat, they'll still fight. Once they bite, they won't let nothing go. That's how they are. They're good eating, too. But, they're tough.

I learned how to skin and stuff birds long time ago. My father used to do that. So, we used to be right beside him looking at him. Even though I'm out of the way, that's how I learned. But I just tried so many birds. You had to get those little downies when they were two days old. That was how the permits always went. The little downies when they were two days old, you killed that, skinned it, take the meat off. That's what we had to do and why I say we didn't stay home all the time. We stayed out in the field waiting for these birds.

We found their nests first and put a little marker in it. When the eggs started breaking up, well, that's the time we started taking care of 'em. And then after the last bird hatched out we'd get it, and then we'd get the mother. The mother had to go with 'em. All kinds of birds we took, even loons or big birds. It took us a long time in summertime. Took us a long time to find all those birds. Had to keep on walking and walking.

Then my dad sent those birds to museums.[26] There were a whole bunch of 'em down at Denver, that's what they always said. Maybe there are some in other places where they collected all these birds. Maybe where the permits came from?[27]

ॐ

While Harry assisted his Dad's scientific specimen collecting, his older brothers helped with some of their father's other ventures. Charles Brower was an entrepreneur, finding various ways to make a living in a place where there were few opportunities. During Harry's boyhood, the Cape Smythe Whaling and Trading Company and the Brower reindeer herd kept his father busy. Brower trained his son David to run the family business and eventually turned over complete control of the store and post office when he was too old to handle it all. Tommy, the oldest son, was in charge of the reindeer herding operation. Robert, the third oldest son, did some of the bird collecting and moved his young family out onto the land to help Tommy with the herd. By the time Harry was old enough to learn the family business, his father had already passed things along to his other sons.

After fur prices dropped during the Depression of the 1930s, reindeer herding grew into a significant part of the Brower empire. Brower's reindeer roamed the tundra around Alaqtaq, across Dease Inlet near Cape Simpson. Tommy Brower was in charge of the herd, but other family and community members helped. Harry was only an adolescent at the time, but drove his own dog team out there and helped watch the reindeer herd in solo four-hour shifts. I asked for details of how they herded, when they corralled the animals, if they harvested them for the meat, and just what it was like to be a reindeer herder.

There were reindeer herds around Barrow way ahead of us [in the early days of the Iñupiat reindeer industry, before the Brower boys became herders]. People like Herman Rexford, Arthur Neakok, they were the herders up here before us. Reindeer herding came from Laplanders. There were not too many people here anyway in those early days. They started it by giving each family one female reindeer. One guy would have a steer [bull] that they used for mating. This guy would get a share from the other people and that's how they started having all the reindeer herds up here. Every fall or every summer when they had to kill some reindeer, they had to get just the increase [they slaughtered the annual increase that resulted from breeding and kept the base herd size the same]. They had to kill one or two for the family.

And then in fall time, it was the same way when they were having a counting and corralling. Everybody went up to the corral. They had to kill some too for each house. Well, you had to save some for yourself to have some left to let the herd grow a little bit. They called it a company herd, all this that belonged to the people [this herd was jointly owned by people in Barrow, and was different from the Brower family herd]. It kept the people going. After the herd grew so much, then they butchered the whole bunch of 'em and started to sell some of the reindeer.

My dad bought some reindeer before they started coming up. And then these Laplanders brought them up here. The government brought up the whole bunch for the town. That's how it was. They drove them up here at the same time. And then after they got up here they took them [Dad's reindeer] out from these herds and separated them way up there.[28] The Wainwright herd had their own mark, so that they won't pass over to the Barrow herd. They had to keep them on their own side.

And to the east, on the other side of Cape Simpson, at Cape Halkett, there were families herding there, too, like Ittas and Leavitts. The whole bunch of 'em. There was a big place up there that had a big store. A tannik [white person], Oliver Morry, ran it.

ᴔ

We used to go up inland to the reindeer herds. All of us would always be up there. Eddie and Charlie Edwardsen, Arnold, me. My brother, David, was never in the herds. It was just my brother Robert, besides Tommy. We were on the herd all the time. Tommy was never out with the herd! He just stayed home. Tommy and his family got a big house up there at Half Moon Three. That's where they stayed. Not on the herd. We were the ones that stayed with the herd and took care of the herd. Every four hours we'd take turns, day and night, staying with the reindeer 'cause they saw some wolves.

We did have corrals made with ice blocks, but just in fall time when you marked up on the ears. You'd just cut the ears up on the fawns and all that so you knew which ones were yours. And then after that they were on the open space. And then you had to walk and walk and walk with 'em. We didn't use dog teams. No dogs, unless we had those sheep herd dogs that he ordered. You just got those sheep dogs and then you had to train 'em. But, after they were trained it was easier. Two sheep dogs could handle everything. And you were supposed to be one person out there for four hours watching two thousand heads of reindeer. But, those two dogs knew what to do just by whistle. But when you were out in the daylight, they just looked at you and you could use your hands or your arms and they knew what you were telling them. They could round up the herd in no time, round up the herd in a one big ball! And then they came back to you.[29]

With those husky dogs it's hard. They don't work like the sheep dogs. The sheep dogs they ordered from the states were much better, because they were trained for the sheep. But once you went out there on the reindeer, they were different than sheep. You had to train 'em up a little bit, but they knew what to do. It's just your signals that they had to learn. They just followed you, as long as they weren't looking the other way. When it stormed, when the wind was blowing, you had a little shelter from the wind by sitting on the ground inside some snow blocks that had

Harry with relatives, circa 1950. Back, left to right: *Nate Neakok, Harry Brower holding Edna Ahgeak MacLean, Sadie Neakok, Mary Adams. Front,* left to right: *Maria Ahgeak, Abe Simmonds Sr., Billy Neakok, Fredrick Quniaq Ahgeak. Flora Leavitt Collection, acc. no. FL015, Iñupiat History, Language and Culture Commission, Barrow, Alaska.*

one part open. It was just a shelter and then these two dogs would be right close to you on your legs, keeping you nice and warm. Four hours was a long time to sit out in the cold. And when you got cold you'd walk around out there.

I was twelve when I first helped with my dad's reindeer herds. It was hard labor. They also had those they call company herds, the ones that belonged to Barrow. And there was some at Wainwright. And there was some at Cape Halkett. And there were some they took from here way up to Canada. I don't know how those are doing up there.

Each resident earned their reindeer by working. They increased, kept on going, once you earned one female reindeer. Then it increased every year with a fawn. And that's why they had to find out if the ones they had were a male or a female. That's why they had to mark them up every year. If it was a male, then you didn't get much of an increase. But if you got a female fawn, then the next year that's gonna give you one more. In falltime, in the corral time, that's when you had to find out what kind of fawn you had.

From the two thousand heads we had to count the fawns first. But in springtime when they had fawns, we'd lose some of 'em too from the cold weather, or the wind blowing. When the snow is really blowing, it freezes up in no time. And then you had to pick up all the small calves that froze to death and skin 'em all up to save the pelt. In summertime you'd butcher two hundred fawns, and in falltime you had about one hundred adult reindeer that you had to slaughter. Then, you'd sell 'em.

It didn't last long when we took over, because there were too many caribou that started coming in. No matter how you tried to stop 'em you'd never get 'em out from the herd. Lotsa caribou started coming in and took over the whole thing: Wainwright, ours, company, and Cape Halkett. The reindeer just went. They took off, disappeared with the caribou and never came back. It stopped around early '40s, I think.30

There was a guy named Mr. [Jens] Forshaug, I think, that was trying to take over the Barrow herd.31 But it didn't work out, so Al Hopson ran the company herd for Barrow. After Al had 'em for awhile, then they had Joe Sikvayugak as their manager and they started having all that trouble.32 After Joe's term expired they had Al again. And ever since then, Al was running it for a long time. Then the reindeer mixed with the caribou and never came back.

ᴣᴖ

When Kupaaq was a boy, the annual supply and government ships came up every summer when the ice moved away from the shore to deliver people, mail, groceries, news, and medical care. Airplanes came and went, although not quite yet on a regular schedule. The United States Army Signal Corps' radio/telegraph station maintained contact with the rest of the world.33

The people of Barrow were beginning to learn more and more about the outside world, and those far from the Arctic were starting to be aware of the Iñupiat, too. Kupaaq's remembrances are only those of a child, but they still offer a glimpse of what life was like at the time. This was just the beginning of a prolonged period of social and cultural change with increased reliance upon Western technology and goods; faster connections to the outside from radio, TV, telephones; daily airplane flights and regular mail service; and stronger influence of non-Native ways.

When the first ship, the *Northland*, came up here we always had fun.34 They had this new movie. They showed it in church. Boy, you see it was really interesting though because we didn't see no movies. No nothing. Everybody old and young went. It was just a cartoon, I think, but that was the only thing we could see. There was no sound. Just moving around, you watch it, that's all.

After so many years passed by, three or fours years later, when the ship was coming back they took everybody that wanted to go down to the ship after church. We had a movie down there on the shadow [side] of the ship. It was better. It had sound. That was the only time that we started seeing the sound movie. I was about nine or ten, probably.

We had a good time. Everybody went I think. They started singing on top of the ship, and going home on the thirty-foot little boat of the Coast Guard ship, *Northland*!

Boy, they did all the work down there on the *Northland*. The dental, and all the x-rays inside the ship. Free! They had to take all the tonsils off. They took mine off, see.[35] They went south and between Barrow and Wainwright they took the tonsils off. And then when they reached Wainwright, they took the people off the ship that had their tonsils off. And when the Northstar [the BIA's supply ship] came up from the west, he loaded up all those people that were in Wainwright and took them back to Barrow.[36] And then he'd be wandering out past Barrow and come back. On his way to going to Wainwright he'd load up some more people and then take all of them down there. And then that *Northland* took these last ones back here himself. They just used to go back and forth around here in summertime doing medical and all that.

Reindeer herd in an ice block corral. Eva Alvey Richards Collection, acc. no. 78-14-439, Archives, University of Alaska Fairbanks.

There used to be lots of crying when they pulled out so many teeth. It hurt! They didn't use nothing. They just pulled 'em out.

The Signal Army Corps was here when we started growing up.[37] The first one was down on the beach. It was a long building, a great big building with no second story. That was a short wave radio that they had in there. And they'd fly up these little balloons [weather balloons]. The name of that weather man was MacGregor. He must be the weather man for them, I don't know. We never asked, but we were always welcome to go inside anytime. We'd always go watch him, mostly in summertime. He always welcomed us and always showed us how it traveled and all that. Just the kids anyway. Maybe he wanted to please us, that's why? Well, we got nothing to do anyway; no TV, no radios, no nothing.

And when Sergeant Morgan came up the Signal Corps took my uncle's house off and they put that new radio station up. They built a house right where my uncle Ahsoak was living, so they had to move his sod house away. They moved it on the other side of the church. They took it apart pieces by pieces and then they had to put them back again the way they looked like.

And after that, they built a wooden frame house on the side of the sod house, next to it. He lived in it after they moved all that sod house. Well, I don't know, they must have had some agreement that they had to wait for all the material to come in for the house before they could build it. It was way bigger than that sod house they had. The sod house it was low and it didn't take too much heat. But that new frame one was eight feet high, so it took more heat. They had a little cast iron stove. It burned anything. Blubber, wood, trash, anything that can burn.

ᣲ

August 15, 1935 is a day well known in Barrow history. It is the day that pioneering aviator Wiley Post and favorite American humorist Will Rogers left Fairbanks attempting one of the first flights to Barrow across the high mountains of the Brooks Range. They had plans to visit Charles Brower.[38] Caught in the dense coastal fog, typical of the Arctic in the summer, they landed about twelve miles southwest of Barrow at a lagoon called Ualiqpaa [Walakpa] to get their bearings. They never made it to Barrow. Their plane crashed into the lagoon upon takeoff.

Clair Okpeaha, an Iñupiaq man camping nearby with his family, witnessed the event and ran all the way to town to notify authorities. The first man he told was Charlie Brower. Barrow men removed the bodies from the wreckage, and Dr. Greist prepared them for burial and transport. Fairbanks pilot Joe Crosson flew up to retrieve the bodies; they were buried in the Lower 48.[39] News of this tragedy quickly spread across the globe from the small U.S. Army Signal Corps radio station in Barrow. All of a sudden, people heard of Barrow.

Harry Brower was eleven years old when this occurred. I was curious to see what he remembered.

In 1935 we were out playing around when Okpeaha came in. He came in to see my father. After that, then everybody start rushing, getting everything ready. And they said a plane crashed down by Walakpa. It was Will Rogers and Wiley Post. That was the time when Okpeaha had to come here running for help, to let everybody know. Sergeant Morgan sent the message out by radio, I think. And my brother, David, and Bill Solomon, and the others that went down there, had to take the bodies out from the airplane that crashed. I was too young. I wasn't thinking of going anyway.

And then in the next year. There was a little two-masted schooner that came up. And we went down there to Walakpa. Pretty near the whole village went, I think, with lots of boats—skin boats and wooden whale boats. And that was the wife of Wiley Post in the schooner. She came to have a memorial. And after that they built that monument which is there now.

↜

Kupaaq and I did not really talk much about people he had known or remembered from his youth, or who may have been prominent figures in town. But one person we did discuss was Marvin Saġvan Peter, who was born at Nuvuk and took pictures of Barrow in the 1940s, '50s and '60s. We talked about Marvin because I specifically asked Kupaaq about him. The Iñupiat History, Language and Culture Commission office where I worked had a collection of Marvin's photographs. I was doing research on Marvin, his photographic images, and their Iñupiaq perspective.[40]

Due to a childhood ailment, Marvin had difficulty walking and used crutches to get around.[41] Many Barrow people remember that Marvin wove exquisite baleen baskets and always had a camera around his neck. Kupaaq remembered Marvin teaching baleen basket making at the school.

In wintertime, Marvin worked at the school, like a janitor. And then he worked afternoons in school showing kids how to make baleen baskets. Not the boats, just the baskets. He was a young guy when we started growing up. Most of the time he worked at the school. He earned a little money anyway like that. And then he worked in the hospital once in awhile. He did what he could do.

He took all the pictures, too. Taking pictures, pictures every time. Before everybody had all these cameras he must be the one that had the camera. I never asked him

*Marvin Peter. Iñupiat History, Language
and Culture Commission photo collection,
Barrow, Alaska.*

what kind of camera he had, but it was one of those flat ones. I didn't see him with
that box camera. Those box cameras were small anyway in those early days.

He never showed us about taking pictures, just about the baskets. And he always
showed us something else, too. He talked to us, you know, about hunting and all
what he learned, what he knows. He used to be in school most of the time, like a
helper. We'd have a special room with him. Split the class half and half. He didn't
like to take this class with lots of students on it, so for the course he had just a few
of us there. After he showed us we'd go downstairs and they let the other ones go
up. The other half of the class did the schoolwork [while the one group was making
baskets, and then they switched]. Just like these guys going to basketball nowadays,
we did the same thing.

We had to go. We got no choice. But, it was fun. You can speak in Eskimo. In those
early days you were not allowed to speak Eskimo in the class. You'd get cornered
every time. You had to stay in the corner. Go get spanked for talking in Eskimo.
And nowadays, they want all the kids to talk in Eskimo. After they had 'em learn all
in English before. And I told 'em, I says: That's a big problem right now. In those
early days we talked in Eskimo. And then when we didn't talk our English words
and tried to talk in Eskimo we'd get cornered; we'd get spanked. And we'd get
anything. But nowadays, you fellas want all the kids to learn how to talk in Eskimo.
It's hard for them, because all these parents that were in school were taught how to
speak English not Iñupiaq. And that's why they teach their kids all in English and

not in Iñupiaq. Like when I talk to my grandson, Gregory, in Eskimo he doesn't understand.

Marvin was doing that teaching for a long time. From that old first school that we went to. And then, when Marvin was working on something else we had old man Qiŋaqtaq. All Qiŋaqtaq did is basket work, but Marvin was different. With him you had to do a little wood work, make little basket sleds about a foot long. You'd just follow what he drew on the paper. Most of all, that Qiŋaqtaq was the one that did most of the basket work.

Marvin, he just told us what he learned from when he was at the Point Barrow way back when he was a boy. Told us stories, I think, from before their father died. He was crippled. I think he was born like that, I don't know. Or I think he got rheumatism, something like that. Ever since I started seeing him he was like that. Sometimes he got worse.

He wasn't doing all the hunting himself anyway [because he could not get around by himself], but Marvin, he went all over. When they were walrus hunting he followed them. When boats went caribou hunting, he went with 'em to try to get a meat supply. He took his share. Once you follow, and then help a little bit, you get your share. Even though you don't shoot, you get your share just by helping.

But not on whaling. It's too rushed, too much work. It was too much for him. When they went out there they just had one set of dog team out there. Just to pull the boat and then to move to the top of the ice when it's breaking up. You had to pull the sled using your own manpower. And then when you're in a rush it's dangerous. You know how it is when they're in a rush. Nowadays, they got these skidoos they can haul everything out real fast. In those early days by walking that takes a long time. Anyway, when they catch a whale they don't miss nobody; if there's a house with nobody who's out there whaling, they get their share anyway. They don't miss nobody.[42]

Marvin did all his own film developing in his own house. Maybe somebody must have showed him how to do it anyway. Might be he learned from old man Dr. Greist, because he stayed with Dr. Greist once in awhile, too, while doing some work for Dr. Greist's wife. She used to collect birds. Marvin, he skinned some birds for her, too, and blow some eggs, those little eggs. He'd empty them. Mrs. Greist collected, but Dr. Greist never paid attention to those. She always had some permits for all kinds of birds. After we collected all the birds for Dad and he said that was enough of this kind and that kind, then we took them over to Mrs. Greist.

Marvin was a bachelor forever, but he used to do all the hunting for his family. Kept him alive anyway. He would get all that groceries and everything. Made money from school and from his little work that he'd been collecting. And then he used to order some groceries through the school. They let him do that. When the ship came up, after they unloaded everything, he'd get his orders in the school and take 'em home. That's how they treated him. Well, when somebody was good they treated him right in those early days. Not anymore, like this. Around here it's just out.

4

"I Walked That All Over"

H arry Brower began working at a young age, and quickly learned to be a
hard worker. He quit school when he was eleven. At twelve, he ran his own
dog team out to reindeer herding camp. His father sent him to Nuvuk (Point
Barrow) to shoot fresh ducks for soup for the men who helped unload the supply
ships in August. At fifteen, he ran one of his father's whaling crews. Iñupiaq
practices at the time dictated that boys learned to hunt and whale as early as
age seven, so Kupaaq's responsibilities were appropriate for his age. He was old
enough to hunt and do other work; he was no longer a boy who could just play
around. Also, he came from a family where hard work was emphasized.

He joined the Alaska Territorial Guard (ATG), when the Japanese bombed
Dutch Harbor and occupied the Aleutian Islands of Kiska and Attu in 1942. The
U.S. military worried about Alaska's vulnerability.[1] Governor Ernest Gruening
established the ATG, and in the spring of 1942 assigned Major Marvin Marston
to put together this local militia for the army and to recruit Natives to protect
the far reaches of the state. Local men were provided surplus Enfield rifles, wore
ATG patches on their parkas, and received training in marksmanship, marching,
and patrolling. In Barrow, Edward Hopson, Sr., who had been in the regular
army, returned to train his fellow Iñupiat for the ATG. Marston, nicknamed
"Muktuk" because of his taste for the Iñupiaq delicacy of bowhead whale skin
and blubber, oversaw the whole ATG and traveled throughout northern and
interior Alaska by dog team to supervise his troops. The ATG was disbanded in
1947 and absorbed into the Alaska National Guard.[2]

At age eighteen, Harry joined the U.S. Army, served from 1942 until
1944, and after his discharge continued in the Alaska National Guard for many
years. One particularly memorable story he told from this period of his life was
about how his National Guard unit was called to help with clean-up after the
1964 "Good Friday" earthquake.

On Pearl Harbor Day, December 7, 1991, I asked Kupaaq what he had
been doing on that same day fifty years earlier. This led to a discussion about
his years of military service.

"What was it like in the army?" I asked.

"Why, you want to go?" he teased back.

---

*(Opposite) Harry Brower and Kenneth Toovak receiving Sigma Xi awards for contributing to
arctic science, Fairbanks, 1988. Photo by Bill Hess.*

"No. I wanted to know what that part of your life was like," I explained, laughing at the idea of myself in the army.

I didn't go over there to Pearl Harbor. I was here. Everybody was scared. I was just getting ready for the ATG. They said they needed some guards around here, too. While we were working we were invited to the school by Mr. Morgan [Sergeant Stanley Morgan] and he gave us a word that we had to watch out from then on. We had to be on guard night and day.

This was before Pearl Harbor. And they said there were some Japanese planes someplace flying around. But, they weren't expecting Pearl Harbor anyway. They attacked that all of a sudden. That's where they started and then they went to Adak, Attu, down there on those islands in the Aleutian Chain.

We were guarding around here in Barrow. When Major Marston took over ATG he took from St. Lawrence Island all the way to here. They had local groups in each village. Women had to be on guard, too; when some hunting went on, the women took over for the men. This way the men could still go hunting when they needed to. They were on the shifts, four hours apart. The group was divided: some men on the end of town; some more on the other end. There were always two or three [men] out at the same time. When on guard you had to walk around, because once you just stand around, it gets too cold. Four hours, that's too long when the weather is too cold. But, towards the springtime it was a little bit better. And I don't know if the Japanese could make it up to here in the cold and the dark.

I went down to Nome in 1942 with the army. I was stationed there for two years with all these other soldiers from all over. We were way up on the mountain at Nome, fifteen miles from town. They had a big camp up there; 8,000 soldiers right there. We went all over. We went out there around the Little Diomede and Big Diomede Islands with a boat.

There were some other Iñupiat there, but they were from all over, like from St. Lawrence Island. I had one for a roommate from Gambell. And every time when he comes up here for whaling convention now [Alaska Eskimo Whaling Commission convention of whaling captains] I meet him and his friends and have them to my house. And there were soldiers at Nome not just from Alaska, there were some from Oklahoma, from California, from all over. They were all mixed up in there.

While we were there at the camp we just did whatever we were told. We even went fishing to get fish for the camp. We'd get lots of salmon when they started running on the river.

For training they'd shoot over you with the bullets with the lights on them. Once they took a shot from the gun there was a bright red bullet coming at you. Once you were on the ground you didn't want to put your head up, because they were shooting above you. This was in practice, but they used real bullets. These bullets got a green color and red color on them. You had to keep on moving, even though they just shoot them above you, see. You had to be trained up, had to learn that when they're shooting at you from another area that you shouldn't stick your head up or you might get shot.

I was in the army 'til '44, in Nome and with Russians. Most of the Russians came over on this side the time when those Japanese bombed Pearl Harbor.[3] We were on patrol sometimes. We had to go to Little Diomede and Big Diomede Island by plane or by boat. We just had to go see and keep on checking on how they were doing down there. With the boats.

"What was your rank while you were in the army?" I asked, looking for more detail.

I don't want to go into the rank! I forget all my serial numbers. But, I did see my major brother. I met my brother James, my brother from my father's first wife [Taktuk from Point Hope], right there. He didn't grow up with us. He was at Nome and I didn't know it. I hadn't met him before. But, the worst part of it was when I met him some of the other soldiers and I just had undershorts on and we were fighting inside our barracks. We were off duty and we'd put all the mattresses from the bed on the floor and were wrestling. Somehow he happened to find out from one of the officers that I was over there, and he stopped by and walked in the door. Here we were and the major walked in. What a funny looking bunch of soldiers we were! We all stood at attention. We had to.

Until he said, "At ease." He just asked, "Which one of you is Brower?"

A major asking you which one of you is Brower makes you jump, so I quickly said: "Here." Boy, after that I thought a little bit, I wondered, "What did I do?"

He started coming up towards me. I'd never seen him before. I'd heard about these two other brothers, but I didn't know how they look like. He had this major uniform on, come up to me, walking. When he was about two feet away from me, he grabbed me and said, "How's my little brother?"

I almost fainted, I think! Then I found out that he was James. And after that it was better; after you find out that you have a major brother. Well, the captains seemed to like me better. James was stationed at Nome, too. He came from down states someplace. Most of the time he was traveling around going every place.

Summer '41 to summer '42 I was at the ATG, and then, the National Guards for few months. Then to army in summertime '42 and was in Nome for two years. Then I got three discharge papers: one from the National Guards; one from ATG; and one from the army. I got a medal from the ATG for being a good guy!

The army was too much. I didn't like it. You couldn't go no place. You were always restricted on the one place. Only place to go was inside the camp. Outside the camp, at the end of the camp, there were only MPs. Good thing I didn't get sent out to fight, that's one big thing. They took some out from here, like Harold Kaveolook, Eddie Hopson, Eben Hopson, and Levi Greist.[4]

After the war was over, I went home. I had to go to my father. He wasn't feeling too good sometimes.

ᔆ

After WWII, wage employment increased in Barrow and money was now essential to provide for a family. One of the ways Harry earned money during this time was to work for the navy's oil exploration program. "I walked the whole North Slope," Kupaaq would proudly say. He knew that not many could make this claim. The mapping project that took him on this journey often came up in our conversations. It fascinated me and I wanted to know every detail.

Other people knew of Kupaaq's walking, as well; his family and friends explained that one of the reasons he knew so much about the North Slope was because he had walked it all.

Before I went to the army in '42, I was working. Working, working, working, all these things. I've worked with the Coast and Geodetic Survey. I've been all over. I've been with the Seabees [navy]. Kept on moving, come home once in a while for maybe two days. Walked across the North Slope on a survey with the Seabees; just for the maps. They were part of the navy. We went from up there at Demarcation Point [Canadian and U.S. border] to all the way down to Point Hope through the mountains. I walked with eleven guys. We did all that mapping. There was another bunch of guys that went up to Umiat and I stayed with them. We mapped things from Umiat. That was after.

And then, I got tired of being alone, so I got Ross Ahngasuk to come along. I asked the commander if I could have somebody from Barrow that I could talk to in Eskimo. And he said, "Whoever you want." So, I asked Ross if he wanted to go. And he always tells that story about the time when we were up there. We had lots of fun!

The navy was mapping, and looking for some oil, I think. It lasted for a while, in summertime. They didn't work in wintertime. In the winter I'd hunt, trap, and travel around. I think I was there three summers. Walking from Demarcation to Point Hope in the mountains was for two summers. And then going through Colville to Noatak was another two summers. We climbed up that Mt. Michelson. That's the highest mountain in the Brooks Range, nine thousand, seven hundred and some odd feet above the sea level.

And then we changed our commander. Commander Rex, that was our new commander. Bill Foran was our first commander.[5] That's when he started looking for the oil at Prudhoe Bay. He sneak on us. His son-in-law and him got the best part of that Prudhoe Bay; they discovered the oil after he worked for the navy.[6]

We started [the survey] from there on the mountains and we ended up at the Cape Lisburne, where the mountains come out to the ocean. There's a navy air force camp right there on top [of the bluff], towards the ocean. On the mountains there was a navy DEW–line with a tower in it with lights in it and a landing strip on the bottom. And then we went back, started on the hills again. And from there went to this side of Killik, big river. And then from there went through the Colville River all the way up to Noatak River. And then after you make it to Noatak, you go down the hills, follow one hill then another and then there's these U-shaped valleys and little rivers.

You were not following the river, but the land. They put it in a map, see, after we got through. That's how all these maps were made. The navy did it. I just went with them. There were eleven of us. We started from May 'til September. That's how much [long] for four years. And then on the fourth year we went through Hula Hula Pass, went up to Arctic Village, then went to Fort Yukon, and then we went to Fairbanks. And from Fairbanks we flew back to Barrow on Wien's [Wien Alaska Airlines].[7]

We walked all that with no dog teams, nothing. Had to carry hundred-pound pack on your back. Never changed. There was a tripod and then there was your stuff, your camping gear and all that. Carried some food, too. There were some times that they dropped food, but sometimes we didn't get all the food that was dropped, because all these brown bears and all the animals would get it. That's why I had a rifle. Me, I'm the only one with a rifle. Since I had the rifle, I had to shoot some caribou for food. And that's OK. Then I had to cook all the meat. Then, we had to throw some of it away and then carry some of what we could carry; not the rest, just part of it. Each of us had to carry so much, so many pounds.

There were no rifles. They sent the others on the crew just with a knife. That's all they carried was a knife. And then, we hit one brown bear. After we got all eleven of us in one place right there, we started walking and this brown bear from nowhere stood up right from the bushes. And this one guy got hold of his knife. He took his pack off and said, "All right, get all your knives out. So, if I get hold of him all of you guys better come over and snap him with the knives." I was next to him. That bear was maybe about as far as two feet away. He stood up and that guy took up everything, grabbed his knife, and he was just ready to get hold of him and the brown bear took off backwards. Away he went, he just took off. When you're not scared of them they don't fool around with you. And there's a lot of brown bears over there.

I wasn't supposed to shoot the bear. Those were the rules. Unless that one of us would get wounded, that's the only time I could shoot it. That was what we were supposed to do.

Then, when we went up to Umiat on those sandbars that was better. A small plane could land on those sandbars. They brought us food, and then some beer. As we hit Umiat we made a camp there and enjoyed ourselves for awhile. From Fairbanks that little navy plane would come up with a full load of hard kind liquor, whiskey. They also brought Bibles. Everybody got drunk and lay around on the gravel. After all that, we started walking again. Pep you up first with all these good stuff! And when we came back to Umiat the same thing happened.

Umiat, that's where they started making this landing field right there. They had all these planes. It was a great big camp that the navy started. We picked out the location right there, because they wanted to drill by that great big hill which they call Umiat.[8] There was a regular gas right there, underneath, but not oil. And on the other slope going up there was a seepage from there to the river, some kind of a crude oil. And from there, there was another oil that you could pick up with a cup and then pour it in a glass. It was a stove oil, that's what they said. So, they wanted to make a drill on that area. And after they drilled they just capped them, so later on they could be opened. They're still up there with a great big valve on it. That was way back in the early fifties or late fifties, something like that, after they got that landing strip and all the camp all fixed up.[9]

We started walking around before anything was built around here. And then we found that good place up there for a landing strip. Every time when they had this great big high tide [high water from spring breakup or run-off after a lot of rain] on that Colville River all the islands would be filled up [covered up by the water]; there would be no islands. All these animals that were around, they would start swimming, even all the eggs would be just floating around. It would happen once in a summer, just right after it breaks up. And then, there was one place by Umiat that was never covered up by the water; it was a little sandbar that goes up this way. So, that's where all that camp was built. It was a good place for a landing strip right there on the sandbar, so smooth, so straight.

There were always lots of moose right there. And, after the high tide would go down there was lots of those great big whitefish. You'd put a fish net out with a two by four and get lots of those whitefish. We did it once in a while. We just watched it first, because once you didn't watch it you'd get too many fish.

When I was on that survey, we'd be sitting around sometimes when we were having a break and we'd start fooling around. We'd make a campfire, but we had no tent, no nothing, no sleeping bags. You'd just lay down on top of the ground and sleep with all your clothes on.[10] And then wake up and just start going again, take off.

We didn't carry no tents, just the little mosquito screen, that's all. Once you started seeing the mosquitoes coming up you'd put those up and then let them pass by. Have you seen this stove oil soot coming out from a stove? That's how the mosquitoes came. All black! All the time they fly around it's just like a tornado, something like that. Once it started coming up to you, then you put that screen tent up, so they just gonna hit that tent, but not on your body. Mosquitoes don't bother you when you're traveling. But when we stopped and the ones that came up like that, that was the only time we had to put up those little screen tents, that's all.

To keep mosquitoes away, Iñupiat use a little wood fan that's all shaped up with a little handle on it. You use it right in front of your face. Lots of little bang, bang, bang, bang, bang, bang when you start hitting all these little mosquitoes right in front of you. And you've seen those little twigs, more like of a braided twigs. Whatever they call those green little ones that come in a little ball. They're lots of 'em up there on the tundra. It's braided, little, brown. They're not flowers. You get one of those and burn it. They don't burn, but they make a great big smelly smoke when you burn it and all these mosquitoes just keep away from you. They don't like smoke. It's called *piḷgaurat* [false heather, *Cassiope tetragona*]. I showed the navy how to work on those with it, because you burn those up and they just smoke. They're awful smelly, but awful good.

Those mosquitoes and little small bugs [no-see-ums or blackflies] that go inside your nose and mouth, that come out in the fall, don't bother me. Maybe because of the smell of me. We got all grass smell, I think. Three, four months we were walking without a bath. What a smelly guys! We never took baths in the rivers. We got no soap! The water alone wouldn't take care of all that dirt. All that stuff that was on us! But anyway, it was always nice to get in and stay in the water a little bit. And then when we hit Fairbanks we'd get clean.

On the job we had to go across all these rivers with floats. We had these instruments that weren't supposed to get wet. There was a little float to keep you, the transit, and all the other equipment up out of the water. You didn't walk across the deep parts, some of the rivers go up to maybe thirty, forty feet wide, even sixty feet wide and five fathoms deep. One fathom is six feet. There are some great big rivers up there that go from the other side [south side] of the mountains to this side [north side] of the mountains, like the Canning, the Colville, and the Hula Hula.

To get across the big rivers, we had a long string [rope] that we went along. One guy would swim with the rope around him first. Once he got across then he got all fixed up, so we could go across. We were holding the rope, so we could pull him out if something happened while he was swimming. The first guy went across along the rope, and then another one went across, and then another. And the last one untied the rope and then we'd pull him out. And I'm the one that didn't float. I needed two floats. I didn't hold too tight on that rope, because I wouldn't sink with these floats. You got a vest with a float on it. Once you got up to where you could hit the bottom, then you started walking and holding up most of the gear and all that. You'd get your pants all wet and you just wear 'em out of the water and they'd dry themself.

ॐ

I have suffered the weariness of hiking for hours on tundra. The ground is soft and wet. Every pull of your boot is accompanied by a loud slurp as the damp muck resists letting go. Energy is drained by the persistent effort to make progress. In some places, the tundra plants form a smooth cushion, in others it is an obstacle course of tussocks—small islands of matted plants, surrounded by standing melt-water. If stepped on in the middle, tussocks provide full support, but step the least bit off-center and the mound collapses. Twisted ankles and wet feet are par for the course. Walking around or over the tussocks means walking through water and stepping over mounds anywhere from six inches to two feet high.

I could not imagine how Harry and the other members of the survey party had the strength and stamina to walk over two hundred miles across the North Slope under these conditions.

"How many miles did you guys walk every day?" I asked.

You walked until your legs got tired! When you got tired that was the only time you'd lay down.

We were all working. We had these, what they call these sticks (stadia rods) that you stand up to get the elevation of the hills and the valley and all that. They had this one great big transit that they set up on the highest hill. One guy would be way, way over there on the highest hill and we would be all scattered, see, with these sticks with the numbers on there, showing one way to that guy over there that was taking all these pictures. The stick got this little lever on it that you used and then you'd see southwest, east, whatever that he had to write down on every book. And when he was done he took a shot with a flare, and all of us would start going one way to that one place where he was, and by the time when we got there he'd be way, way over on the other side again.[11]

But when you were left behind, no matter what, you had to catch up. When you were on the last pole everybody took off. And by the time when you got caught up with your friends they'd be sleeping. And then by the time when you started taking a nap it was almost time for them to have a breakfast or something. They'd take off and then you'd have to follow them again. That one guy does that and then we'd all take turns doing it. It was much better when we took turns, because after you'd done this, then you were free. There were eleven of 'em until you'd get the last turn again after all these other guys did it. Took us a long time to get around to your turn again.[12]

But, once you were on the middle part of the group you were lucky! You could do whatever you wanted to right in the middle of those eleven guys. All these others were all scattered out, and you were right close to the guy that was taking all these pictures with the transit. When you were right in the middle you weren't holding the pole or anything. You were just waiting for this guy at the transit. You'd just take a good rest, right there! Well, you were always the closest to the guy that was talking and taking all the pictures of what was which way, the west, southeast, that he started telling by this transit.

꒚

We were making maps and we happened to hit that amber.[13] I had a camera. I wanted to take a picture of it, but the navy guys I worked with said no. They took my camera out. We couldn't even take a chip out of it. It was a eight foot diameter and it got a brass plate on it.

Not realizing that there was amber on the North Slope, I asked, "Where did you find it?"

He just giggled and said, "It's a secret."

Other people don't know about it because they didn't travel like I did! Even Kaktovik, they couldn't know it because they never go up there. They don't go to the mountains that high, they just go to the first little mountains. Those little foothills, they call them mountains. And on the other side, there's a big valley. And when you goes in there you hit the real mountains right there. That amber was up in the valley. Nobody knows this, except me.

There were stones up there on the river in one place, so I just picked one up. I picked one that when you carry it, it won't get too heavy. I just took a small piece. And the biggest part I miss is those glass marbles up the river. Well, they looked like a diamond. Once you were way, way off when the sun went down over there and they were rolling in the water at the edge of the river, they made all kinds of sparks [sparkles, possibly quartz crystals]. Well, I picked one of 'em and I was carrying it and I told 'em, I said, "I'll get the big one when we pass by coming home." We never made it the same way! Heck! Some of 'em were big as your fingernails, all round. They looked like a glass, but they were all kind of a bluish inside. I don't know if they were rocks or glass or what.

That one I picked up, I lost it, because it took me all summer long to carry it in my pocket. I just had one pair of pants! Ah, so dirty! Had only one pair of pants from May 'til September. You didn't stop, kept on going and going and going, carrying stuff, making maps. They didn't want to make aerial photos so we had to walk. I did this [mapping survey] in '45, '46, after I got home from the Second World War.

ॐ

The Naval Arctic Research Laboratory (NARL) was a central feature in Harry's adult life. He was first hired as a carpenter, but scientists quickly realized that he held a great deal of knowledge about the animals and environment. In his twenty-five years at the lab, Harry joined many scientific projects and assisted numerous scientists. Many of these researchers still remember Harry for his arctic skills, his patience in sharing what he knew, and his sense of humor.

Also during his tenure at NARL, Harry worked in the field and on floating ice research stations (ARLIS I, ARLIS II, T-3, Fletcher Island). These were small groups of buildings placed on large, flat ice floes in the ocean pack-ice where researchers studied ice conditions and sea ice dynamics, among other things. Harry traveled on an ice breaker to and from these ice stations and through the pack ice into Canada. He also prepared all of the lab's bird specimens. There are still birds at the University of Alaska Museum in Fairbanks with Harry Brower's name and hand-written collection data on the original field tag.

As previously mentioned, Harry is most known for his help with bowhead whale studies and the North Slope Borough's whale research program. Even after he retired in 1979, Harry would periodically stop by the North Slope Borough Department of Wildlife Management to see what was happening and to share what he had seen recently.

Harry had a varied work history besides just working for the navy. He was a janitor at the hospital and school, and was a carpenter for the National Weather Service and the DEW–line. But his years at NARL stood out. This is what he talked about most.

*Naval Arctic Research Laboratory, Barrow, 1950s. James Ahyakak Collection, acc. no.
AHY085, Iñupiat History, Language and Culture Commission, Barrow, Alaska.*

I was working before the navy came up. There were thirty-six big ships that came
up here to build up that whole camp up there. Before the NARL was up here it was
just a navy camp. Nobody from here helped. It was just the navy itself who built up
that. That was in the early forties.[14]

Before I started working for the lab, I worked for the navy right after the war. Then
I worked on DEW–lines. See, after the buildings for the DEW–lines were built up
around here at the shop, they put them in the sled and they had a great long Cat train
to all these DEW–line sites. When they started hauling all these buildings on a sled
they were looking for a trail. They had to mark those trails with the flags a hundred
feet apart for the Cat train to follow. Once we had to make so many flags and then
fly them on the airplane and throw 'em up, throw 'em up, throw 'em up. Just marked
the trail, because the Cat train got everything else they needed in there with them.

There was a big navy camp up at Tupaaġruk for drilling for oil. We built up that
building up there and I went up there with a Cat train. I went as a carpenter. The
trail was already marked and everything. I also went up to Point Lay and worked
on a great big hangar. It was on the other side of the lagoon from Point Lay. It was
way up on the solid ground up there with a great big landing strip. One time one
airplane landed with one wheel. When he took off, one wheel just rolled off, but
he took off anyway. Coming back, he landed with one wheel. He got his wheels
up. They were ready for it, and when the plane stopped they had a big box for
the wing to land on top of. And after they got it all fixed up, they had this wing
so it wouldn't fall off. It was all blocked up, and then they started working on the
airplane, on the wheel.

I went up there to the NARL when they already had the all-metal houses [Quonset huts]. I started in '57 as a carpenter. After we were there for awhile, then they started building the new lab [completed in 1969]. I helped build all those wood buildings there. And then, I started going off and on, and off and on [back and forth between Barrow and being out in the field]. I went out on the icebreaker with John Beck. Then he went to work at the carpenter shop as a machinist. He worked with us for fifteen years, and then when he retired he went to Seattle.

While John [Beck] was up there, I had to be working with him, but we always had a little fight, John and I. We each wanted to run everything our own way. He couldn't run some of these people, because they didn't understand when he was talking to them in English. They were elderly people. I had to talk to them in Eskimo to let them understand what they had to do. If John was all by himself he'd just get real mad, 'cause they didn't understand him. Well, he was getting better and better, and then he just got tired and retired. I was running part of it and he was the head man, ordering all the things. He retired and I became the head man. I took over the shop. That was someplace in the '70s. Then the shop burned up.

They always come over and still ask me about when we built up the new lab. How we worked on it, what the inside was like, were there any fire stops and all that. The main office was right in the middle. It was where Max Brewer [former NARL director] and John Schindler [former NARL assistant director] had all their offices. All that north side was the labs. And on the farthest wing was where they had all the people living, the bedrooms. There were women on the ocean side, and men on the south side wing.

Sometimes when I was working with these scientists that are all over, walking with them for so many months, I couldn't remember their names. Sometimes they'd be

A building on a sled (wannigan) pulled by Cat trains to remote sites. Floyd Akin Collection, acc. no. 78-133-217, Archives, University of Alaska Fairbanks.

The new lab building Harry Brower helped build in the late 1960s. Photo by Karen Brewster.

"Eskimo's Outhouse" at an oil exploration field camp, circa 1950s. Floyd Akin Collection, acc. no. 78-133-215, Archives, University of Alaska Fairbanks.

mixed up. Sometimes there'd be one guy, or maybe fifteen of 'em and they go round, coming and going, coming and going, coming and going. When we were making all these maps it was the same group, but not these scientists. After that mapping, they were some guys looking for like flowers and all these animals that they could see or the birds nesting. That's what some of 'em did.

One time we were looking for where some of those shrikes nest. We followed the Colville River all the way down to the bend going down to Nuiqsut and we finally found them there. That's where they nest, up there. They were about twenty miles south of Umiat. We followed that river because we'd been seeing all these birds all over on that area. We'd been trying to locate where their nest was and then when we went way, way up there, just before it started going down on the bend, we started finding the nests.

Shrikes, they were in the willows. They eat meat, like lemmings. But they don't eat when the meat gets a little bit old. They like fresh, fresh meat. Once you shoot a caribou, they'll come up to you for the meat. They're about a foot big and their wings are spread about a foot and a half.

Falcons are all over on the bluffs, too. All kinds of 'em, like the ones they call peregrines. They're blue color. These little blue ones are the worst. They come up to you with their legs out. Gyrfalcons are another kind. They're kind of grayish color. They're all kinds of 'em on the Colville. So many of 'em. When they're sitting they're about three feet high. They're a big bird!

Some of the falcons get to be about two feet high, the tall falcons. And they start going down in size; the blue ones are the smallest ones. Boy, they really get mad in no time once you get closer to their nest, mostly when they got these young ones. When one or a couple of 'em are hatched already, boy, they go to you like this: they fly from the side with their legs out in front and then they go up to you! Then you just push them with a stick when that other guy is working on the little birds, the downies. You are trying to protect him from that big bird. We used to have fun! The scientist was tagging the young ones with a band that once the bird grows up there'll be a little space in there, so the band won't get tight on their feet. They had numbers on 'em. They measured the birds when they were full grown, I guess. But the birds, their legs won't get fat, not like these animals that have a collar on their neck. But, I don't know what the scientists did after we got through with the birds. I never stayed up there.[15]

かな

Dr. Max Brewer, who was scientific director of NARL from 1956 to 1972, initiated construction of remote field camps for scientists to use as bases for their research projects. This was safer and logistically easier than sending parties out to remote sites with tents and supplies, and it quickly and simply extended systematic scientific study beyond the boundaries of Barrow. One of these camps was at Peter's Lake [Lake Peters], a secluded spot high in the central Brooks Range.[16] Harry Brower helped to construct this camp in 1960 and spent other summers there assisting scientists.[17] Although Harry was out in the field with scientists a lot, he was particularly fond of Peter's Lake. He spoke of its beauty and the adventures he had there.

When I was working for the lab I was at Peter's Lake, too. Before they built up that Prudhoe Bay. Before they found oil up there in the early sixties, something like that, the oil companies had already started showing up. After we got it all built at Peter's Lake, then the oil companies started coming in. That's where I've been flying around with the chopper.

The navy first started the whole thing of oil exploration. When I was working up there mapping for the navy and at Peter's Lake, there was not even one road or not a one building at Prudhoe Bay. Then, the oil companies came along when I was at Peter's Lake. I met this young guy, Hendrickson was his name, who had a small chopper. It was his birthday present from his father. His father was running this whole company up there.[18] He was the only one young guy that was going with his father. He found me at Peter's Lake. He was flying around and landed there. We talked and then I asked him, "How far are you guys?" He said they weren't too far down.

I said, "There's nobody around here that takes care of me all summer long. No airplanes. Why don't you come and pick me on Sunday, so we can have a suppertime then?"

I was just getting everything ready and waiting for him, and here he showed up. We took off, left the camp, and I went down to the oil company camp and met his father. He said, "You two young guys you can do whatever you want to, but don't keep out of your jobs too long." He just told me to be sure to be careful. We had fun. Every day that young guy he came up to see me, and we'd fly around over the mountains looking for all kinds of little animals, just watching them. That was the first time I started flying around with the chopper. With that oil company at Peter's Lake when they started trying to locate some oil and they made a camp there near Prudhoe Bay. This guy he told me that his father said there was a great big oil right there. So, that's where they started looking.

On the bottom of the slope at Peter's Lake there's about nine buildings right there that I built. The lab, the kitchen, power house and a bunkhouse that about forty people can sleep in. And then there's the labs and all that; hundred and three labs, I think. These were for the scientists, the navy, or university, or whoever called himself a scientist. Some came from Japan, too. We had a nice place up there, a nice location.

I was up there all summer long with all these scientists for close to five, six years. Sometimes I'd come home when there was nobody to go up there. When there was somebody who came from States, from Canada, or anyplace, I had to be up there.

We got a great big Whitney engine up there for electricity in the light plant. I had to take care of them, everything, and sometimes, I cooked too. When there were some ladies around, I didn't cook.

The navy had their turn at Peter's Lake. Now they have it for a U.S. Fish and Wildlife [Service] cabins up there. The ones that use it are from Fairbanks, most of 'em.

I built it after I was married. I got married in '45 while I was still running around [in the field for the navy]. I took off after I just say, "I do." I fly away! I run away! Came home after three months. She just didn't want to lose me, I think, that's why she wanted to get married. I didn't stay home. I was twenty-two and Annie was one year younger than me. We had fun, but sometimes she'd get mad at me, because I never came home. I'd only come home after six months when I was out, out in the field. When I was out there I wouldn't come home all summer long from May 'til September. And then, from there I'd go to the icebreaker; go down south towards Nome on the *Staten Island* and *Burton Island*. Those were the two Coast Guard icebreakers. We were way up on the Canada with the icebreaker. They didn't stay up here all year around, just in summertime.

Being apart like that works when you're brave enough. Some of 'em get jealous when their husband's working over someplace. If there's a lady in there, working out in the field, the wife gets jealous of her. But me, I was working with all the navy; there were no women where we were. But, sometimes we could see one of our commander's girlfriends. He always took her out in the field when we were camping where there was a landing strip. And that's the only time we'd see a woman. Annie and I would have fun when I came home! Sometimes you'd come home only for one day, that's it, and the next day you'd be out.

I had to have that job. I was the one that was taking care of everything for my family. If I didn't go up there I was gonna lose my job. And I said, "Hard to find job in those early days." I got paid from the navy a lot of money! Sixty-two dollars a month in those early days, '46, '47. And then later on I started getting hundred and fifty a month. That was a great big money. Fifty cents an hour that was a big money! Sometimes got three dollars a day. And them guys around here called me a crazy guy. Eddie Hopson was the worst one who said I was working for the cheapest outfit, while they were getting paid so much more a month working construction when they had the Arctic Contractors here. They were getting over two thousand a month, while I was getting hundred and fifty a month. And I told Eddie, I said, "Well, we'll see later."

I always told Eddie when he started working on the big projects: "You'll be sorry one of these days when I start getting all these retirements."

I worked for the navy until I retired. And then, the reason why I worked is for that good retirement. So, I wouldn't have to think about work. Ah, if I wanted to sleep all day, all day, all day and never get up out of my bed then towards the end of the month the money would still start coming in. That's what's happening right now.

Well, I tried talking to some of the boys that I worked with that if they kept on going little bit farther, then when they stopped working their retirement would come in handy. They didn't believe me, except Arthur Neakok. For some reason he went along with me and now toward the end of the month he starts waiting for his retirement check.

After so many years the navy asked me if they could increase my retirement. They've been asking me for so many years, so after saying no, then I finally said yes! When I'm brave enough for the tax I say yes. My retirement is good. Before retirement, the navy helped me, too. When I first got the house I didn't pay the freight. I paid the Seattle price for the lumber and the navy brought it here. Free freight, that was pretty good.

I started working at the lab in 1957. I retired close to '79. I worked for the navy for twenty-one years, mostly at the lab, not including the times I've been on the icebreaker. But, anyway, when I retired they sent me from Kodiak a plaque with my name and navy symbol on it. They also gave me a pin that got a blue diamond for twenty-one years of service. It says University of Alaska, because the lab was under the university.

꜡

One of the things NARL was well known for locally was its Animal Research Facility (ARF), which had live wolves, marmots, wolverines, foxes, and even a polar bear or two in cages. It was like a small zoo and people from town often came out to watch the animals. Biologists, physiologists, and veterinarians observed, monitored, and studied the animals for such things as mating behavior, temperature regulation and hibernation, or diseases that might threaten humans.

For twenty years, Pete Sovalik cared for NARL's captive animals. Like Harry, he was an expert Iñupiaq naturalist whom scientists relied upon for input and advice about the animals of the Arctic.

Harry talked about helping Pete take care of the animals. He especially remembered the polar bears.

And then we had one polar bear at the NARL for eighteen years [his name was Irish]. When we first got it he was, oh, about a foot and a half long. It was a little baby one, maybe about seven months or so. We'd feed him any kind of meat and play with him every day, until he was way up to ten foot. That's how big he grew up to be. You could feed him from your hands, he was gentle. He didn't bite you. You could talk to him. He'd just sit there and listen to you talking, just like human beings. That's what I always say, anyway. But, he liked to play, even though he grew real big. Well, he was born playing with us, not all of us, but a few of us.

He was really scared with Pete Sovalik. I don't know why, because Pete was the one that worked on it most of the time; took care of him, went inside his cage and cleaned it up and fed him up. And most of the time I played with him, too. He wasn't scared of me, because he knew what I smelled like. The only thing that you had to take care of was your scent. If somebody else who he didn't know or like went on the wind side of him, then he'd start growling. He didn't like the smell of it. The scents are all different, I think.

When he got big they tranquilized him and then took him out hundred miles from here on the ice with a chopper and let him go.

One time they got a full grown female polar bear at NARL, too. Her name was Britt. Inside the cage we made a house with a grass in it and so it'd be dark, so she could stay in there. But, for some reason the scientists had a spy in there. They put a hole on that plywood roof so they could see inside. And from there they had got some kind of a scope in there that they watched the polar bears with to see how big their babies were going to be.

Female bears stay in the cave anyway when they have the pups. She doesn't go out for at least about three months. She takes care of the kids all by herself. She don't eat, no food, no nothing. That's a problem, but they survive. Once Jack Lentfer found this out when they found a polar bear with a little cubs on it, they'd been checking on it inside the house we made.[19] They had a vent that they could spy through. She never went out from that house for three months. She had two cubs, and then in springtime, something like March or April, then she took them out. She had the cubs like in January or February.

I don't know how long polar bears live.[20] Jack [Lentfer] never said anything about it. When I was working with him, he'd always take that little tooth which was just on the back of the bear's big tooth in front. He said you could find the age of the bear from that. The one at NARL was in a cage for eighteen years, and he might have lived longer after they flew him out back to the ice.

⠀⠀⠀⠀⠀⠀⠀⠀⠀⠀⠀⠀⠀⠀⠀⠀⠀⠀⠀ح

With the influx of more jobs, money, and people into Barrow in the 1950s and 1960s, there was a ready market for goods, supplies, and services. Residents had extra income to spend, which fostered the entrepreneurial spirit. Many private businesses popped up to fill the niche—Shontz's store opened, and a branch of the Miners and Trappers Bank was established. Teenagers sat around the counter at Al's Cafe munching burgers and pie. And there was the movie theater, something Barrow does not have today.

It was the 1950s. That big theater Steve Hopson had was not too far from the Native Store, it was just a few feet away. I don't know how come it broke. Nobody took good care of it, I think. But, Steve was going real good when he had it. I used to run that theater for him, for one year, while I was also working at the NARL. The movies came up on the mail. There were all kinds: war movies, gospel movies, or religious movies. Everybody in town would go in there.

When we were running that movie in one night we used to make a lot. We gave Steve and Terza [Steve's wife] the money while they were in Fairbanks. We sent them money pretty near every day. I was running it, and then I went to work at six o'clock in the morning at the lab. I worked 'til five o'clock, came home and took a nap in between five and seven, and started that movie again at seven o'clock. And then, quit about midnight. On Saturdays and Sundays I didn't work on that movie. It was fun.

There was a first and second show. After midnight they'd get these movies that there was nothing but elders, these old guys, who were watching them. And I used to laugh at them. Some of them, when the people in the movie were starting to take their clothes off, they covered their eyes. And they'd say, "What happened? What happened?" And then you'd see them watching it again. You see, they paid for it, but covered their eyes. Well, I don't know why. They were just serious, I think. So, anyway that makes it fun, I guess.

The bottom part of the building was a coffee shop, which Annie was taking care of. Both the theater and the coffee shop were really going full blast, and that was why she always got mad. We didn't get nothing. She said, "They didn't give us even a penny for working all that. All that work for nothing."

And then, one year they wanted to do the same thing and she said, "No!" After we tried it, it was too much work, especially with them kids along, too. It's fun though once you run it.

Harry and Annie Brower in Anaktuvuk Pass, circa 1960. Courtesy of Ronald Brower, Sr.

"No Rest for the Wicked"

K nowing family and nurturing kinship ties are key elements of Iñupiaq culture.[1] Iñupiat believe it is important to maintain familial relationships and readily do things to keep them up, like stating who they are related to when they introduce themselves, sharing food, visiting, hunting together, and caring for the infirm.

In April 1945, at the age of twenty-two, Harry Brower married Annie Hopson, the daughter of Steve and Eunice Hopson, whose Iñupiaq name was Qaġġun. Annie and Harry's first child, Eunice, was born in April 1946. It was the same year that Harry got his first whale as captain of his own crew. They soon had a household of other children: Eugene (b. 1948); Ronald (b. 1949); Charlie (b. 1951); Price (b. 1952); Dorothy (b. 1954); Harry Jr. (b. 1958); Teresa (b. 1960); and Vera (b. 1963). Harry's three oldest children spent their early years in a sod house at Iviksuk, a long-used fishing and camping spot on the Inaru River.[2] Harry and his brother, Arnold, ran their traplines from this spot. As the children grew, they helped feed the dog team, hauled water and ice, took care of their younger brothers and sisters, and traveled with Harry to learn to hunt, trap, and survive in the Arctic.

It was not easy to raise a large family in Barrow in the days of few jobs, low pay, and a heavy reliance on subsistence hunting. While working at NARL, Harry continued to hunt and whale, and also trapped foxes for extra income. Trapping was more or less lucrative every year, depending upon the fur market, until the late 1960s when the demand for fox fur decreased and prices plummeted. There was also the movie theatre Harry and Annie ran for her father. All of this kept him away from home and his family. As hunters, Iñupiat men had always been away from home for long periods. However, wage employment placed another demand on their limited time and kept them away that much more.

As if this was not enough, twice Harry had to take care of his family alone—once in the 1950s, when Annie was sent to Sitka for tuberculosis treatment, and once in the 1970s when she went to Greenland to study their educational and political system.

(Opposite) Brower Family, circa 1970. Back row, left to right: *Charlie, Eugene, Harry Sr., Price, Dorothy, Ronald, Annie, Johnny Nageak. Front row,* left to right: *Harry Jr., Vera, Teresa. Courtesy Eugene Brower.*

Annie died of cancer in 1984. She was well known across the North Slope and the state for her many years of service on the North Slope Borough School Board. She was also active in local political affairs and community events. She is remembered for her strength, determination, generosity, sense of humor, and fine sewing skills. John Schindler said, "With Annie it was a constant stream of jokes. Harry would just sit there and smile. You very seldom got words out of Harry when Annie was around."[3]

Providing for his family was important to Harry. He worked hard to raise his children well and to provide for them. When they were adults, he helped them in emergencies and readily shared his subsistence harvest. Harry's house and belongings continued to be the center of the family. Sons came over to borrow a drill or use the table saw, or ask for the big set of keys he kept in the cabinet over his desk, so they could get into the garage to work on a snow machine. Family members would stop in to see what was for supper. Grandchildren were dropped off to play. Daughters came over to do his laundry and clean house. They all gathered at Harry's for lunch every day to enjoy their favorite Iñupiaq food.

Dr. Tom Albert said, "You can measure a guy by looking at how his offspring have done. Harry's children are successful and are real nice folks. Not many people can say that. Harry was proud of his family."[4] Harry and Annie's children's activities have ranged from the political (mayor of the North Slope Borough, president of the Ukpeagvik Iñupiat Corporation, directors of North Slope Borough departments, Barrow Whaling Captains Association president) to the professional (firefighter, nurse, subsistence specialist, accountant, small business owner, pilot, museum director) to the artistic. Their sons have all become accomplished hunters and whalers in their own right; two of them are whaling captains, and all of them hunt throughout the year. They all absorbed the lessons of hunting and sharing, and continue to practice them and teach them to their own children.

Despite Kupaaq's devotion to his family, he and I rarely talked about them. He didn't tell me what Annie was like, or things that happened with the two of them, other than their wedding. What I do know I heard from their children and other people who knew her. Nor did Kupaaq and I speak about how he raised his children or the relationships he had with them. He might mention something one of them had said or done lately, where another was traveling, or that he had spoken to his daughter in Montana and was expecting a package from her. And I did not ask much. I felt it was none of my business, since Kupaaq, not his children, was the focus of our work. But I was able to tell how important his children and grandchildren were to him because of how he interacted with and spoke about them.

An important aspect of Kupaaq's early family life was his father. As the grand patriarch of the family, Charles Brower was a looming figure in Kupaaq's life, even though he was already in his fifties when Kupaaq was growing up. He also became a role model later on when Kupaaq himself became a father. Charles Dewitt Brower passed away February 11, 1945, at age 83. Despite his age and the fact that his son, David, was in charge of the business, he still spent every day at his store. Asiaŋŋataq had died a few years earlier.[5] His father's death was deeply imprinted in Kupaaq's memory. Forty-six years later, he relayed the events to me in vivid detail, as if they had just happened.

My dad died suddenly. I was there the day he died. He'd just had his lunch and was gonna sit on the easy chair after the meal. After he ate his meal that's where he'd sit and take a little nap. I stayed down there most of the time with him in the store.

He was just sitting there, and all of a sudden, Boom! The door fell right on the floor. All these three brass hinges on it were broken in half. It was a great big door that was right in front with about two and a half-inch-thick solid sticks [logs]. It was the door for the ship. It had these great big half-an-inch-thick brass hinges on it.

I was in the store. There was nobody else around. I didn't know he'd passed away, until I heard that door fall. Then I found out he wasn't breathing, so I started heading home. My sister Maria and her husband, Joe Ahgeak, were home.

I came in and said, "Maria, I don't know what happened."

I looked at her for awhile, then said, "Father passed away." They started running down to the store, but he was already gone. He had a heart attack. He just put his head back on the chair and that was it.

The door had fallen off all by itself after he died. Nobody touched it. The whole thing just fell. All three of those half-an-inch-thick brass hinges were broken. That's it. Somehow it fell.

When my father died, I made the grave for him. David wasn't feeling too good and the rest of my brothers were all out. Arnold was in the army as a parachuter. And Tommy and Robert were at Half Moon Three.

I had to use my own power to dig my dad's grave [in the frozen ground]. I used a railroad pick. It was February. After I used that railroad pick I couldn't get my hands off of it. They got stuck in there. Somehow I had to use my face to push them off [the handle], and then I got them straightened out. They were stiff in there.

While I was doing that, there was somebody who came above me and said, "How come you never told me?" I looked up and there was this old man that had a little sod house over there by the cemetery. His name was Israel Aqargiuluk. And, he said, "If you had come and talked to me and just asked for a help I would be willing to help—I wouldn't ask for anything. Your dad has given me enough food for a long time." It'd be just for my dad helping him for the last years; he wouldn't ask for anything.

Then we started. We got through on May.[6] The grave was solid rocks in there, frozen. And it was just two of us. While we were digging my father's body was frozen and in a coffin at the back of the store.

After we finished the grave, I told my brother, David, I said, "No matter what you fellows say, I have to get some flour, milk, coffee, and everything for Israel from the store. You don't have to write 'em down. It's for helping me with the grave." David said, "OK." So I got him everything what he wanted. That was pretty good when you got somebody to help you.

While father was alive we all get along, but after he died that's the time when everything went haywire.

When Annie Brower was stricken with tuberculosis in 1951, the doctors sent her to the hospital in Sitka for a year.[7] Kupaaq had young children to care for. He took them with him in the dogsled when checking his trapline and in the boat when traveling inland for summer fishing. Annie's grandmother, Lottie Ahlaak (Aalaak), also accompanied them on the winter trapping trips. Kupaaq talked about Annie being away and taking care of their kids by himself.

Annie was down at Sitka. She stayed at Mt. Edgecumbe over a year. She was resting down there for a while in the hospital for TB. I was left with three of our kids: Ronald, Eugene, and Eunice. I had to raise the kids myself, but I just keep on going, going, going.

One time, I had all my boys with an aluminum boat. We were on the Elson Lagoon here, Dease Inlet, and I had to drag the boat with a rope. I was walking on the shore way up right close to the Oarlock Islands. I had come home dragging the boat following all these U-shaped curves and bays of the coast. It took pretty close to two weeks or so. We were fishing, caribou hunting along the way and put all of these we caught in the boat, too. We had just enough meat to keep the boat up out of the water; didn't want too many or else it was going to be too hard to pull.[8] I pulled it by myself. I didn't have dogs with me. Eugene was about seven. I had Eugene, Eunice, Ronald, and Charlie, I think. I wasn't as small when I was young as I am now. I was lively! I could outrun a polar bear!

That's how I raised the kids. I'd be out traveling with 'em with the dog team. We went fishing in falltime and I put 'em inside the sled and then I'd go trapping with 'em. I'd take them along and when we came home the house would be cold, so I had to build up a fire and get them guys going inside the house. We had no electricity, no nothing! We had only those kerosene lanterns. We heated with wood, driftwood, and then when the coal mine on the Meade River started coming along then we bought some coal and used some of that.

And after the house would get warm and the kids started taking all their clothes off, I'd go feed all the dogs. Or sometimes I had to cook dog food and then feed them about two o'clock in the morning. It was lots of work; even washed all the clothes by hand. I did all of this by myself, but the older kids helped a little bit. That was a big problem. I always tell 'em nowadays is no problem when you can just throw away all the diapers and you don't have to look for a something to heat the house. All you do is turn the knob, that's all, and it clicks and all the lights go

Annie and Harry Brower in their living room, 1984. Courtesy Eugene Brower.

on! And with a snow machine, too, you just stop it, that's all, and go inside, not like with a dog team.

Back then there was no place to work. All you could do was just try to get some foxes to sell the skins. This was in the late forties, early fifties.

ᒉ

In his last years—when Barrow was damp and alcohol was legal to possess but not sell—Kupaaq took a glass of wine every night for medicinal purposes. "It helps me sleep better," he explained.

Kupaaq and I did not talk specifically about alcohol in his life or how it affected his family, and given the sensitive nature of the topic I never asked. However, his stories and his actions showed that he did not consider alcohol a problem in and of itself—a forbidden fruit—or that it had been a destructive force in his life. I knew he drank and smoked cigarettes before I knew him. He went to parties at NARL and had cocktails at dinner with scientists. He told stories that happened in bars in Anchorage, Fairbanks, and Seattle, and mentioned buying cheap beer at the navy's commissary. He baited his fox traps with liquor, and even brewed his own beer.

But, I could tell that the current level of alcohol abuse and the resulting tragedies in Barrow distressed him. He told me with sadness that he had started locking his door at night for safety reasons. Once he saved a young man from freezing to death when he discovered him passed out in the snow beside the house. He also strongly stated that drinking and whaling did not mix.

One evening when Kupaaq and I were talking about raising his family, he told me in a matter-of-fact way that he had brewed his own beer. Apparently, he was not concerned with the modern stigma against alcohol use promoted by the strong Native sobriety movement.

I used to make my own beer. Sometimes when you just had it in the open place, it would take too long. It had to be warm in order to get it going real fast. This was when we didn't have no heaters like these today. We had these wood burning ones that went out and everything would freeze. So, instead of it getting frozen you had to keep it inside the blanket or something, inside the bed.

This one guy was showing us how they did it long time ago. They mixed flour with molasses, and then like making a sourdough starter, put sugar with it and you mix it up. It would be like in these wooden kegs. And then, let it get all gassed up, see. Let it drip. When the water started dripping from a little hole, that's when you tasted it. Well, sometimes it would take about six months. Boy, that's a real good! That's good beer!

But this other guy, he said he learned it from one of the commercial whalers. He added water with raisins and yeast and sugar, mixed it all together, and kept it tight. From that yeast all these raisins would start swelling up and get real, real fermented in there. And then these raisins would start breaking up and then they'd pop up that cap off! With the raisins it would go real fast, less than a month if you kept it warm. It made beer, not wine. It had a different taste on it, like wine with a yeast and raisins and sugar and water in it, not like the one that was mixed with flour, molasses, water, sugar. I've had quite a bit of those.

One time, I was sleeping with the beer and it got so hot it exploded. It blew the whole cap off! It got too strong, I think, real fermented! Once it explodes like that while you're sleeping, that's the worst part of it. When you're having a nice good sleep, dreaming of something else, and it goes Boom! Ah, your bed is all wet! Smells like a beer! Annie wasn't here, so I had to sleep with somebody! It's nice anyways to do something while you can do it.

Nowadays you wouldn't have to sleep with it, because you have all these warm stoves going all the time. You have to keep that beer nice and warm when you make it. But in those early days, you didn't have a stove like these now. Once you went to sleep the fire would go out and it was going to get frozen in no time. In the morning everything would be frozen, even the tea kettle with the water in it, it'd be just cracking up inside from that ice. That wood burns real fast, so once it starts going down it just goes out, and the heat starts going down. Once they had this stove oil, it was pretty good, but when the weather gets real cold when you had a tank outside the stove wouldn't burn. The stove oil out there would freeze, because the oil was a real heavy kind.[9]

"I Never Get Scared of Nothing"

Typical of any Iñupiaq boy of his generation, Harry was born into a world in which it was important to learn how to hunt, and he did so at an early age. His first teachers were his mother, Asiaŋŋataq, and her brothers, Taalak and Ahsoak. He followed when Asiaŋŋataq went duck hunting at Piġniq near Point Barrow. He accompanied Taalak on trips inland to check the trapline. He joined Ahsoak in late spring when he went down the coast to hunt seals. He learned from the older men when he went whaling with his father's crews. And like other boys his age, he practiced his aim by shooting lemmings and small birds like the phalaropes he gave to one elderly couple as a special taste treat.

When Harry became a teenager, his father counted on him more and more to help support the family through hunting. One August, Harry shot all the ducks needed to make the soup the Brower household prepared for workers unloading the town's annual supplies from the ships. Harry's older brothers and brothers-in-law also taught him hunting skills while he was still quite young. He recalled following his brother David and brother-in-law Joe Ahgeak when he was "just a little bugger." Even when he became an adult, Harry regularly hunted with Joe, and their other brother-in-law, Nate Neakok, often joined them.

Harry had a special bond with those who taught him how to hunt, trap, navigate, and survive in his homeland. People like Vincent Nageak, Sr., who showed Harry how to set fox traps, were key to his future success, and he continued to consult them as long as they were alive. In Harry's later years, the tables turned and he became the expert who showed others, especially his sons, how to find their way across the seemingly featureless terrain, where to have the harpoon strike a whale, and the best way to set a fox trap.

Harry hunted to feed his family, his whaling crew, and the community. He spent much of his "free time" hunting, fishing, and trapping out on the ocean and tundra. "Over the years my dad was most happy when he was out hunting," Eugene explained.[1] He knew his surroundings intimately and became respected as an expert hunter. Some say it was as if he had a sixth sense when it came to hunting and knowing when a whale was nearby and ready to give itself. He closely observed the world around him, had excellent teachers, and had the patience to move through the natural world at its own pace.

(Opposite) Harry Brower in his hunting parka, circa 1980. Photo by Tom Albert. Courtesy Eugene Brower.

Hunting stories are important for Iñupiat men. They share their pride in a good hunt or the suspense of a close call. Knowledge about animals, survival, the environment, and hunting skills are passed along to younger listeners. Like fish stories among fishermen, hunting stories bond people together. The tales build on each other when a group of Iñupiaq hunters get together.

Kupaaq, like many other men of his generation, was not only a skilled hunter, but also an adept storyteller. He provided just the right amount of descriptive detail to set the scene realistically, threw in a smattering of dialogue to break up the story, and used suspense and drama to carry the listener's attention through to the end. His stories came to life. It sounded as if they had just happened, instead of occurring years earlier. His polar bear hunting tales were especially thrilling.

Men used to hunt polar bears (*nanuq*), but nowadays this is rare.[2] A hunter is more likely to kill a bear when he happens to encounter one or when a bear becomes a threat at whale camp or in town. Polar bear meat is still enjoyed as a delicacy, especially by elders. These animals can be anywhere from six to twelve feet long, so one supplies lots of meat. A polar bear hide makes a warm tent floor mat or is transformed into lush mittens, mukluks, parka ruffs, or even fur pants.

Kupaaq had his fair share of excitement pursuing these dangerous and unpredictable animals, but he remained calm. "I never get scared of nothing," he explained to me.

After Joe Ahgeak and my sister Maria got married I used to go out hunting with Joe. And in one year we got twenty-seven polar bears. We were just lucky, I think. All these people were hunting out there, but the bears always came up right through us. Sometimes there would be three in one day.

And one day we saw some polar bears way on the other side of the ice from where we were. And Joe told me, he said, "You better take care of the dogs. I'm going out there, down to that point of ice by walking."

I said, "OK. I'll wait for you. I'll take good care of 'em. I'm not going to make them holler for anything."

I had the first gun I had, a .25-20. I was all alone with the dogs, watching the dogs. And one of the dogs started making all that little noise around there, right close to me. I was always saying, "Shh, shh," but he wouldn't stop. Then I looked backwards and there was a polar bear on the back of our sled [standing behind the sled]. My .25-20 was right there on the sled, but I was up with the dogs [at the front of the team], so would have to go back through the dogs to get it. So I went right through the dogs and grabbed my gun from there.

But it wasn't a real big bear, only seven feet. I got it with two shots and it didn't run too far off. And Joe didn't know it; he was too far away to hear. I skinned it right there while I was waiting for him to come back. That was my first polar bear right there. I was fifteen.

And finally Joe went bang, bang, bang, bang, bang, bang. After that he started waving at me, so I left the polar bear where it was and just took the dogs up there to him. I wanted to smile, but my golly, I was trying to keep it all secretly to myself. But, he could tell and said, "What happened?"

"I shot a polar bear. I left it up there. I already skinned it."

He got three of them right there and I got one. We skinned all the polar bears, and then while I was still down there on the ice, he loaded up the sleds and took the meat up to the safe side of the ice [the grounded, shorefast ice that doesn't move with the wind and current as the pack ice does]. He made two trips. Then on the third trip we took everything else up there and loaded up some, oh, not too much meat. But, we got the skins in there and took them home. That was long time ago, about '38, '39, someplace. That was the time when the price for polar bear skins was starting to go lower and lower. They were priced by the foot.

꒰꒱

Before we had started tape recording our sessions, Kupaaq told me about the biggest polar bear he killed. He showed how large the skin was by pointing to the place on the kitchen floor it came to when laid out. "Thirteen feet," he said. Many months later, I asked Kupaaq to tell me the story again of "that really big bear you caught all by yourself."

In one spring, when all winter long the ice was closed, everybody was low on food. There were no seals. You had to look for seals in their houses inside the snow [pupping dens carved in the ice] or at their breathing holes in the ice.

In March, one day at about two o'clock in the morning, I told my wife, Annie, I said, "I'm going out there."

She said, "What for? You won't see nothing out there."

Well, I said, "I want to be out there before the day breaks."

Even though she got mad at me, I just kept on going. I harnessed up my dogs and took off. I had two rifles with me: a .25-20, and that old army rifle.

I was sitting there on top of the iceberg and finally I saw this big polar bear coming up. And I thought, "I'm not going to let him go." The ice was so smooth and the sun was coming up. Then I put my binoculars on to see how his face looked. He was going right into the sun so he never opened up his eyes! I thought, well, must be his eyes don't want to open up, or something is wrong with him. But, I started sneaking up on him. Then I sat on a real smooth piece of ice, just waiting for him. Well, I could shoot him even though he was still a little distance away, but every time when I looked at him he was just using his nose, waving it in the air. And then, he'd start walking again. He still never opened his eyes. I thought they were closed forever.

So, finally he was as far as maybe five feet from me. I was sitting on the ice hiding, and he was walking, and I was going to hit him right in the head. Well, you know on that old army rifle you had to give the trigger a great big pull to get it to fire. I forgot all about that when I got excited, I think. I pulled that trigger, and I ended up pulling my gun sideways a little bit. So I shot him right through the collarbone. He opened up his eyes and he stood up on his hind legs. I had to start putting another shell in there and when I made that noise he saw me and looked down. He started coming downwards after me. The only place I could take off was between his hind legs. I grabbed my gun and he was still coming down on me, so I pulled the trigger and just threw my gun. I ran in there under and between his legs, but one of my legs got caught a little bit. I pulled it out and I didn't even look backwards. I ran and ran and ran and ran.

Finally, I started looking backwards. There was no polar bear on the back of me. So, I went back and got my .25-20. I started walking toward him again. I thought to myself, "This time I'm going to kick him in the butts!" They always used to tell us not to go in front of a polar bear when he's lying down. He wasn't moving, so I went around the back side. I had seven shells in this gun, so I was going to shoot at him, right in the head. And I started thinking, "Oh, well, let me look at him for awhile." Then instead of opening the top eye, he opened his other eye that was laying on the snow and looked at me with that one eye.

Then finally he started putting his legs under him like he was getting ready to get up and go after me, I think. "Well, you're not gonna get me," I thought to myself. So, I went around again and I kicked him on the butts! Then he got up! And I had this .25-20 right in front of me, about as far as a couple of feet. I had to put all these seven shots right in his head, because, well, the head was about six inches away from the barrel of my gun, anyway. And I shot him right through one of his eyes and the bullet went inside his brain. That's what knocked him down.

But, later on I got scared. I wondered what would I have done if I didn't knock him down with those last shots? And finally, I happened to think about my old army gun, wondering what happened to it. Well, it was all bent up, it had no handle, the stock was all broken up. It was the one that the polar bear fell down on the top of when I shot him the first time.

Then I started skinning that polar bear. Boy, that was hard! Later on—oh, about two o'clock in the afternoon—when I had the skin off him half-way, I was sitting right there resting with my dog team a bit further up from the bear and I saw something moving around. Then I went back to the bear to keep working. I started looking again at what I'd seen moving and finally I saw somebody was crawling at this polar bear. They would put their head up, look at the bear, then they'd start going again. I looked at him—oh, he was about a hundred yards away or so—and I started walking around the polar bear. Then the man stood up and came up to me and scolded me for not letting him see me before. After seeing my gun, he scolded me a lot. He said, "What would you have done if you got caught by this polar bear?"[3]

Boy, I wasn't thinking about nothing. I wasn't scared of that polar bear. I wanted to get something to eat anyway, because if I went home with something I knew that I was going to be happy to feed all the people around here. That's what I was thinking.

That night I came home about midnight. After I skinned the whole polar bear with the help of that guy, I gave him half of it and I took home half of it. That was a big polar bear with lots of meat. When I came home, Grandma Lottie Ahlaak [Annie Brower's grandma] was sitting right there. She was an old lady. She didn't look you right in the eye when you first came home from hunting. She looked at the boots to see if there were blood stains. The first thing when I walked in right through the door she said, "Uh, oh, he got something."

I tried to clean up my boots as clean as I could, but she could tell the blood spots were there. And I told her I shot a polar bear.

And Annie said, "I thought you said you were going to run home if you saw a polar bear!"

I'd always told Annie, I'd said, "I'm just going to run away from any kind of a polar bear that I see, it's too scary."

This time, I said, "No. Well, the skin is out there if you want to look at it."

"I'm not going out there all by myself. I'm not going out there, just to look at the skin."

And so I took her out and together we took the skin off the sled. It was pretty dark out there.

After I got home people started asking me all these questions. How did I get it? How I shot it? How far? Then Vincent Nageak came along, and he told me, "You lucky guy!"

"I'm not lucky. The bear almost got me," I told him.

He said, "Uh oh, I never told you to get that close when I was showing you."

"Well, you always told me when you're scared that you don't have to shoot the polar bear at a distance." Then I learned my lesson. And after that, seems like all these other polar bears that I shot were nothing.

When I took a shot at that bear, I pulled the trigger first and then I went underneath it, but he was still alive. And well, that's how the man should be when he goes hunting. You have to be lively. For some reason, I never get scared of nothing, anyway. Maybe it's after raising polar bears as a boy.

That wasn't the first polar bear I shot, but that was the biggest. It was almost thirteen feet. That scary old guy! I just used that .25-20, but nowadays they use big guns! They've got all these seven millimeters, three hundred Weatherbees.

That thirteen-footer must've weighed close to two thousand pounds. Maybe more than that, I think. I had nine dogs. They pulled their load, but they got tired coming home, too. We were way out on the other side of the Point [Point Barrow].

After I got that big one, this guy came along who wanted to buy the skin. The skin was spread right here on the kitchen floor. He was down on his hands and knees looking at the head from the floor. I was standing at the back of him. I just touched him and said, "Boo!" And he fell face down on top of the skin. That sure made me laugh!

That skin was worth lots of money though. I sold it for a thousand dollars. That was lots of money then. It was someplace in 1949 or early '50s. I don't know what the guy who bought it did with it.

But I don't want to shoot no more polar bears, I think. It's a lot of work. It's too heavy, when you're trying to cut it up and move it around by yourself. You have to work on one side, the top, then you have to turn the whole thing over the other way again.

Not all of Kupaaq's hunting stories were dramas of close calls. He also told some funny ones, such as the one about the time when he and his brother-in-law, Sam Hopson, went hunting geese. Geese, ducks, and other birds return to the North Slope in May and June to have their young. As bare spots of tundra emerge with the thaw, geese congregate in these snowless areas, especially along riverbanks and lake edges. The geese are usually hunted with shotguns as they fly by, but they can be killed in large numbers if surprised when resting on the ground. Goose hunting is generally a family affair—there is time for joking, game playing, and visiting when the geese are not flying or the weather is bad.

When it's windy the geese don't fly. They just sit until the wind starts dying down. Boy, we sure have fun this one time! The wind was blowing, the geese were just curled up, so I walked up to them. They didn't hear me. And when they all stood up, I started shooting them! I had five shots in the barrel. I got fifteen geese. I tried to carry them about a mile to bring them home, but boy, those were heavy when you carried them home. So, I left them up there and went home empty. When I got home I started my Ski-doo, drove it up there, and took all those geese home.

When I came home the first time, my wife, Annie, hollered at me about where I was going again so quickly. I said, "Oh, I'm just gonna take a short trip." And when I got home again after not being gone very long, she said, "Where did you find all these geese?!" Anyway we laughed! The kids started plucking couple of 'em and we made some fresh soup.

By the time when I was done at the end of the day shooting all those geese, my arm was all blue [bruised] from the shotgun. Sometimes when I'm shooting too much that twelve-gauge shotgun kicks me down. It sure really kicks. And here I am on the ground with no ducks from the trigger! It's always fun anyway. That was a five-shot shotgun. Sometimes I had to shoot four or five geese at a time, and if I didn't knock them all down I had to keep on banging. But the last shot I'd always shoot just for celebration, I think. I'd shoot the last one for nothing, even when there were no birds around. It just goes bang for nothing.

⌇

To hunt successfully in the Arctic, it is critical that you can find your way around. This is especially true in the winter months when everything is white and there is little daylight, or when visibility is diminished from fog, blowing snow, or what locally is referred to as "white-out," when the light, clouds, and snow interact so the ground and sky merge into a whitish sameness.

Kupaaq explained to me how to navigate in the winter using the snowdrifts, which generally form in the same line according to the prevailing wind direction.

Around Barrow, a northeast wind is most common. The drifts form in parallel lines like the knuckles on your hand in a southwest to northeast direction. The tips of the drifts spread out downwind. You must cross the drifts at the same angle throughout your journey if you wish to stay on course and arrive at your destination. You need to know what the wind direction was in the most recent storm so you know which way the drifts are running.

I could not quite picture this from my chair in his living room. The next day when I went out cross-country skiing, I carefully looked at the drifts on the tundra thinking about angle geometry and what Kupaaq had said. I tried to visualize his explanation, but could not quite get it. I realized how much the confines of his living room hindered us. I needed to have him out there standing on the drifts to show me what he meant. But Kupaaq was not well enough for that kind of traveling anymore.

It was not just my lack of first-hand experience that limited some of our discussions. Iñupiaq teaching and learning encourage showing, watching, listening, and trying things oneself. Kupaaq would have shared his knowledge better where he normally used it: at whale camp, traveling across the tundra, chasing a caribou, or pursuing seals along the ice edge.

One weekend in May, I asked another friend to explain snowdrift navigation to me. With a lot of mental focus and hard listening, I started to understand. Now I saw the regular pattern of the drifts, and could picture how cutting across them on my snowmachine at a constant forty-five-degree angle would guide us home. But maintaining the same angle over miles and miles of wide open, flat country is not easy. I was not ready to throw away my compass just yet.

Using the stars, constellations, the sun, the moon, and the wind are other important Iñupiaq navigational tools. Kupaaq discussed these methods only briefly, but did express concern about traditional navigational skills being lost. I am sure there are more Iñupiaq names for stars and ways to use them that he did not cover. He had a hard time talking about the stars and constellations in English, because he only knew the Iñupiaq names.

The handle of the Big Dipper [*Qayutaniq̇tuk*] goes 'round.[4] It changes during the night. It turns to the south. And there's a Little Dipper that never moves from the Big Dipper; it follows the Big Dipper. And there's a big light, a big star that is always bigger than all these other stars. It's only one way, comes from the north. And there's a polar bear up there, the star they call a polar bear.

If you learn all of those stars, then it's easier to travel. I learned that from an old man, too. We had to sit out there when the stars were all out. He took me out and we sat on top of the sled. He started talking to me all about what he knows. Siġvan, Steven Siġvan. They call him old man Siqvauraq.

When we were trapping up there inland, he used to take us out and tell us all these stars. He said we had to learn these stars if we were to travel a lot. So, that's how I learned 'em. There's all kinds of stars up there. He showed me the Eskimo names for them. He could speak English, but it was better for him to speak to us in Eskimo.

If I tell the kids today the Eskimo words, they won't understand 'em. That's a big problem. Some of the stars are *Nanuq* [Ursa Major], *Paatchuktuurat* [Pleiades], and *Qalugauraq* [Ursa Minor]—there's all kinds of 'em up there. I never studied their English names. And there's a star *Aagruuk* that comes up from the east just before the daylight starts breaking up.[5] You can see it from the ground. And they know that when they see that star, the daylight is coming up—in those early days they call that star *Aagruuk*; that means just before the daybreak.[6] But in someplace like Wainwright or to the east, they've got a different name for it, too.

But when you say it in Eskimo, even around here, they don't understand it. They just call you a liar. But, there are some guys too that know it. And then one time we had this great big argument on the CB about it! That old Jonah Leavitt, he gave us the advice, he said, "If you don't know nothing about stars you shouldn't say anything, because these two guys are telling you what they learned from an old man that I know of." He must have learned the stars from that old man, too. This guy on the CB said the names that we were calling these stars were not the names. But, old Jonah he got him all fixed up.

Siġvan never told us from where he learned the stars. These old-timers just knows them. I don't know where they learned them. Siġvan just told us the names, where the stars were, which way they came out, and which way they were standing. He never told us stories of them. He showed us how to find our way with the stars. Even though you talk to these guys nowadays, they don't look up when they're trying to navigate themselves when they get lost.

If you follow just the handle of the Big Dipper you're gonna go 'round and 'round. But the Little Dipper, it never moves from the Big Dipper. It's always on the one side of the Big Dipper all the time. If you keep it on that side then you'll find your way. It's hard to explain in English after they've [the elders] told you the stories in Eskimo anyway. It's when you're trying to explain everything in English when you're not a preacher! And most of the time, it's hard to say the right word in English for the ones they talked about in Eskimo. That's why some of these people, when they ask them, they don't like to tell stories.

There's all kinds of stars up there if you know the names of 'em. Some are real close to each other, like those three stars all lined up that you can find easily. They call those the three shepherds. They're called *Imnailiqirit* in Eskimo.[7] They must have got that from the Bible story or from the Christmas story or something like that.

But, I don't know how Siġvan noticed all of these figures up there. He always pointed to them up there, but it was always hard for us. I can find out some of 'em by looking at the stars. There's some that sometimes show up real good.

And when the northern lights are on it goes only one way: west to east. I don't know why. Once it starts moving, it just keeps moving. The faster it goes, I think the closer it gets. Does it? The colors start showing up real good. It's looking for a football, I think![8] I haven't seen it for long time, because I never stay out now. When I used to travel a lot, I used to see it a lot, but nowadays I stay home.

In the summer, when there're no stars there's always the sun and the wind to help you find your way. When it's really calm, that's how people get lost. They don't know which way they're going. Even though there's no wind, there's the sun showing. You have to know the sun's path when it starts moving around. You have to know where it is in the sky at what time, like that the sun is getting weaker in springtime when it goes towards six o'clock P.M.

ᎠᏦ

Kupaaq especially needed these navigational skills for his long forays inland to check his trapline, which ranged as far as fifty miles inland from Barrow. Kupaaq fed, clothed, and housed his family for many years off trapping income combined with periodic jobs and hunting. There is no longer an outside market for foxes, and wolf and wolverine are preferred locally for parka ruffs. They have thicker fur, are more durable, and shed frost better than fox. Hunters today obtain pelts mostly for personal use rather than for sale. They shoot wolves, wolverines, and sometimes red, cross, or silver foxes while chasing them with snowmachines.

Kupaaq enjoyed life out in the wild country so much that he spoke fondly of his trapping days, despite its hardships.

I just kept on going with the kids [when Annie was away in Sitka for TB treatment]. That's all I did, take care of the kids. But, I still traveled a lot. That was the only way you could make a living, by trapping. I couldn't work [at a job] with all these three kids, so I might as well do some trapping.

The fur price was pretty good in those early days: eighty some-odd dollars for a white fox. This was in the early fifties. Sometimes you'd come home with twelve white foxes. That was a lot of money. And then towards the end of the trapping season, the price went over a hundred dollars for some reason, I don't know why. Everybody wanted to buy my skins. There were lots of fur buyers who came in trying to get all the furs from the Natives. There were all different kinds of fur buyers for each company who bid themselves higher and higher trying to get the most fox pelts.

Fox trapping season was from December to April 15. They changed it once to November 15, but the foxes were all still too brown from the summer. So, they took it back to December. The best skins are always coming in from February when the sun is up. When the sun is up the foxes start getting more whiter. They turn real white, when you're turning black [tan] from all that sun in the springtime!

To check my trapline, I'd take off from here at six o'clock in the morning and come home about ten o'clock in the evening. I'd be setting traps and checking on my trapline. After I'd set them up, I'd go from here through Tupaaġruk, way up to Tupaaġruk River, then go up to Half Moon Three, and then come home through those islands in Dease Inlet and through Avak Creek. From Avak I'd follow the shoreline of Elson Lagoon checking on my traps. And by the time when I got right up close to the DEW–line, then I started heading home.

I'd check over 200 traps in one day. Sometimes I'd get fifty or sixty foxes, sometimes only thirty. Ninety-six was the most foxes I got in one day on that route. You wouldn't always get all white foxes. Sometimes you'd get a blue fox once in a while, and sometimes you'd get red foxes, too, when you went farther up inland, way up by Half Moon Three and Tupaaġruk.

When I was first trying to trap, the foxes don't want to get in my traps. And finally, one Sunday, I told Vincent Nageak, "You always say you love me. If you really love me, show me one time how to work on the traps. I'll watch you work it. How you do it your own way." I got him right there when I told him, "If you really love me you have to show me."

He said, "That's a hard word! I love you." So, he grabbed up the traps, got his snow knife, and said, "Let's go out. I'm just going to show you only once. So if you're dumb, you're not going to learn nothing from me."

I watched him carefully. He hid the trap after he worked on it and took everything off from around it. That was the only thing he showed me. So when I went out to check on my trapline, I still remembered how he worked on it. Then I started changing all my traps and about three days later I went out to check on 'em and I had twelve foxes in the traps.

There's a little trigger in each trap that goes up and down. Where they've got that spoon inside the trap, there's a little thing that holds it up. If you don't take good care of this part, if you put it on the wrong way, then every time when the fox steps on it that little thing that goes up and down is going to pull the feet up and that bar will close and it will miss! That's what happened to all my traps. So, I turned my traps around. Then I learned it.

The little spoon is right in the middle of the trap. Every time it's up, it's sticking up about an inch from the bottom of the trap in the middle of the trap. And every time when the fox steps on that little trigger the trap closes. It's got a spring on the back of it and it closes up, so it won't pull the leg off.

You can use anything for bait, any kind of meat, fish, or blubber. But I don't like blubber, it gets on the skins, the fur, and it stains a little bit. It gets a kind of yellowish color on it once it's stained. Or you can even use just a piece of a ground. Chop the ground, get a little piece and put it by the trap. The foxes will come over and look at it because it's black. They'll look at it and then they'll come closer and closer and they'll forget the trap. I used Kleenex or tissue paper to cover my traps.[9] Once you learn how to use these, it's better than the snow. We also use snow. You make a little place for a trap in the snow—oh, about a couple of inches deep—and cover it up with that nice icy little snow from in between the top layer of snow and the ground, that real soft snow right in the middle. You get that one and cover up the trap, get it all less than a half inch thick. And then, the fox will come around and just step on it. That's it, the fox is there. You don't put bait on those ones.[10]

Sometimes use a good expensive booze for bait, like when you had this 128 proof Old Granddad. You pour that whiskey on top of little pieces of caribou skin and put it on the trap. And once that fox gets in the trap and throws that piece of skin away all these other foxes will be playing with it, see. And instead of picking the skin up, moving it to here, to here and then to here, you just put another trap over there by where the skin is without moving the skin. Put this one trap up and put a little black spot right there, something a little black, and once this one trap gets a fox the other fox will come along and go on to this first trap you put there. And every time when the fox moves the skin someplace, if it's showing up, you just put another trap there. Every time once you get a fox, the snow goes up from the fox circling around. He pulls up and piles up this snow.

It's lots of work though. But, it's nice. Sometimes I got three hundred foxes a year. But one year, I did pretty good. I got over nine hundred white foxes in one season. I treated them pretty good; got the foxes all drunk. I heard somebody was talking about using like these Old Granddad, hundred and twenty-eight, hundred and ninety proof whiskey on 'em. You pour that whiskey all on your traps. No bait, just

Fox furs ready for sale. Eva Alvey Richards Collection, acc. no. 78-14-611, Archives, University of Alaska Fairbanks.

the whiskey. They like it. Then I bought a couple of bottles of wine that cost seventy-five dollars a bottle. I spent a hundred and fifty dollars. When the foxes started mating, I tried using that wine for bait. And that's the time I sure really got foxes. I got 997 white foxes out of those two bottles. Not quite up to 1000 white foxes. I had 200 traps laying out there for one day. Sometimes I'd take home ninety-six foxes in one trip, sometimes only sixty or seventy.

I poured the wine on the snow right close to the traps. I used just enough so when they stepped on it, started smelling that, it wouldn't take long to attract them. You pour it about three inches from the trap. When a fox comes up he's gonna step right there on the trap just enough to smell that. Pour the whiskey three to four inches away from the trap, so it gets him on the foot, on the leg, when he steps there.

I think the scents of the female urine when they're mating is like the wine, 'cause they go real crazy for it. That's what I found out. But, I tried this strawberry wine, one time, because it was kind of a reddish color when you pour it on the snow. For some reason, the smell of it didn't last long. I think, there wasn't enough alcohol in it. It was too cheap, that's it. The foxes didn't like it.

At the time the fox prices started getting lower. The price had been up to thirty-four dollars a skin, but that was way back. And then when I got over nine hundred white foxes it helped. Once they start adding up they adds up pretty good. This was in something like the '60s. And then one year it was really nice, you'd get a hundred dollars for a white fox, a hundred and seventy for a red fox, a hundred-ninety for a blue fox and a silver fox for three hundred. That was the time when I started trapping.

But most of those early ones I got I didn't take care of. My old uncle was having a hard time, so I gave most of 'em to him. I told him to skin 'em and sell 'em for himself, not for me. I said, "Just work on 'em and just use them for yourself. Don't think about me." He passed away way back in '49 something like that. That was when the fox prices were high. These fur buyers were really crazy for 'em. They even came up here to buy up all the foxes that they could find.

One time, I had about two hundred white foxes laying around here. The ones with the blubber stain on 'em—well, they were good for nothing anyway—so, I skinned the legs off, took the tails off and just dried 'em up. I worked on 'em and just put them in a bag. And then this fur buyer came around.

I asked him, "How much do you want these furs for? They're really thick fur, but they got these blubber stains on 'em."

He said, "Here, let me see."

So I told him, I said, "How much do you want 'em for?"

He looked at 'em for awhile, he said, "How about thirty dollars apiece? Just count them, count how many skins there are."

So, I said OK. I bet he was happy. I didn't know they dye them any color when they're making coats. When they dye them that stain comes out. That's why he said, "Thirty dollars apiece, just count 'em, just count up how much." He knew he was gonna dye them. But, I didn't know until I found out way later. I didn't mind! After he gave me a check, I just threw it to my wife to spend the money any way she wanted.

৵৲

I never hunted for wolverine to sell 'em, just to use them around here. But wolves, you'd get a bounty for 'em.[11] There was a fifty-dollar bounty when you shot one of 'em. But when you shot a female with all these pups already inside her, they'd take the pups out, send them out, and you'd get the fifty-dollar bounty for each one of them, too, even though the pups weren't full grown yet. They said if you hadn't shot that wolf, those pups were gonna be born and start messing around with some of these big bull caribou. They said there were too many wolves around, that's why. There were lots of wolves, sometimes there'd be a hundred in the bag for the bounty. For the bounty, they just took the bone of the lower left leg for the proof. I wonder why the left one? They didn't take the skin from you.

When I got my Ski-doo I was trapping out there and got four wolves in one day! I thought they were dogs when I first saw them way off. But, I looked at them again and saw that they were not dogs. There were seven of 'em. I got four of 'em. And then about a couple weeks later, me and my nephew went up and we hit those three wolves that we hadn't gotten before. We started chasing them and they started spreading out, but we had these two Ski-doos. I shot one of 'em and my nephew went around the other way and he shot a black one. That last one was left right in front of us and we just came up from an angle and we got that one, too. They were eating all our foxes, tearing up the foxes in our traps, that's why we were trying to get those three.

And then, a couple years later there were some wild dogs mating with the wolves. One of the female dogs had a red collar and she had some pups up there. We got all the pups again and shot the mother with a red collar on. We shot all of 'em. I had to kill all what we saw, because they were gonna ruin everything, again [get into the fox traps].

Boy, that was nice when you got one of those. I got one good wolf skin. I shot it right through the head, so I didn't ruin the skin. He was running and I took a shot at him right about two feet ahead of him. My shot ended up going right through his head! He was a long distance from me and was running away from me, but I still got him. And the fur was real, real long. Annie used that wolf skin for her great, big ruff on her ground squirrel parka.

ᣠ

As a hunter, the natural world was important to Kupaaq. He found beauty in a landscape that outsiders consider cold, harsh, and desolate. He was concerned about what happened to the North Slope's environment. He saw the area change. The grassy tundra of Barrow got covered with gravel for roads, driveways and building pads. His arctic homeland became less remote, and was being drilled for oil. He saw ocean dumping and other carelessness by the navy. These environmental changes saddened him.

As late as the 1970s, Kupaaq still trapped white foxes, even though it was no longer particularly lucrative. He liked to travel around the country and the little bit of extra money he made was helpful. But oil development at Prudhoe Bay was in full swing, and there was heavy equipment activity even in the remote tundra.

I just don't tell nobody all what of I see, anymore, because after I sued Husky Oil and Ritchfield Company, I don't pay no attention to them too much. But, I'd told them so many times not to fool around with what I was doing in my hunting area, my traplines and all that. They didn't believe me. They just broke up my foxes. They ran over the frozen foxes in my traps with a Cat train and all that.

And I told 'em, I said, "You fellas better watch out. You fellas might be in big trouble."

"Ah, that Eskimo won't do nothing to us. He don't know nothing," that's what they were thinking. Then I took some pictures and had a private lawyer for myself. It wasn't a big thing with many people and attorneys together, I just got one private lawyer!

I didn't have money, so I told him, "If you can help me, if we win, you can take whatever you want."

He said, "You got proof?" I said, "Yes." I showed him the proof.

He said, "I'll take it." And we started the court case. These attorneys for Husky Oil Company and Ritchfield Company came from Texas, and then we had a court in Fairbanks. And the judge asked my attorney, "You got any proof?"

My lawyer opened his briefcase, and took these pictures and handed them to the judge. He looked at them and he asked those two guys that came from Texas, he said, "You got any proof?" He asked them what they got to say? And then he called 'em, said come on up to his table. He showed them the pictures, said this is the proof, and had them look at this Husky Oil name on the Cat train.

They had enough of it when they saw I got this good proof. That little camera that he was showing around gave me a good proof. I took the pictures of my damaged traps with a Ski-doo light. I had my Ski-doo with me and I went right up close with my Ski-doo and then click, click, click.

It was a big sum of money for the kindergarten to start with [for someone who was a first timer at suing]. You see, I started the wrong way; I got mad. But, once you get mad you can do anything, I think. Well, I did pretty good on Husky Oil and Ritchfield Company, but my attorney didn't even take half of it. He just took what he wanted. I told him whatever he wanted I'm satisfied with it, even though I didn't get too much of it myself. It was just to scare them off. Well, he did pretty good on both of 'em. We got 70,000 dollars each. This was the early '70s.

Husky Oil was around here in the '70s. They started working around here with the ASRC [Arctic Slope Regional Corporation]. And then they know where the oil is. They had a great big camp at the point on the ice where the great big airplanes could land. Then they stopped coming around here. They got into trouble too much I think. They were here for quite a bit. Harry [Harry Brower, Jr.] was working with them for awhile. And every time when I said something, if I hadn't heard about Harry who was working out at Lonely [Point Lonely], or anyplace with the Cat trains, I'd call Husky Oil and they'd give me information right away.[12] If they didn't know where he was, they said, "We'll fly with a chopper and locate him first and then call you back." This was after I'd sued them.

༃

On a cold November evening when the wind had kicked up into one of its typical arctic blows, the topic of drilling for oil in the Arctic National Wildlife Refuge (ANWR) came up. Kupaaq wondered what the current status of it was in Washington, D.C., and with Congress. As we discussed the refuge, Kupaaq shifted to his views on other aspects of oil development on the North Slope.

I wonder what they gonna do? Gonna drill up at the ANWR? The time when Governor Hickel was in Barrow after he'd been at ANWR [in June 1991], I told him, "You never walked up there. You just put your foot on the ground and one on the helicopter! That's how far you walked!" He don't know, but I know what it's like up there 'cause I walked that all over.

After I walked all over, then the oil companies they spoiled that place up there at Prudhoe Bay. They say, they don't block nothing up there, but I always tell 'em after you fly around up there with a little airplane over everything it sure looks awful from the sky. You can see there's buildings, cars running, roads all the way to either direction and pipes all over. I don't know how many miles of area that they had covered.

That Saġvaġniqtuuq [Sagavanirktok] River was the best one. There were no camps, no nothing right there. Boy, it was so beautiful. There were glaciers there that you could cool off at. You could just go down there to the glacier and then sit right close to the edge of it and get your cup out and drink cold water.

Then on the other side of a high spot on the Saġvaġniqtuuq there was that red clay [red ochre]. It's a grounded sand with red. You wet it and you can have a red paint.[13] I got a piece of that kind from way up on top of the mountain at Anaktuvuk Pass. It comes out from the mountain and then the sun dries it. That makes the best color that you can have. It's real red! And it lasts a long time.

Oil drilling is gonna mess up the ocean. They're not gonna hunt no whales after all that solution from the drilling and all that what they've done starts flowing up to the ocean.

People in Kaktovik didn't know it, but later on after I started talking to them they started flying with the chopper and found out for themselves. And then when Isaac Akootchook was here in Barrow he came over to me—his name is Kupaaq, too, my atiq—and he said, "Atiq, you were right.[14] Good thing you've been telling us about everything that you've gone through. And now, when we start flying with the chopper, I've seen it. Now I believe you. Now I start finding out."

"I've been telling you guys not to just say yes to ASRC or anybody on oil drilling.[15] Because if you said yes to even ASRC, you're giving your land away, your property for hunting."

Kaktovik said because they needed some money from the Arctic Slope Regional Corporation they had to go along with 'em on oil drilling. I said, "No way! You're not supposed to just go with the Arctic Slope, no matter what. Don't just say yes. Go against it! They're just gonna swipe all your land and trade you for the ugly looking land."

Around Prudhoe Bay it's different than by Kaktovik, 'cause the whales go way out when they go by Prudhoe. By Kaktovik, that's where they migrate close in and from there they go way out through the barrier islands until they hit Cape Simpson, and from there they start coming in towards Barrow.

When I was on that icebreaker all summer long with the navy, I learned quite a bit about that area, too. We started from Point Barrow, just drifting, and we went way out, way out. And then we hit forty miles out to the north, northwest, from the point [Point Barrow]. From there, you can travel all the way up to Herschel Island. When you hit Herschel Island, going into the Mackenzie River, then you start seeing all these whales. They were way off by the other side of Barter Island. This was in summertime. And then when you go up to the Mackenzie River and Banks Island, you start seeing all these whales with the calves. On the end of the Banks Island, that's where all these whales were all scattered. Way up there is where they had most of the calves. A few of 'em had calves coming in when they pass Barrow in the spring; there's few of 'em that we caught that had calves or fetuses.

"A World of Possibilities"

K upaaq's outlook was rooted in a value system and world view that he heard about in elders' old stories. Iñupiat separate their oral tradition into two distinct, but often overlapping, categories: *Unipkaat* and *Quliaqtuat*. *Unipkaat* are explanatory tales, and occur in a more ancient time where magical events, human/animal transformation, and time travel are the norm. An *Unipkaaq* story might explain why there is daylight, or why a geographic feature has a particular name. It might contain unusual creatures, like a ten-legged polar bear, a giant, or animals that talk and behave as human. Or characters might have unusual powers, like a hunter who travels to a distant land and returns home after what seems to him like years to discover that his physical body never left home.

Quliaqtuat are personal experience stories that describe specific historic events, or things the teller has done or witnessed in his or her lifetime. Sometimes these stories are funny, such as the one in which a man thought the first airplane he saw was some kind of frightening new big bird. Sometimes they are instructional, such as one in which a man describes how he survived when he got lost on a trip. And sometimes they are sad, such as one that tells how an ancestor died from starvation.[1]

While a devout Christian, Kupaaq grew up hearing stories that reinforced that the world is alive with human and non-human, natural and supernatural interactions that should be paid attention to. Stories present a way of respecting and living in both the physical and psychological worlds. From stories, Kupaaq learned about how to hunt whales, how to wait for a seal at its breathing hole, or what to do in case he got lost, but he also gained a broad understanding of Iñupiaq thinking and ways in which his people explain the world. He came to believe that there are certain things whose truth or falseness cannot or should not be questioned. A woman turning into a bear was accepted. A man learning how to sing and dance from an eagle mother was not considered outlandish. This opened a world of possibilities for Kupaaq. It also helped him understand seemingly inexplicable sensations he had as an adult, like knowing that a whale was about to come up and sensing when there were people in trouble.

Once he came upon an overturned airplane that had crashed on a frozen lake and brought the pilot home alive. Another time he found his hunting partner, Antonio Weber, who had followed a light on the tundra he thought was

---

(Opposite) Harry Brower sitting at his table telling stories, 1991. Photo by Karen Brewster.

Kupaaq's snowmachine light, but it was not, and the two got separated. Kupaaq and other local hunters attribute the light to a ghost traveling around inland carrying his lantern. Eventually, a search party found Antonio where Kupaaq thought he might have gone based on the direction they were traveling.[2] Then there was the evening Kupaaq was restless at home; he sensed something was not right. Despite bad weather and poor visibility, he got in his snowmachine and headed onto the tundra. He ran into a non-Native man who had become disoriented in the storm while out hunting caribou, and could not find his way back to Barrow. Kupaaq helped him get home safely.[3]

The presence of the supernatural and the power of the non-empirical world found in Iñupiaq oral tradition allowed Kupaaq and Iñupiat who knew him to accept his moments of intuition.[4] They describe it as if he had a sixth sense. As his niece and sister-in-law, Mable Hopson, said, "It was instinct. It's just that when he gets that feeling, I think he follows up on it. If he thinks there's something wrong, then he does something about it. Goes out."[5]

Kupaaq shared with me some of the old stories he heard as a boy, and told me a little bit about his own experiences with phenomena he could not explain. "I never saw any *aŋatkut* [shamans] anyplace, but I've heard lots of stories about them," he said.

I had read and heard about shamans in past Iñupiaq culture.[6] *Aŋatkut* sang special songs to encourage animals to give themselves to a hunter, provided magic charms to hunters, established taboos to ensure successful hunting, and cured the sick. But *aŋatkut* could also use their powers against people. They controlled with fear. They demanded favors. They hexed people.

The current generation of Iñupiat elders was raised in Christian households. They had little or no direct experience with *aŋatkut*, and were reluctant even to talk about the subject. Kupaaq told me some of these stories, albeit briefly. He did not seem to doubt that it was possible for people to travel through time and space, to transform into animals, or to have magical powers, as occurred in these stories. I heard lessons about respecting animals, helping other people, listening to and sharing with elders, and about paying close attention to the environmental signs around you.

In Iñupiaq there's a story about an old lady whose name was Nuyaaġġiq. She was a good lady when she wasn't feeling bad, but once she felt a little bit kind of funny, or worried of something, a great big tooth would start coming out through the front of her. She told people not to look at her when she was like this.

And later on, she'd turn into a brown bear and take off. One day, they say she didn't get everything quite off before she started coming inside and her big teeth were still there. And some lady yelled, "Ah!" And that lady heard it, went back out, and then later on she came back normal. I don't know how far she'd been traveling when she was a bear.

She always knew when her grandson was walking way off someplace, where he went to. But, before her grandson went out she'd tell him "if you see a brown bear right close to you, don't try to shoot him." It might be her, because she'd just watch this young guy hunting way off someplace. Sometimes she'd just watch him from across the river. This was how she always knew what part of the earth he'd been on and where he was. By the time when he got home, she was always home, just waiting inside the house. She always just told her grandson that she was always right close to him, just watching him.

Aŋatkut they'd turn into everything, I think. They could even fly. Oh, when I was about seven or eight there was a little sod house way down there by the far end of Barrow, across from Levi Greist's house, this side of Ahsogeak's house, by Kugrok Ravine. And there was nothing around there. There was an old couple that lived in that little sod house right there. Towards the early fall when it starts getting darker and darker we'd be playing out and people always tell us not to get too close to that house at night. Because when it got dark, this man, Kuutchiuraq was his name, was gonna fly right through the chimney. He'd go visit Point Hope. He had this little axe made out of jade that by the time when he started coming out the chimney, that jade would be all red hot. That axe would be tied up on him. Once he took off he'd fly with it and visit Point Hope. That must be his engine or something. Before the day started breaking up, he'd always come back inside the house.

I've never seen it; we never went to visit them. But in summertime when there was lots of daylight we used to get lots of all kinds of little birds when they first started coming in, like phalaropes and all that, and we'd take them down there to those two old people. Those two liked to eat those phalaropes. That's how we treated them, with the birds.[7]

When the day was long, lasted for all day and all night, they used to stay outside their sod house. The man used to tell lots of stories of what he'd seen and what he'd gone through. He'd never just keep it to himself. He told us stories where he'd gone to visit his friends down at Point Hope. He'd fly around just to go have fun with his old friends. He just went out there just for the fun, not trying to harm nobody. It was just like taking a short trip on an airplane and then coming home. But, it's cheaper!

I think he's got a special song, in there. His old wife she used to tell us that he was all tied up. They'd tie his hands behind his back. And then, he'd be sitting on the floor and they'd tie him around his legs with a rope, so he wouldn't come out. Then they'd turn the lights off. He'd start making all these little noises, like singing a song or something like that, and then she could hear these wings flapping. He'd finally go out right through the vent [qiŋaq, air vent in the roof]. The last thing she'd see was that jade hammer all red go out right through there, and that was it. He'd take off! She never worried about nothing.

Once he was on the air he could fly! And then he'd come back and after he was inside the house on the floor, that was the only time they untied him. That's what he always did. They don't keep it hidden, but the only thing that he didn't like to tell us was the song. It was a special song, I think. If we ever learned it we might start flying around, too!

In springtime when they used to go whaling, when they just had a harpoon [with no explosives], a guy just threw his harpoon from the front of the boat then kneel down and start singing. In about fifteen, twenty minutes the dead whale would come up right in front of him. That's a powerful song! The only time they could sing that kind of song was when they strike a whale. They never told anyone those songs; they weren't passed on. If a son became a captain, he had to get his own song. I never had one. I didn't want one.[8]

Ꭾ

For the Iñupiat, the landscape is imbued with supernatural events—events that shape people's understanding of places and influence how places are used.[9] For example, people may learn not to hunt at certain places because of the fear of ghosts. Or they learn that a place's appearance is the result of events that took place a long, long time ago. Where I saw just old sod houses or flat tundra, Kupaaq saw stories.

They say there was a grandmother and grandson living together in one of those old sod houses at Piġniq [Birnirk, six miles north of Barrow]. All these whales were running out in the lead in springtime, so she took her grandson out there. They got a whale with no boat, no nothing. That old woman had fur pants that got a little belt around them. She took that belt off and tied it around the whale's mouth. She told her grandson that they were gonna go home with the whale, but he was not to open up his eyes until she reached their sod house up there. And then when they got there she told her grandson to open up his eyes and there they were, right in front of their house. And just with that little belt she'd pulled the whole whale way up by her house!

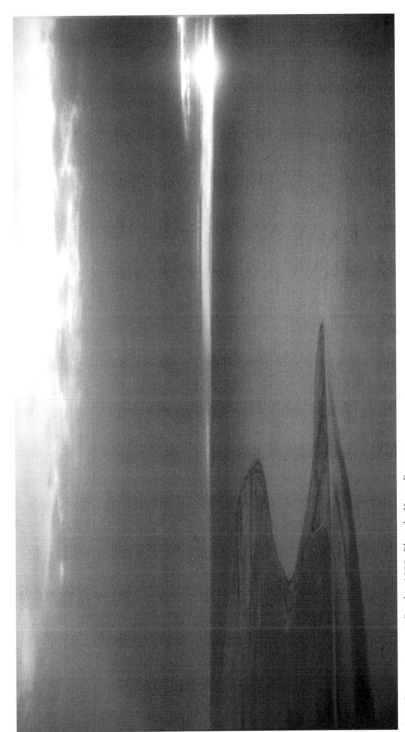

Point Barrow at sunset, October 1989. Photo by Karen Brewster.

People say that this whale that they brought home, they had the whole whale for food for themselves. They never say that this old woman and her grandson shared, but they never hunted after that. They say they got enough food. Why not? With a one great big whale, even though it's a small whale, that's big for just two people. That's lots of food. She must have been *aŋatkuq*, maybe her belt or something?

And they found all these whale bones when a man named Ford dug up those old sod houses at Piġniq.[10] We went duck hunting up there every spring and we were camping up there when they were digging that part. And they had these whale bones all in one piece over by where that story happened. The whale bones, vertebras, ribs, the head, and everything were there. I don't know how they got it all there.

There was a old couple up at the Ikpikpuk River way up on the high hills when we were up at the herd taking care of the reindeer when I was fourteen, fifteen years old. They had a little sod house up by the edge of the river that they spent summer and winter in. We used to stop and visit those guys. He was Amaġuaq and Natchiġuna was his wife. We used to sleep right at their place. But, I don't know, for some reason that old lady would cut little pieces out of your parka, or your snowshirt, your boots, or anything you were wearing. I don't know why she took a little piece. We never asked her. Maybe she was *aŋatkuq*? But, we're still alive, anyway![11]

There was a grave way up where I used to trap. It wasn't a grave, it was just a box, a casket made out of driftwood. But he was alive. He'd put a lantern on in the evening. The dogs when they saw this lantern you could just never get them off of his scent. They wanted to go up there 'til you hit that box with your sled. Then you'd turn around and start heading home.

It wasn't just me who saw the lantern. All of us who goes up there. He'd get everybody lost up there following that light. They say it was *aŋatkuq*. I never think of nothing. I never get scared. I never think of what's gonna happen. I just enjoyed myself traveling, that's all. Maybe that's why it makes me feel better when I'm traveling all alone.

There is another place farther up this way on the Inaru River where at night you can hear a guy hollering and driving his dog team. You can hear him holler, but he won't ever come up to you. At moonlight we waited for him one time for pretty near an hour and a half, but we never saw him.

One time me and my nephew were traveling up on the high hills with the dog team. We made a camp, put up the tent where there was a little hump, a hummock with not even a grass or snow on top of it. It was the best place to put our tent. We stayed over night in there. Every time when we took a step, there was a sound coming out of the ground. After the daylight came up we took the tent off and chopped the top of the hummock off. It was a old house with these great big wood supports on it. They were made of the willow, I think. We looked inside and there were a couple of guys laying in bed, just like two guys sleeping in there. That's how they say they used to bury them, just put them in a house and seal up the house.

And then while we were coming home, my nephew said, "I've been seeing things." He saw a white caribou and brown bears running around. I didn't see them. And about a half a year later he passed away. I was just thinking that it might be that place because, the time when those people were alive they might have had some kind of a devils around them. We didn't look to see if they had any charms in there with them. We just saw them down there and we covered it back. But we must have got their spirits out that were locked up inside that house for so long, because of my nephew starting to see things. He might be the one that they got into, not me. Maybe spirits will look at you and then start saying this is the place where they're supposed to be!

"He Gave Himself"

H arry Brower grew up in a world dominated by whaling. It is what guided his personal development, directed his choices, and influenced his beliefs, values, and actions. I believe it is necessary to know about the modern practice of whaling in Barrow to better understand and appreciate what Harry knows and says about it and how central it was in his life.

In late April or early May, whaling crews set up camp on the shorefast sea ice out at the edge of the open lead; here they wait for whales migrating north and east to their summer calving grounds in western Canada. In Barrow, the handmade skin boat, called an *umiaq*, is still used for spring whaling.[1] Whalers also now use fifteen- to twenty-foot aluminum skiffs with outboard engines to chase a wounded whale or to tow a killed whale back to the ice for butchering. The *umiaq* remains the boat of choice for the actual pursuit of a whale, however. It is lightweight, easy to maneuver, and slides silently through the water.[2]

Being out on the ice waiting for and pursuing whales is the culmination of a year of preparations. In July and August, men hunt bearded seals (*ugruk*) for the boat cover. In August, September, and October, whaling captains fish and hunt caribou and ducks to feed their crews on the ice in the spring. In February, crews begin to prepare their equipment: the boat frames are repaired or built; the men scrape the hair off the *ugruk* skins; and the women sew the skins together with braided caribou sinew, using a special waterproof stitch. The men stretch the new skin coverings over the wood frames and put the finished boats outside in the sun to dry and bleach white. New paddles are carved, freight sleds are built, and guns are cleaned. The women sew and repair warm parkas, fur socks, mukluks, and parka covers. In the middle of April, the men use ice picks to cut trails through the jumbled sea ice. Gear and supplies for a crew of six to twelve men and boys living on the ice for a month are loaded onto twelve-foot wooden freight sleds, and pulled out to camp using snowmachines. The captain or an expert crew member meticulously hand-fills the bomb cartridges with black gun powder, and they are carefully stored in a padded box for the bumpy trip across the ice. The boats are strapped to flat sleds. Finally, candy is handed out at the captain's house when the crew takes off.

(Opposite) Successful whaling captain, Harry Brower, Sr. in front of a whale his crew landed, 1980. Photo by Tom Albert.

Women sewing bearded seal skins together into a skin boat cover, Barrow, Alaska, circa 1990. Photo by Karen Brewster.

By the beginning of May, crews are spread out along the lead. They camp in eight-by-ten-foot canvas-wall tents heated with propane stoves. The skin boats are poised at the edge of the water, with the darting gun, float, and shoulder gun carefully placed in the bow. The men take turns sitting by a windbreak (*uquuttaq*) waiting and watching for whales.

When a bowhead is spotted close by, crewmembers jump into the boat. The harpooner sits in the front, the gunner just behind him, and the steersman at the back. Extra men help paddle. They quietly and smoothly push the boat out onto the water, then paddle hard toward the whale, trying not to splash or hit the side of the boat as they approach the animal from behind.

When the harpooner is lined up with the blowhole, he throws the darting gun at the back of the whale's head. A large round bright pink rubberized-plastic float is attached by rope to the harpoon point, which sticks out the front end of the darting gun. The float helps to locate the whale and slows the injured animal down. The harpoon point penetrates six to eight inches into the blubber, then the point swivels to a right angle, preventing it from pulling back out of the entry wound.

A trigger arm sticking out the front end of the darting gun fires an explosive bomb into the whale. Preferably, the darting gun is thrown so this bomb ends up in the brain, heart, or other vital organ and kills the whale instantly. After impact, the five- to six-foot long wooden handle of the darting gun disengages from the harpoon and is retrieved from the water. The handle is handmade and

A newly re-covered umiaq *drying in the spring sunshine, circa 1990, Barrow, Alaska. Photo by Karen Brewster.*

carefully shaped. It must be just the right weight to give the bomb momentum to enter the whale, but be light enough to float afterwards. If the whale does not die from the single strike of the darting gun, follow-up bombs are fired from a heavy, brass shoulder gun. This wide-barreled, short-handled gun and the darting gun are both carryovers from the commercial whaling era. After the initial strike, other nearby crews aid in pursuing and killing the whale.

Whalers aim to kill the whale instantly with just one shot. As with any hunting, sometimes this does not happen and the injured whale tries to dive and keep swimming. Sometimes whales get lost under the ice, the identifying floats come off, or they swim off and cannot be found. However, all efforts are made to kill and retrieve whales quickly.[3] A lost whale counts toward the International Whaling Commission (IWC) quotas just as if it had been landed and butchered. Sometimes lost whales resurface within a few days, after bloating has made them buoyant. Called "a stinker" (*avataayyuniq*), this type of whale is retrieved and butchered for the *maktak* which is the only part still edible. If the carcass is more than a few days old, even the *maktak* is spoiled, and nothing is edible.[4]

When a bowhead whale is killed, all the boats line up and tie onto a single tow rope to bring it ashore, and slowly move toward a flat spot on the ice. A block-and-tackle system is secured around an anchor bar cut through the ice. Thick ropes are run from the pulley to the whale, and a long line of people slowly pull the massive weight out of the water. The successful crew hoists their flag atop the captain's house to signify that a whale has been caught. Each crew

Pulling a whale up onto the ice. Photo by Karen Brewster.

Butchering a whale in the fall. Photo by Karen Brewster.

has a flag of its own design, and a larger version is flown at the butchering site to help identify the spot for people coming from town.

Any crew wanting a share helps tow and butcher the whale. The whale is cut up into specific shares: crew shares for the other crews; the flipper for the harpooner; a share for the captain to feed the community at feasts; and a share for the successful crew. The captain marks where the different shares should be cut, and butchering begins. One or two men stand on top of the whale making deep cuts with a long-handled, sharp cutting tool, called a *tuggaun*. Long strips of pinkish blubber and black skin are peeled away. As a slab is cut away, five or six people grab it with curved meat hooks on long ropes and drag it away from the carcass. The same is done for the large chunks of meat. In addition to the meat and *maktak*, the intestines (*iŋaluaq*), heart (*uumman*), kidneys (*taqtu*), tongue (*uqaq*), and sometimes the gums, where the baleen is attached to the jaw (*mamaaq*), all go to the captain to feed the community. One side of the baleen (*suqqaq*) is divided among the successful crew and captain; the other side is divided among the boats who helped tow.[5]

Butchering a whale is a serious and hurried affair. Ice conditions or weather can change at any moment, and the whale can rot if not cut up quickly. Groups of people swiftly pull chunks of whale. Sharp cutting tools and hooks fly about. Older men sit on the sidelines sharpening tools for the cutters. Women cut up and serve fresh *uunaalik* (boiled *maktak*) and make hot tea and coffee for the workers.

When the butchering is complete, the piles of meat and *maktak* are divided equally among the crews present. They haul their shares back to town on sleds pulled behind snowmachines. The women of each crew divide their share equally among crew members, and then individual households cut their shares into usable portions. The *maktak* is eaten freshly boiled, or frozen raw, frozen boiled, or pickled. The meat is either frozen raw, or boiled and then frozen.

Finally, the whale's carcass is pushed back into the ocean to return its spirit to the sea. This is in appreciation for the gift the whale has given to the people, so it will tell the other whales that it was treated well and they should return the next year.[6]

Barrow whalers also pursue whales in the fall when the bowheads swim south. The ocean is usually free of ice, so they use skiffs and cruisers to travel long distances to locate and chase whales.[7] The whales are towed back to town by a line of boats, pulled ashore using D-8 Cats, and butchered on the beach. More onlookers come to the easily accessible fall whales compared with the spring, when butchering sites are often many miles out on the sea ice. Crew membership and ways of earning shares also vary slightly between fall and spring whaling.[8]

꒱

On his way to becoming an *umialik*, Kupaaq learned how to approach a whale and how to dispatch the harpoon to kill it quickly. He was shown how to read the ice to tell when it was safe and when it was time to pull up camp and move to secure shorefast ice. He learned how to act so a whale would give itself to him. He was taught how to pick the best spot to wait and watch for whales.

Like his fellow captains, Kupaaq had to get other men to follow his directions, abide by his decisions, and join his crew. He knew *umialgich* were responsible for the entire community, so they were encouraged to act as law-abiding and respectful role models. Even when he was in the hospital dying, he told his sons to go out whaling because as whalers they had a duty to the town. To Kupaaq, being an *umialik* was central to who he was.[9]

Kupaaq believed in a connection between humans and whales. He knew about whales and their behavior. He sensed their presence when nobody else was around. As a captain, he believed nurturing this relationship was one of his primary responsibilities. It bound him to these great creatures of the sea. He believed the whales listened, and that a whaler would suffer if he spoke badly or showed them any disrespect. He did not assume he would get a whale. He could tell when a whale was giving itself to him versus when it was not the right one to be taken, as he described in a court affidavit:

It's hard to explain what it's like when the whale gives itself to you unless you see it. The whale is given to you out of nowhere. Many times I've caught a whale I did not see in advance…all of a sudden right under my boat on the edge of the ice, the whale would appear. When this happens, no matter what you do, it's yours—it has been given to you. You could shout at it, try to chase it away, but it will stay there.[10]

Kupaaq spoke about whaling often, usually telling me about particularly memorable hunts. He told me stories from his years of whaling to teach me what whaling is all about and how it is done, but also to show me what the whale and whaling meant to him.

There was a time when they used to have an open house before they went out whaling and they'd serve that tail part.[11] It was in March, mostly on Sundays. They announced it before everybody went out that there was supposed to be a big feast over at the house of the captain that got the whale the year before. So he had anybody that wanted to come over; it was a time to eat some of that tail part of the whale. And then everybody that came out of the church would go over there, but there were no kids allowed. I tried to go inside, but they wouldn't let me go, even though my mother was in there.

On Sundays, when I was a kid, we used to have a whole bunch of these elder people at our house at lunchtime after church. They'd be a great big round group of them sitting on the floor. They'd be eating and talking away. Then one day before they went out I finally said to them, I said, "When I start hunting whales, I'm not going to feed the old people first. They eat too much. I've gotten kicked out so many times when I've been a boy that the first thing you know is I'm going to have all the kids eat first, if I catch a whale; when I catch my first whale."

I was fifteen years old when I had my own crew for my dad.[12] Then later I had my own crew. It had taken us about three or four years as our own crew, before we caught that first whale. In 1948, I got a seventy-foot whale. It was the first and only whale that was caught in Barrow that year. That was my first whale. I shot it with a shoulder gun. I flew over fifty feet backwards! We didn't have no other bombs so we used kind of a bent bomb in there. Me and my brother, Arnold, both of us had to push the bomb into the barrel of the gun. Both of us were pushing on it and these two great big whales showed up. There were nine of us by the boat. There were these guys that used to do all the shooting of the whales [harpooners] standing there and I told them, "Who's going to shoot the whales?" Nobody said anything, they just stood looking at each other.

There was a great big whale coming up to the edge of the ice and nobody wanted to grab the gun. I looked backwards; the ice was all smooth behind me. And this

Strips of blubber to be distributed as shares. Photo by Karen Brewster.

Peeling away strips of blubber when butchering a whale. Photo by Karen Brewster.

great big whale which was right in front of me put his head up and then started going down in a dive. So I pulled the trigger, and that was the end of a whale that I saw! After I pulled the trigger I wondered, "Where was my crew? Where am I?" It was all white around me, nothing to see, but I was still holding my gun! I looked around and realized I was on the back of the tent! When I took a shot at that whale from the front of the boat that was still on top of the ice, the blast from the gun threw me. I flew all over everybody and landed on the back of the tent. For a while I couldn't believe that's where I was! I was OK, 'cause I had this great big, heavy parka with the fur on the outside. I had these little fawn skins for my outside parka, but I got the caribou skin with the fur turned in on the inside.

Then I walked over and said, "Where's the whale?"

"He went down." They told me it went under the ice, went right straight up when I took a shot at it.

So we waited and waited. My brother David's crew was camped right next to us, on the back side of the point of ice where our camp was. About thirty minutes later my brother's crew started hollering. That whale came up, came out dead, right through the ice there by my brother's camp.

Boy, I sure really flew from there when I took a shot at that whale! [The extra kick came from using a bent bomb that didn't fit right.] Then, because I was the one that was running the boat [the captain], I told my brother, Arnold, I said, "Next time you're going to take a shot at the whales."

We butchered that whale for three days.[13] We used four block and tackles to pull it up onto the ice. Every time when we pulled on it and a little bit more came up out of the water, we had to take the top part of the *maktak* off. We'd leave the bottom one. The *maktak* was about four feet thick. We had to take all the top off and then keep on pulling because it was so big. It was getting heavier and heavier, so finally they cut the head off. You just tie the whole head all around the top in between the baleens and tie it up on the ice. It floats from the tongue. We pulled the body up first, and later on after we got the body all done, then we started pulling up the head. It was just like a thirty-foot whale, that's how big the head was! The baleens were fifteen feet long. It was a seventy-foot whale. We measured it with a hundred-foot tape we had. That's the biggest whale I ever shot.

But for two days I had nothing but kids come eat fresh whale at my house, no old people. And after all the kids were gone, then the elderly people started coming up. One of 'em just said, "Well, he said it before. Now he did it." They don't say nothing about it once I start feeding everybody. That was lots of work. We had a feast and cooked for three days.[14]

About two years later we lost all our whaling gear under the ice.[15] The ice took them out after we'd gotten just one whale. We got caught on the moving ice, the piling ice. Each man had to try to survive for himself. I told them just before we started leaving the boats and everything, I said, "Don't look backwards, just go ahead and try to save yourself. Don't look at the others. If they get caught, don't go help 'em, just keep on going. Let's see how many of us can make it." Boy, when the ice is piling up like that you have to travel up on top of it and jump around. Scary! That's why I told them, I said, "You kind of have to take to yourself. Don't look backwards. Don't help nobody." We just threw away all the gear, 'cause we weren't going to be able to save it anyway. We were right in the middle of that moving ice. Most of the dogs were all caught in the ice, too. They were let loose to run around and try to make it through on their own, but we still lost quite a bit of our dogs.

All the other crews were out, but most of them got on the safe side of the ice before it started moving. We were way out at a point of the ice at the open water. You have the current, the wind, the ice coming in real fast. We were too far out, that's why even though we were trying to come home the ice started breaking up already. We made it; all of us got back safe. When we hit the safe ice, the first guy to make it was my old uncle. He came up to me first and I told him I said, "My God, I wonder how many of us are going to be saved?"

Whale camp at ice edge. Courtesy Eugene Brower.

And he told me, he said, "Don't worry. We'll find out. Leave it up to Him [God]. If He wants us all alive, we'll have to be."

And for sure enough all nine of us were all saved. And I said, "Forget the gear and let's go home." We didn't even have a gun, nothing. I told them, "We'll try, once we can, to get all the replacement for our whaling equipment, boats and all."

But, it took me a long, long time to replace every one of 'em. This was in the early fifties when I lost everything. I finally got all the gear put together in '71, and we went out whaling in '72. And then I think it was in 1974 when we got a whale. We had new bombs, new equipment, everything. I lost all my brass guns and everything that I had from what these old whalers had left behind [the equipment that his father and other commercial whalers used]. And when I started buying up everything, they were all too expensive. It was nine hundred dollars for one shoulder gun, and I was just making three hundred a month from the navy. So, it took me a long time to get everything going again for my own crew. All my kids had to go to school at Mt. Edgecumbe.[16] But, I made it. I bought my father-in-law, Steve Hopson's, old gear. I bought the whole works cheap.

ॐ

One evening, I asked Kupaaq to explain the various whaling tools and the order in which they are used.

"So, they throw the harpoon first and then the darting gun?" I asked.

"No, they're together," he said.

After going back and forth like this for quite a while, Kupaaq grabbed his parka and headed for the door. I thought maybe he finally had enough of me, but I put on my boots, grabbed my own parka, and scampered after him. We went to the shed behind the house. As he talked, he pointed to whaling implements hanging on the wall above us that he had tried to describe to me earlier.

Despite this hands-on lesson, I remained confused. It was only years later, and after many explanations from other whalers, that I gained a better understanding. Yet without actually going out whaling, I will never truly know.

I was waiting for a whale one time. I had the gun and everything ready. The whale was coming up. He was about six to ten feet away and he stopped inside the water. He looked at me and blinked his eyes. He looked at me for at least maybe ten minutes and then he started coming up real slowly, even though he was still looking right at me. And when he was about two feet from the top of the water, he stopped, looked at me for awhile, and then started moving his tail. While his head was looking at me, he got up closer, and turned a little bit sideways. He put his eye on top of the water and looked at me. And after he got it all fixed up like this, I shot him inside the water right through the mouth. And when the bomb exploded, the whale just floated up. Even though I was waiting for him, he just wanted to be given to me, I think. He just started coming up, coming up, coming up to me and looked at me, just like that.

We were waiting for two whales one time and I told the guys of my crew to strike the smaller whale. And then from nowhere, another whale came up and pushed that first whale backwards away from us. We hadn't struck it yet. It pushed it backwards. And I told the boys, I said, "No, just put away your shoulder guns and harpoon. No way we're going to shoot it. That whale doesn't want us to get that smaller whale." So, we waited for another one. These were small whales, about less than thirty foot. I've never seen that again. For some reason that second whale said don't get that whale and was just like pushing it backwards. It's always amazing when you've seen quite a bit of how all these animals do all the things that they do inside the water.

During one conversation, Kupaaq and I talked about a crew in town headed by an elder woman whose husband had been the captain and when he died she kept on running the crew. Her oldest son and daughter did much of the work of running the crew, but she was still considered the captain. I knew another crew like this, and wondered how common it was for women to go whaling.

It is generally believed by outsiders that women do not go out whaling. Instead, they describe the women's role as sewing clothing and the skins for boat coverings, preparing food for the crew to take out on the ice, cutting up and distributing shares for the crew when a whale is caught, and organizing the feasts. These tasks and the women's role are essential elements in the whaling cycle.

As one whaling captain told me, "Once we hit shore, she's the boss." His wife had power over share distribution and feasts. Running their crew was a joint effort. He was in charge of the affairs of the hunt and on the ice; she controlled matters related to food, people, and sharing. In addition, nowadays some Iñupiat women help run crews, go out on the ice, are in the boat, and help butcher.

A long time ago, women were not allowed on the ice, because it was considered bad luck.[17] I asked Kupaaq about this:

"In the old days women didn't go out, did they?"

"That's way back anyway," he answered, meaning it happened a long time ago.

But, during these times, women were considered spiritually linked to the whales. A traditional Iñupiaq story tells of a girl tending a seal oil lamp inside the belly of a whale who lets the flame go out, and both she and the whale die because the light powering their mutual souls was extinguished. Just like with the hunters, women's behavior was controlled by strict taboos so as not to offend whales and to encourage them to give themselves. Even though this appears to be an old belief, Harry told stories emphasizing a special relationship between women and whales.

Whalers at ice edge watching for whales. Photo by Karen Brewster.

There's a good story about this one guy who was a good whaler. He'd get whales many times in the springtime. And then there was a guy in another boat who always wouldn't come quite close enough to the whales to get one. And so they traded wives! Then the second guy he caught a whale. The wives then went back to their own husbands after the good luck charm was up!

One time this one guy struck a whale, not a real big whale, and we used twenty bombs on it. It still went away, took off, gone. After all those bombs that we used on that one whale, and I don't know, maybe we were after it all day, yet it was still alive.

And then this one old man told us, he said, "Well, somebody had said something." But I wasn't really sure what he was saying.

Later on, we had a hold of that same whale, but he took off again. He took the whole float and all the line with him under the ice. And later on we heard that the wife of the captain who'd struck that whale first had said that when they catch a whale it's too much work. So people said that the whale didn't want her to work too hard, so he just took off. Then what that old man had said made sense. They say these whales always listen to the people. Sometimes we've even seen some whales in February around here [usually bowheads are not seen until April]. People would say these whales came here just to find out what people were saying about whales. The whales are listening, that's what they always told us.

Then there's another story about when these two elderly people got their last whale. The last time they went whaling they got one whale with one bomb and it was just the two of 'em. Just the two old people got the whale. The wife got hold of the rope and her husband harpooned the whale. And that was it. With one bomb the whale wasn't going no place.

That would be a pretty good share when you divide a whale for just them two. They didn't have to tow it, because it was there right at the edge of the ice. Only when they had to butcher it did others go over there to help. That was lots of meat for them two guys, but their kids helped take all that meat home using a dog team. This happened way back in early '50s.

I've gotten a whale with one bomb like that maybe three or four times. But these people were really old when just the two of 'em were out there. It was Numnik and his wife, Qupaq. Them old guys they knew how to throw the harpoon anyway.

Sometimes a whale is harpooned right from the ice. Kupaaq, and later his son Eugene, explained the technique of pushing one man out in the boat to a whale near the ice edge and killing it with one throw of the darting gun. Eugene explained that when one person is pushed out in a boat the whale should be killed with a single strike from the darting gun because it is too dangerous to shoot a shoulder gun from the ice when a boat is above a whale like this. This is because the bomb could accidentally explode in the water under the boat before reaching the whale, exploding shrapnel could hit the man in the boat, or the force of the explosion inside the whale could cause the whale to thrash about and flip the boat.

Kupaaq told me about a time when he was that sole harpooner pushed out in the boat.

One time I held onto a whale all by myself. The boat was on top of the ice, but they had to push me out into the water. It wasn't that far. There was no weight with it, only me in the boat. They have to push you out, see, with just the harpooner sitting in the front of the boat. You don't have to paddle when they push the boat, because it's going out only half-way and the front part of it's on top of [above] the whale. If you were to throw the harpoon from the ice, it would be a little bit too far away, but when you push the boat half-way out or so, then you're on top of the whale and can kill it. The other crewmembers aren't supposed to go inside the boat, but they use a rope that's on the edge [gunwale] of the boat to keep a hold of it and push it around from the ice.[18]

I was in the boat on top of [above] the head. I just threw the harpoon and held onto its rope [the float line]. That's it. There was the bomb from the darting gun and the float attached to the harpoon that went into the whale at the same time. I just used the harpoon [darting gun], that's all, because there are no shoulder guns allowed when you do it this way. I got it with one shot. Also, I didn't need to shoot the shoulder gun, because this one was half dead anyway. He gave himself to me.

Once you're holding a whale from the boat it looks funny, because once he starts towing you there's no weight in the boat. It's just you in the front holding the rope on the float, so the boat would be going down with the front getting pulled toward the water and the back sticking up. But you have to keep an eye on it, too, when it stops.[19] When the whale stopped, I was about oh, four, six inches away from the water when the boat stopped going down. And they had to come up with the other boat to help me. They started climbing up on top of the back of the boat trying to lower the back end. When they push you out, that's it, sometimes this happens.

When you're on top of the whale, it's not dangerous when you just put a harpoon in there and kill it right away. But if somebody with a shoulder gun shoots from the ice after that, I'll be on top of the whale, see. That's the dangerous part. There's no way of shooting it with a shoulder gun when there's a big boat on top of the whale. There's supposed to be no boat on a whale when you take a shot at it, because sometimes he lets his flippers fly and you can get flipped over. Or with the shoulder gun itself, sometimes the bomb explodes before it reaches the whale, see. It happens all the time.

But nowadays, when they have to put that float on first that's what makes a difference. When you're trying to put the float on first it's too dangerous with the gunner shooting the shoulder gun from the ice.

ᒎ

On November 29, 1991 Kupaaq and I were looking through some of his old photo albums. As we flipped the yellowed pages, Kupaaq talked about the faded or cracked photos, some of them from as far back as the 1940s, others as recent as the 1980s. Naturally there were pictures of whaling, spring whale camp on the ice, and of whales he and his crew had landed. Kupaaq pointed to a photo of himself posing in front of a bowhead lying on its side, hairy fronds of baleen peeking out of its mouth and said:

That's the whale I shot all by myself. The boat was out, but there was another shoulder gun and a harpoon right there on the ice. So, I shot that whale with the shoulder gun right there from the ice [before quota rules]. In those early days without the quota nothing bothers you, see. You could take a shot at a whale with just a shoulder gun, and then put your harpoon in later on. Nowadays, they told us not to shoot the whale with the shoulder gun unless you put the float on first, see.

And sometimes, the bomb explodes inside some of the guns. When a bomb explodes like this someone usually gets hurt, like one time there was one guy left with no belly on him. Another guy next to him was holding the gun and the bomb exploded as it was going out.

And then there was another time when they were going after a whale with a boat and this guy was going to shoot at the whale and the bomb exploded inside the barrel of the shoulder gun. The guy sitting to the back of him was hit by part of the gun and got a great big hole in his chest. Nothing happened to the guy holding the gun, but the guy that was paddling the boat, that's the one that got hit.

You hold onto that big, big handle of the shoulder gun and the barrel is pointing away from you. See, that barrel is what always explodes, not this handle part. The barrel flies away and sometimes it just rips the whole gun. That's why these bombs have to be fixed up real good. If it's loose in the barrel a little bit, that's what always happens [the gun explodes].20 They got so many of these accidents down at Point Hope; we've had quite a few of 'em around here, too. But, it's not good to look at; it's sad to think about.

It's the quota, that's what makes it different, see. In the meeting about the whaling [the International Whaling Commission] they said there were too many whales being lost, so they put all these rules on; too many rules. Rules like you have to put the float on first, because too many whales were lost when shot without a float on them.

Sometimes just with a darting gun, it's not enough. Sometimes a harpooner will shoot a whale with both a shoulder gun and a darting gun. They're both right there in the boat with him.21 You have to look to throw the harpoon at just the right spot. Sometimes they just rush trying to put the float just anyplace and it doesn't do anything to kill the whale. That doesn't count. That's when they have to start shooting bomb after bomb into the whale to finally kill it. Nowadays, they have to try to get it with the shoulder gun and a bomb from the darting gun after they put the float on first. The more bombs you put in there the better it is nowadays [so you kill the whale faster and you keep from losing it].

You say you've struck by putting a float on the whale that holds, but sometimes it comes off. Sometimes when they put the float on, the float hits the water and then the harpoon pulls out of the whale. When this happens, there's no float on the whale and that's a lost whale.22 Or sometimes they can find this same whale right away if there aren't many whales running, see, and then get it.

Once you don't follow these rules that they put in, they gonna ask you all these questions. You have to give all these answers when you catch a whale for the reports to the AEWC [Alaska Eskimo Whaling Commission], because they're real worried that they follow the rules.

There was one guy once who made a mistake. He was trying to catch a whale all by himself and lost it without saying nothing.23 AEWC was going to go after him, but he confessed. Under the rules that they give us, they'll take all your whaling equipment away from you and you can't whale for five years. You can't even lend your equipment out to try to get a share from the other boats when they get a whale. It's really strict.

The whale is divided during butchering, and then shared with the community at feasts, potlucks, and celebrations. The day after the whale is caught, the captain's wife and other women of the crew serve boiled *maktak*, meat, intestines, kidney, heart, and tongue along with stewed fruit and bread or *uqsrukuaqtaq* (fried

Umiaq *at ice edge. Photo by Karen Brewster.*

bread dough known as Eskimo donuts). Anyone in town is welcome to get a plate of food at the successful captain's house.

When spring whaling is over, usually in the beginning of June, a successful whaling crew hosts a small feast on the beach called *Apuĝauti*, which celebrates the return of the boat and its crew. Fresh duck or goose soup, cake, and hot tea and coffee are the standard fare. *Mikigaq* (fermented whale meat, *maktak,* and blood) is also sometimes served. In earlier times, *Apuĝauti* was held when the crew first came off the ice and the crewmembers were served. Today, it is held later in the season and the crew feeds the community.

In late June, the end of a successful whaling season is celebrated with *Nalukataq*, a day long feast featuring the blanket toss and Eskimo dancing that goes on late into the night.[24] The entire community gathers to eat such favorite foods as duck, goose or caribou soup, *mikigaq*, boiled whale heart, intestines and kidney, frozen *maktak* and whale meat, and fruit and cake. Visitors come from other North Slope villages and as far away as Anchorage and Fairbanks to enjoy the good food, the visiting, and the fun.

The circular blanket is made of the *ugruk* skins from a boat cover, with sturdy rope handles attached around the edges. The blanket is raised about six feet off the ground by heavy ropes held aloft by criss-crossed wood stanchions. People rush to grab a handle, then pump the blanket up and down over their heads, throwing the person standing on the blanket high into the air. The throwers take turns jumping.

Cooking and serving whale meat and maktak *in Kupaaq's kitchen at a successful captain's feast, 1991. Photo by Karen Brewster.*

A successful captain also distributes shares to the community at Thanksgiving and Christmas feasts held at the churches. Successful captains in the fall do not host *Apuġauti* or *Nalukataq* feasts, so they give away larger portions of their whale at Thanksgiving and Christmas than do the captains who catch spring whales. Like at *Nalukataq*, each family goes home with shares of meat, *maktak*, fish, and other subsistence foods. In addition, a successful captain shares his harvest with distant family and friends by sending them packages throughout the year. Kupaaq often said that all that he shared would eventually come back to him. To give was to receive.

One time, my wife, Annie, was down at Juneau and we were out whaling. We got the first whale that year. It was about a thirty-foot whale. And when we came home, there was Charlotte [Eugene's wife] and Mary Jane [Litchard], Ronald's [another of Harry's sons] first wife, and other women cooking around here. We told them there was this one part of the whale to be saved for the *Nalukataq*, and not to cook that. We showed them this other pile and said, "You can cook from this part. You can cook all of these here, but not those other ones."

And while we were there Charlotte came and said, "There's no *uati* out there." [*Uati* is the captain's share of the whale to be used for feasts.]

"Oh, no!" I said. I went out and there was just only the little flippers left, that's all. We got nothing for *Nalukataq*. We got nothing to put into the ice cellar. Everything was already cooked.

Blanket toss at Nalukataq, Barrow, Alaska, 1990s. Photo by Karen Brewster.

Steve Hopson, my father-in-law was over at the house watching TV. So, I told him, "Steve, we got no *uati*, nothing left. We'll have to catch another whale, because those flippers won't help us anything. Just the flippers isn't enough for *Nalukataq*." So we put the flippers away inside the ice cellar without cutting them up to save them for *Nalukataq*. And then, we were ready to take off again down to the ice.

When we went back down on the ice, all these other crews already had the best part of the ice for their camps and to put their boats. So I looked around and I told Eugene, I said "Well, let's just put our boat right here. There might be a whale someplace." So, we put the boat right there without putting up the tent.

And then I told 'em, I said, "Well, maybe you fellas should put up the tent." And while they were working on it, putting some mattresses in there and every-thing, Price [Harry's son] pointed out to the water and said, "Right there, Dad, right there."[25]

I looked sideways and a whale was just swimming towards our boat that was resting on the ice. He didn't go down, he just stayed on the surface. Three of us got the two shoulder guns and the darting gun and that whale was just still coming, coming, coming. I told Eugene, I said, "Well, that's the best spot I have to shoot it at, right through the mouth again. I'll try it right there."

So, the whale was coming right there toward me and I pulled the trigger on the shoulder gun [this was before the quota rules]. Eugene threw the harpoon and I think Sam Hopson had the second shoulder gun. All three of the bombs exploded, pretty near at the same time, too. And then that whale, I was looking at it, and his mouth just closed and he started turning, turning sideways and he was dead. Before even we finished putting up the tent we got another whale! That fast! We sure got the right spot on the ice for our camp. In no time that whale just came up. That was a thirty-seven foot whale.

When we went home Steve was still watching TV over there and I told him, "Hey Pop, we got a whale again!"

He looked at me, "That quick?" Then he started crying. After that he, stared up for a while and said, "Well, I just think about that one word that you said to me: we got no more meat for *Nalukataq*, so we might as well go out there again while the whales are running. And He [God] heard you."

That year we had the two flags up at *Nalukataq*.[26] I think it was in the '70s or early '80s. It was before Annie and Steve died. She died in '84 and he died about a year or so before her. So that whale might be in '79, something like that.

I wrote down all the whales I caught, like how big they were or what the date was. It's written in a book.[27] We got twenty-two to twenty-five whales for this house with our crew since 1972, something like that. This includes spring whales and fall whales. I think it was just those two years we got two whales. And then we killed so many more whales for other crews, by helping to chase them and put more bombs in after they'd struck.[28]

And then one year when one guy was camped over there down off Hollywood, and we were camped up by the navy camp [Naval Arctic Research Lab], they put a float on a whale down there.[29] They shot it from the ice. So we took off into the open lead from up where we were. We went right straight out from the ice, way out, instead of going down along it toward them. When he struck a whale, his whale always would go right straight out away from the ice edge. That's how it was. So we were way out there and we called them on the radio to tell them we hadn't seen that whale with the float yet up there. And then Eugene said, "The float's right there, right in front of us." Before even the whale came up, the float was right in front of us, about twenty feet away. From there we just followed the rope on the float that was coming up, and there was the whale starting to come up. I handed Eugene a gun and said, "You might as well shoot it with your shoulder gun."

Pretty soon, he said, "Where should I shoot it? How far?"

"Right straight towards the head on the back of the front flippers, so that the bomb when it goes in there, it might hit one of the bones. Right there, because when it explodes it's gonna break up the part of the vertebrae or the ribs."[30]

Sure enough, he took a shot at that whale right from the back towards the head, and the bomb exploded. He killed that whale. Then the other crew's harpoon handle that hadn't come off just floated up from the whale. The whale got tangled up in the rope, but once he got loose he didn't have any power to move around that fast anymore. So, we picked up that darting gun handle that was attached to the rope; it was just floating. And we started holding the float to keep hold of the whale.

I told Eugene, I said, "Let's wait for a help. He's not going no place." After Eugene shot that whale, it just never went down. It just floated because he was shot right through part of the kidney.

And then two boats came up to us to help. We were just holding the whale by the float! That other captain finally came around and told us, "How did you know he was going that way?"

"Well, I know which way your whales are going."

So we hit the right spot out there in the lead to meet that whale from way up where we'd been. Those guys who shot that whale first were way down there to the south and we got it way out right in front of us towards the north. When that float came out they said you could hardly see that float out there from the ice; it was more than a couple of miles, I think. That was a great big open water to go through, but it wasn't rough water.

We've killed quite a few of those whales that they've already put the floats on and then we chased them. We always get the right angle, I think. When they come up they're always right close to us. We see the float. Once a crew sends a message that they've struck and are chasing a whale, then we always all go out to help. When someone says they've put a float in a whale, then all the other crews are supposed to go help look for that one whale.

But now, last year when the quota was getting lower [near the end of the season and they had few allowable strikes remaining], they were trying to strike any old way even though they were supposed to be looking for the ones that were struck already. And then they were short three or four whales; they couldn't find which was which. Some crews went after other whales instead of helping to find the lost ones. And there are some crews who don't even want to get out from the ice—they just want to stay in their tent—and then get a share when the others catch that wounded whale.

Kupaaq's crew after landing two whales in one season, circa 1975. Left to right: *Harry Sr., Eugene, Ronald, Charlie, Price, Harry Jr., and Annie. Courtesy Eugene Brower.*

And I told 'em, I said, "Everyone has to help!" Well, they mention it's a different way now, that they only have to come help after the whale is killed, after the whale is on the ice and has to be butchered. If they don't show up then to help butcher that whale, they're going to be left out. That's the rules that they had. They say if they don't show up when they start butchering, they're supposed not to get a share. They don't say nothing about helping to kill or find someone else's whale. The captains talk about everybody going after the same whale after it's shot, but it doesn't work. There's some sneaky guys. Like one guy last spring he struck a whale even though they were talking to the crews that they should all go find these three lost ones first. Then he struck another whale and lost it. It was foggy and they kept going after whales anyway. That's what happened to it.

Sometimes there are some crews that when they strike a whale from the ice they just stay in their tent and let the others look for it. And when they've found it, this crew got a whale just by sitting on the ice. That's what some of 'em do. Like this one crew, they struck a whale and another guy found it just floating without a float on it. The float came off and the whale was dead. He was just going by in his boat, saw it, and put a harpoon on it. It ended up belonging to his brother-in-law, who he let have all that whale. It would have been different if it was not his brother-in-law's, if it was somebody else's whale, I think.

Most captains respected and admired Kupaaq's skills and knowledge. When he suggested they let scientists measure and take specimens from each landed whale, as part of the effort to document scientifically the bowhead population for the International Whaling Commission, the other captains agreed. This support by a strong leader gave the scientific program just the boost it needed to become successful. But at first it was not easy.[31]

When this one young guy first got a whale he was trying to kick us out [from measuring and taking samples]. They'd started drinking after they got that whale, after we got that whale on the ice. They shot it with a float and all these boats were chasing the whale, and we finally got it out there and towed it back home. And that's the time when I was really mad. That's the time I started talking to them. There's no drinking supposed to be out there, but they still did it.

I told him, I said, "Nobody's going to stop me from this. You're just beginning as a whaling captain and that whiskey is not for killing whales. You're supposed not to touch it during whaling. You're doing it right now, but nobody's gonna stop me from measuring these whales. Whoever got a whale, I'm gonna be with Tom Albert [veterinary scientist studying whales] helping him."

That young captain gave Tom a bad time, but I told Tom don't listen to them, just do your work. I'll be with you. If they start doing something, I'll be right there. It wasn't always easy, but we made it.

And then the next year we had a meeting with all the captains. I went over there and I said, "All of you whaling captains I had to say one thing to you guys. If you fellas catch a whale out there, forget that whiskey out there. You can go home and drink it inside your house, but not down there. That's really in a bad business. You might never see a whale again." Then the next year that same young guy came and he apologized to me. It made him feel a little bit better, I guess. He said, "I'm sorry, Harry. I found out that I was making a big mistake. The next time when we catch a whale I'll try to behave myself. So you can tell all the whaling captains the same thing, because that's the only way we might get more quota given to us."

And I told him, I said, "After these studies you might get a free book [scientific reports] about these first whales that were caught, about what we've gone through measuring whales." They took some specimens out to universities and wrote all these reports about what they've gone through. And then when they gave him one of those big books, he came over to me and said, "My golly, you sure was right, Harry! They did give me a great big book free."

"That's what I thought, because that was what was supposed to happen. I knew about it, because the scientists talked to me. I always knew them before you younger guys."

And Tom Albert always calls me when he has to go to those big meetings. He says, "Harry, can I use your name?"

"Just go ahead. We've gone through with this already so many times anyway. If you have to use my name, go ahead, use it."

Those captains were trying to stop Tom from measuring the whales. But, I had to fight for it. I got that Tom and Mike Philo out there with me.[32] But I was really busy during whaling in those days. I went out there when the scientists started counting whales on April 14, and then I had to be out whaling with my own crew, with my boys out there. I had to keep everybody going. I had to take care of those guys that were counting and measuring whales. I had to drive my Ski-doo way up to the Point [Point Barrow] to see how they were doing, talk to them, and then come home. When they caught a whale, I had to go over to where the whale was and help the scientists. I told Eugene I always had to be looking for Tom. This was in 1978, 1979, 1980, I think, something like that.

Barrow Whaling Captains Association, 1982. Photo by Ted Bell.

We did a good job on whales, on the quota. They could get it higher, but I told them we got too much of a quota. It's gonna be the same thing like before the quota was on, when everybody gets too excited and tries to be the first one to strike even though they might make a mistake. They'll just say, we've got lots of strikes so we can do whatever we want. People weren't as careful before there was a quota.

One reason why that quota started was there was one guy who was camped way down the coast so he'd be ahead of everybody when the whales came up. He kept on shooting all these whales that passed by going close to him just with the shoulder gun. He didn't use any floats. He did this so if they found his bomb in a whale that was killed by someone else, then he'd get the whale. This way he could get all the whales he'd shot at.

The scientists were using a microphone that goes under the water, under the ice, to see which way and how many whales passed by. Every time when a bomb exploded it was recorded. And that guy shot twenty-seven whales, but got nothing. We found one whale floating towards the Point and took it ashore. It belonged to him; there was one bomb of his in it.

After this guy lost so many whales because he didn't put a float on, that's the time when they started getting all these quotas; when they started fighting about the whales and putting all these rules on.

156 Chapter Eight

One October evening, Kupaaq and I talked about dreams. He said, "Sometimes these dreams are the best dreams. You can travel anyplace all in your dream in one time. And then when you're dreaming with scary old things, little things, then you wake up."

I remembered a story he had told me before about a whale showing him events in Barrow while he was actually in the hospital in Anchorage. I had assumed it was just a dream or a partial delirium when he was ill. I had heard about people on morphine having vivid dreams that seemed as if the events really happened. I explained away an unexplainable experience in the only way I knew how, by applying Western, scientific thought. From Kupaaq's perspective, it was a supernatural experience from which he learned a great deal.

Kupaaq's children who witnessed this and were told the story have a hard time explaining what happened. Eugene, who was at his father's bedside the whole time, explained:

We thought we were losing him. It was like he went into a trance. We called his name, pinched him, and got no response. Then Dad snapped out of it and told us about the things that happened in Barrow. I called my brother, Harry Jr., who was in Barrow, and these things really happened. I don't know who all Dad told this story to. But I don't retell it much because it's like sacred. Dad really shocked us with that. I was so amazed with how close to the whale he was. He could feel the bombs going into the whale. The whale was his life, so he was this close to the whale who took him away.[33]

After hearing about this near-death experience, I teased Kupaaq, "One of your nine lives?"

He had been in the hospital numerous times in recent years when it looked as if he might not make it and then he would recover miraculously.

"One of my nine lives!" he replied.

On this night, when I tried to relate the experience to dreams, Kupaaq quickly assured me this was not a dream, and went on to describe what happened to him in 1986.

That whale took me all the way from Anchorage to Barrow. I wasn't dreaming! I was dead! He took me all the way over to Barrow where these guys were shooting at the mother whale. He talked to me; he told me all the stories about where they had all this trouble out there on the ice. And he told me which people he'd seen and what they'd done. He pointed at my boys.

When they struck a whale Harry [Jr.] and Ronald went out with the boat to start helping the crew that struck it. The first thing that whale pointed to was Harry and said, "This is the guy, with the red beard, who met my mom and from the front somehow he just took a shot at her. Then she and I tried to go the other way, but the boats started coming up again from the back. And he's the one that shot my mother." He said, then when he looked backwards his mom was just floating. She was dead. He told me, he got no place to go; nobody loves a calf. Then he pointed to Harry and said, "This is the guy that gave me a place to stay."

And later I found out they had the whole little baby whale in our great big ice cellar. Nobody ever mentioned it to me until just before Thanksgiving when Tom Albert and Craig George [a biologist with the North Slope Borough Department of Wildlife Management] and Harry came up to the house. They wanted the key for the ice cellar. I asked them, "What're you gonna do?" Finally they said they were going to get the baby whale up. I don't know where they took him, sent him out to be studied someplace, I think. It was the whole complete baby whale down there in our ice cellar, not even cut, and they'd never told me about it.

And later on, I remembered that word of the baby whale: "That Harry, he gave me the place to stay." I figured it out later that the baby whale was there in the ice cellar until those guys took him out to study him. I told Eugene, "Now I know what that baby whale had told me in Anchorage. He's got a place to rest, that is what he meant. That after he took me back to Anchorage he had to go back to where he was supposed to be resting."

I swam with that whale, but I never had no trouble breathing, like I do now. He took me anyplace. I followed him and nothing bothered me. He told me stories about where his mom and he were shot, how they were wounded, suffered, and all that. And I told Eugene, I said, "I always tell you guys not to hunt after May, because that's when all these calves are born. I told you most of the calves are born after May and in June after they pass Barrow." And then just about the last words the baby whale ever said were, "If me and my mom had passed Barrow and we got over to the other side of it, then we would be spending all that summer up there. Then we would come back the same route as she brought me through Barrow." But, that calf didn't make it. They got him and his mother out there in springtime.

After they killed him and his mother he came over to pick me up from Anchorage and then took me back after he showed me all that went on in Barrow. I was in the hospital two weeks and a half and when I opened up my eyes there was all my family with me there in the hospital. And from there I started coming up alive. Soon after I opened my eyes I said, "Eugene, let me walk."

He held onto me and said, "No, no, Dad. You're not gonna walk. We'll have to ask the doctor first."

But I said, "I'm strong enough to walk."

The doctor came up and Eugene told him, he said, "Just a couple of minutes after he opened up his eyes, my dad said he could walk."

The doctor was really surprised and said, "Well, if he wants to walk, we'll try it." He put a clip on all these tubes that were put into me and I stood up. The doctor was on one side and Eugene was on the other side. I started walking! I got out of my bed, and I walked.

I didn't go very far and the doctor said, "Harry, that's too much. Let's go back to your bed."

I said, "I'm not tired."

When I woke up, I told Eugene that the whale said there was an accident when they were pulling up his mother onto the ice. The rope broke and it hit three guys. Since Eugene had been with me in Anchorage, he didn't know about any accident in Barrow. At the same time I told him that, Eugene called Barrow and then sure enough it was true. And he asked me, "How did you know?"

"I was watching you," I said.

After I got strong enough, all these reverends came to see me. I started asking them what was the meaning of this story that I'd gone through. Nobody ever said anything to me, even though they graduated to be reverends and ministers, except this one old man, named Eric. I'd known him ever since '69. He was from the Assembly of God Church. He always came to see me when I was in the hospital. One day when I was in the emergency room at the hospital he told his wife, he said, "Honey, you can stay home, but I'm going to the hospital. Somebody's pulling me from the hospital. There's somebody in the hospital that wants to see me." And for sure enough, I was in real pain when he walked in. He grabbed me and said, "Harry, I didn't tell you to come back this way."

And I asked him, "How did you find out?"

He said, "I know. The good old Lord told me, so I decided to go look at the hospital."

This time when I recovered he came to see me and said, "Harry, I thought you'd never see me again. I thought you were gonna be gone, but you're back again."

"Yeah, I'm back. But I'd like to get the meaning of the story I have to tell you of why I came back."

He said, "Go ahead, tell me your story."

So I told him the story and he said, "Well, the good old Lord can use anything when He wants to have somebody back. He can use all kinds of animals or anything, not just the human beings, to show someone something he has to go through, so he can tell stories of what happened and do something about it."

Then this other guy who used to be around here, Reverend Wilson, I told him the same story when he came to see me. I didn't tell him about what that Eric told me. He said the same thing like Eric did, he said, "The good old Lord can use anything He wants when He wants somebody back on the earth. He can send anybody back to earth in anyway."

Eric came back the next day and said that He [God] sent me back so I can tell all my boys about these animals, to tell them that they don't have to fool around with these big whales. So I told Eugene, "In springtime, I'm going to give you the deadline of May 27 for whaling. That's how late you fellas are gonna go whaling. When it comes up to 27 of May, even though you didn't catch nothing yet, you have to come home. You've seen me, what I've gone through, Eugene, with that baby whale, so that's a deadline I'm gonna give you."

I told my boys that story in Eskimo, and Harry Jr., he said, "Dad, how do you know?"

I said, "I've been watching you with this whale. I've been telling you guys that I've been watching you even though I'm in the Anchorage hospital. I've been watching you at Barrow when you fellows were killing that mother whale and that baby whale who knows you guys."

My boys never told me, but I knew what they had done. I just told them what they had done. I was watching! And here they were, most of 'em were in Anchorage and I was here at Barrow. Anchorage was where my body was, but I was way off, out of my body wandering around with that whale. Boy that's a good lesson for everybody, I told 'em.

I told the captain of that one crew about it, because he's the one that struck that mother whale first. "You're the one that got me into trouble," I told him.[34] After they struck that whale, my boys went off to help them kill it. Harry's bomb finally killed that mother whale. The calf was just born; it was a baby one about fifteen feet long. It was still alive, lively, but it just couldn't survive by itself, so they had to kill it. But once they had that baby one killed, nobody wanted to take care of it. So Harry told them that they could put the baby whale inside our big ice cellar instead of just leaving it out there on the ice. So after the scientists found a place that wanted to work on it, they pulled it out just before Thanksgiving and sent it out. They sent it down to one of those places where they worked most of these experiments with whales.

Well, that captain said to me, "I'm sorry, but don't say it's me. That's just going to be a lesson for everybody that they have to remember." His crew has to remember, too, I think, because it seems like when they don't catch a whale they act like they're the only ones that has to strike the whale; that they needed that whale.[35]

And I told that captain, "No, it's the opposite way. The quota is given to us and all these strikes are divided up to each whaling captain, but the whale is given to each boat. If the good old Lord wants you to catch a whale, He'll let the whale come right up to you, see, and if He doesn't want nobody to strike He won't let nobody." Some guys are always trying to fight back on this and go after whales they shouldn't [whales that are not meant to be taken or are not giving themselves to them].

Also, they're supposed not to get a mother when there's a calf with her, because it's too dangerous. They say if you have to kill both of 'em, you're supposed to strike the mother first. If you strike the baby one first, the mother's going to get mad and fight 'til death. Like one time in Nuiqsut, they struck the baby one and they didn't know the mother was under the whale. She fought a lot and flipped the boat. If you kill the mother first, the baby one doesn't run away, but sticks right close to the mother.

⌇⌇

By the time I knew Kupaaq, he was no longer going out on the ice to whale. But this did not mean he sat idly by. He oversaw preparation of all his crew's gear; he directed who was to do which tasks; he gave advice and suggestions to his sons and other crewmembers; he kept in touch with what was happening on the ice through the CB radio; he made the decisions about share cutting and distribution; and he supervised all activity around the home base when his crew caught a whale.

It was obvious that Kupaaq really missed whaling. He had been a harpooner—a respected and important position—and a good one at that. He would get antsy during whaling season, always running around or being busy with something so he would still feel involved. He kept close to the radio so he did not miss anything. I knew I could just stop in to see Kupaaq and he would tell me what was happening with the whalers.

One evening during fall whaling, when we were anxiously awaiting word about a whale that had been struck but not yet killed, Kupaaq began to reminisce about his whaling days. With pride and nostalgia, he told me about the last whale he struck.

Even after I got my own crew, I was still a harpooner. Even after I showed Eugene about running the crew, I still harpooned a whale the last time I went out whaling. Even though they said I was too weak to throw a harpoon, I said, "No way!"

It was May 27. They told me that they were going home, going to work. Eugene, he told me, "They have to go back to work. Let's go home. There's no whales anyway." Most of the other crews had already gone inland geese hunting.

So, everybody went inside the tent to get ready, to have some last tea and pack everything up. And I was out there by the boat all by myself. The CB was so quiet, nobody was mentioning seeing any whales. I was just going back and forth, walking around right there at the water's edge. And finally, something got me [a feeling about something]. So I started walking right in front of the boat, going down to the open water. I looked downwards and here this whale was right there floating under the boat. So, I shot it. And there was that harpoon without the darting gun, just the float with it, lying there. They'd been getting it ready to put away. So, I threw the harpoon, oh, maybe as far as five or six feet, and the float was just floating there. [The float was attached to the whale, and the whale died right there.]

A guy coming from another crew was riding a Ski-doo by, so all these guys in our tent didn't even hear me when I took a shot at that whale. They were inside talking away. This guy came along with a Ski-doo and opened the tent, and he told them, he said, "Your dad got a whale out there! Right in front of the boat!" Then everybody went out from the tent. There was Eugene with no stockings, no boots, no nothing. He was chasing his boots [trying to put his boots on while running]. He ran to the boat and he grabbed me so much. He said, "How did you know that the whale was coming up?"

"Well, I didn't know, but he gave himself. He was hiding around on the ice and came up to me and that's it. I didn't have no time to go to the tent and tell you guys." I knew I was going to get him anyway.

I got him with just one shot. Once I'm on top of the ice, it doesn't take me too long to get a whale. That's the last one I got. The last time I went out was in 1980. I started having all this dizziness and Ronald brought me home, but when I got better I went out again and I got this last one. I didn't do all the work of cutting it up, though. I just talked to them and showed them what to do. And then after that, Eugene started taking over the crew. I'd just talk to them on the CB from home. They've learned anyway; they know what to do.

Kupaaq at his last Nalukataq, June 20, 1991. Photo by Karen Brewster.

Harry Kraft Brower, Sr. passed away on April 22, 1992, at the Barrow hospital. His sons were out whaling. They had not wanted to go out while he was sick, but he told them to go. He didn't want them to sit around town and wait for him to die. He preferred that they were doing what he wished he still could, what they enjoyed, and what they had to do. "My dad told us to go out whaling. Not to stay home. Because as whalers we were hunting for the whole community," Eugene later explained. Charlotte, Eugene's wife, sat and prayed with Kupaaq during his last moments. The rest of the family soon joined her.

A couple of days later, the Utqiaġvik Presbyterian Church was packed for the funeral. The people of Barrow stopped whaling and paid their final respects to this distinguished *umialik*. As a cold northeast wind whipped across the tundra, the casket was lowered at the small Browerville cemetery overlooking Barrow's lower lagoon. Kupaaq was laid next to his wife and near his father.

On September 26, 1992 Aalaak Crew landed a thirty-eight foot whale. This was the first whale the crew caught without Kupaaq and the last to be served from his house. The lower jawbones from this whale now arch over his grave, telling all who pass that here lies a great whaler.

It was unsettling being in Kupaaq's house celebrating a whale without him. I had this eerie sensation that he would walk in at any moment. I remembered what Kupaaq told me once about death and the afterlife. He believed in God and Heaven, but in keeping with his lifelong mixing of Western and Iñupiaq traditions and his deep connection to whales, he had other plans for himself when he died:

That [Heaven] must be a good place to go! They always go someplace, I don't know where. I'm going to go there the other way! I'm going to go into the water, go join the whales. That's the best place, I think. You'd travel, travel, travel. You could feed aaaall the people for the last time.

His wish came true. He fed the people of Barrow one last time.

EPILOGUE
Through Other Eyes

Throughout this project I was painfully aware of how little I really knew about Harry Brower, Sr. I only knew him for three years. There was so much about his life and his knowledge of the Arctic that we never got to talk about. So I turned to his oldest son, one of his sisters, his brother-in-law, and some of his long-time coworkers in the scientific community to help teach me more about Harry and his life.[1]

Eugene Brower

Eugene Brower (Aalaak), born in 1948, is Harry's eldest son and second oldest of his nine children. Eugene lives in Barrow with his wife, Charlotte (Iqsraq) in a comfortable five bedroom house near the lagoon on the Browerville side of town. Their grown children, grandchildren, extended family members, friends, and whaling crew members are frequent visitors to the house.

Former mayor of the North Slope Borough and president of the Barrow Whaling Captains Association, Eugene is currently deputy director of the North Slope Borough Fire Department and is a successful hunter. Although he inherited his father's whaling gear and has proved a successful whaling captain in his own right, Eugene waited to take control of the crew until after Harry died.

Eugene is broad-shouldered, wears his dark hair trimmed nearly to a crew cut, and walks with a determined stride. Like Harry, Eugene tells stories to make a point. He speaks in a confident, deep voice with his father's same rhythm of pauses and emphasis.

Eugene learned to whale from his father, who taught him how to predict what the whales will do, how to chase a whale safely, how best to kill a whale, how to read the ice, how to choose a good spot for their camp, and how to be a strong leader. They whaled together for over twenty years.

The thing that really stands out the most is when he struck a whale by himself. While we were having dinner, he was saying grace, and we saw Price [one of Eugene's younger brothers] take off. He was onto a gun. He was trying to pull the shoulder

---

(Opposite) Harry with his sons, circa 1980. Left to right: *Harry Jr., Eugene, Charlie, Price, and Ronald. Courtesy Eugene Brower.*

gun on a whale. Part of the whale was underneath the young ice that was about a couple of feet thick. I ran to the harpoon that was on the ice and my father got into the skin boat and he said, "Wait. Wait 'til I put a harpoon into the whale."

So nobody did anything until the whale got underneath the boat and he struck. And that thing [the harpooned whale] went straight down; it dove straight down and we couldn't pull it.

He said, "Well, boys. Over the years I've asked for a lot of things. I'm gonna grab this rope, the float line rope with my hands and pray. I'm gonna ask that we pull the whale without losing it."

Oliver Leavitt's and Arnold Brower, Sr.'s crews came over to help. And we pulled and we pulled and we pulled. Finally, we broke that whale loose. And when we pulled it up and they put another harpoon into it, the harpoon that he had thrown, just the first barb of that harpoon tip, was in the whale. And after they put that other harpoon into it and we pulled it over, that first harpoon just came off.

And he made a believer out of us when he said, "These hands of His can do a lot of things." And that's what stands out the most.

ᵌ

I never saw my father really get mad at anything. One of the stories I can tell you about him is during the land claims issue. These guys brought a whole bunch of maps over to my parent's house, and they told him, "What would you say the boundaries of the Arctic Slope were?"[2]

Without hesitation he went from Demarcation Point following the foothills all the way down below Point Hope, and told them, "This is the North Slope. This is the Iñupiaq country."

And those people—so called Native leaders of the Arctic Slope—have never acknowledged him. They try to take a lot of coverage, say this is Arctic Slope country, and my father was the one that made the boundary.

He told them, "This is what you fight for. Below that, that's Indian country."

He was never acknowledged, because these people tried to take so much credit for that. Because of his vast knowledge of the Arctic, having been with the survey crew—when these people weren't even born—and having walked this country, he knew where these sites that [these guys were] talking about were. Based from the information that they got from him, they made themselves the authors or the ones that knew the country after first talking to him and getting the information from him. That was one thing that he regrets for not being recognized.

That was the man behind the scenes; he helped make what Arctic Slope enjoys now. And that's how the boundary he made got to be the boundaries of the North Slope Borough. He was never in the limelight. He just stayed behind; he let the talkers do the talking. But he was hoping at least one of them would acknowledge him; would say that the information came from him.

In comparison, Harry's role in the fight to protect Iñupiat subsistence whaling in the late 1970s and early 1980s has been more widely recognized:

My father has been very successful as a whaling captain. He was a well respected whaler in this community. Matter of fact, he helped Dr. Albert get situated when Dr. Albert first started working for the borough as a scientist on the study of the bowhead. He was meeting a lot of opposition until my father spoke up to the group and told them, "Hey, help this man out. He's going to be here to help you, to help us out." And after that the whalers reluctantly opened their doors to Dr. Albert, and now Dr. Albert is a well-known bowhead scientist.

My father had a talk with him and from the way Dr. Albert presented himself, my father believed him; he knew he was going to be here for a long time. For a man to leave his prestigious position back at a major university back east had to be quite an undertaking.

I think because of the attack we had from the IWC and having been exposed to scientists before—having worked with them over the years—my father believed science was the way out, was the way to prove to the world that the whales were not on the decline. Based on his own personal knowledge and observation, he knew they were on the upswing. But he knew that the people outside wouldn't believe us just because we were saying it. We needed people with the degrees, or the scientists, to say what we'd been saying all along.

He saw it before we did. We were too busy rabble-rousing. He was using science on science, science against science. He was using what the scientists were saying about the whales being on the decline, and that the other scientists said, "No, they're on the rise." He was using their degrees against each other, because he knew that they wouldn't believe us. The people outside in the scientific arena wouldn't believe the Native peoples; they thought we were just blowing hot smoke.

Kupaaq was also known for his artistry. As a boy, he watched his father and Iñupiat elders make things from ivory. He dabbled at ivory carving himself, but never spent much time on it until he got older and was not out hunting as much.

After he retired, Kupaaq had more time to develop his artistic talents. He carved realistic animals and created jewelry out of ivory. He fine-tuned his art of baleen boat making and developed his own system for putting the boats together. He soaked and cleaned the long strips of baleen outside in a long, narrow, galvanized metal tub he built on the side of a shed. He traced the templates onto the baleen and cut the pieces out with a table saw. Like a production line, he had piles of each type of piece on his workbench. This way he could put together many boats before he had to clean and cut more baleen. He paid attention to detail in every step; cutting the pieces out of long stalks of baleen, sanding the edges smooth, tying the pieces together with fishing line, and varnishing the finished product to a mirror-like shine.

Kupaaq's boats not only provided an important source of extra income, but making them gave him a pleasurable way to fill the long days of retirement. Being an artist also offered him a way to maintain his Iñupiaq identity when he was an old man who could no longer hunt. According to Eugene, Kupaaq taught himself:

When he was in maybe his late forties or fifties he started carving. It was something to do to pass time in the evenings. He got to be quite a carver. His first pieces of work weren't really good to look at, but with time he refined his technique of carving and making baleen boats. Each carver's got his own pattern for the boat pieces. He learned how to break a piece of baleen in half to make the baleen boat with it and then he refined that. He also learned how to use different things to make the boat look like a sailboat, like the colored portion of the baleen for the sail. He did that himself. His baleen boats got to be quite a sale item that people wanted to constantly buy. He got to be well known as an Eskimo artist. He got to be quite renown in that area.[3]

Kupaaq's son, Ronald, recalled how his father encouraged his own artistic abilities. When Ronald was twelve and sick with rheumatic fever, Kupaaq gave him a set of oil paints to entertain him while he was home-bound. Later, Kupaaq taught Ronald how to carve ivory. As Ronald explained, "We had a little competition going on about making things. On whose was better. Then I convinced him to enter a local art show. He won first place for his boats. I won for oil painting. So we both won. I thought he was mighty proud of that. You know how he'd beam when something was going good."[4]

Eugene and Harry often camped and hunted together, especially as Harry got older and could no longer travel alone. They made their last trip together in 1991.

Over the years my dad was most happy when he was out hunting. In his later years, he wanted to go camping or go hunting, because that was when he was the most happiest. That was what he liked to do. Over the years I'd asked my brothers in the summertime to take him hunting; he liked to go caribou hunting, get his winter supply. And they always had excuses. And I was the one that took time off from work to take him. Even almost at the point of quitting my work to take him up inland to where he wanted to go with his boat. I'd have to make a quick emergency request to say my dad wanted to go camping, and he wanted to go now. And my younger brothers couldn't take him, so therefore I had to go with him. Those were the most precious times for me. Instead of being my father, he got to be more than a father. It was like two brothers, in a sense. And I would tease him. I used to be so afraid of him, but over the years of taking him camping we get to be real close and I used to just kid with him.

In one of the last trips he made out with his aluminum boat the year before he passed away, we went up to Alaqtaq River. I was steering the boat and I could see all those antlers up there above me [on the river bank]. I told my dad, "Dad, there's caribou above us."

He said, "Where? I can't see 'em. You may see 'em, but I can't."

I said, "Dad, you're getting so old that maybe you should just run the boat while I go up and go shoot."

Harry Brower's handcrafted baleen boats. Photo by Karen Brewster.

About that time, he said, "Beach the boat."

So I beached the boat on the riverbank. He stepped off—he just had his little moccasin shoes on—and he started shooting. I killed the outboard and got the anchor. I was going to go run up and anchor the boat along with carrying my rifle.

He said, "Just put your rifle away. Bring your thermos bottle up and give me some coffee. And I'll help you skin the caribou."

He made seven shots, that was it. I got up, went over the bank and said, "Where's the caribou?" In my mind, I said I won't have to really pack them, they will be real close to the shoreline.

"Oh, oh, I only shot the ones I could see!"

He just dropped seven caribou about a hundred to a hundred and fifty yards away from the shore. And that was my pay-back from him—my punishment—for calling him an old man! I had to skin 'em, cut 'em and haul them myself, while he said he was going to go on guard duty. He had a thermos bottle of coffee, sugar, and some crackers, and sat by the riverbank and talked to me about what I was doing. He said that I was a spoiled brat and all this stuff.

What he was really doing was egging me on, because I was getting mad. These were big bulls, a lot of work, and he just sat there. I picked the hindquarters up by myself, threw them onto my back and carried them onto the boat. Then went back and got the front quarter. I'd fall, then I'd get up, and walk down over to the boat, then go back and get another one. All seven of them I did by myself. By then I was mad; I was pouting.

He said, "Well, let's go back to our tent."

And on the way down there another herd of caribou started coming up close to the river. He said, "Son, you want to go shoot some caribou?"

I said, "Hell no!" I didn't even stop. I just kept on going and went to our tent.

And he got up later on and he said, "Son."

I said, "What?"

"Poor baby! You poor baby! You want to go home?"

That got me out of my pouting mood! I said, "Nope. I don't want to go home. We're up here already."

We had the caribou he wanted, so we broke camp and went to different places he wanted to go along the river. We went up to the Chipp River, going through Tasiqpaatchiaq Lake. We went up and saw the different sites he wanted to see. Then we came back down to the mouth and went into the channel to go up to the Tupaaġruk River. Went up and took a look at it and came back.

He said, "You know, this might be the last time I'm up and seeing this country."

And then I never gave it a second thought. He took me where he wanted to go. He showed me where he wanted and I took him there. That's the last time he went up there.

Sadie Neakok

As one of Harry's older sisters, Sadie Neakok's memories tell us about Harry's younger days. Sadie (1916–2004) was born in eight years before Harry. She left Barrow to attend high school when he was a small child, and he was almost a teenager by the time she returned. Despite this gap, Sadie's comments are useful, because Harry's own stories do not include much from his childhood. Sadie completed two years of college, was a teacher, and was Barrow's magistrate from 1960 to 1977.

When we talked, Sadie was a small woman in her 80s, with short, permed gray hair. She has thick, stout hands, exactly like her brother's, that still serve her well for sewing fancy parkas, kneading bread dough, and cutting up seals. In a deep, gravelly voice Sadie energetically recreates the past in entertaining stories of vivid detail. She is a bit of a local celebrity and unofficial historian, because of her talent for storytelling, her extensive knowledge, and the fact that her life story has been made into a book. Sadie tells a bit about the atmosphere around the Brower household when she and Harry were growing up. This shows the influences that made them into the adults they became.

I was born to a family where my father was a white man and my mother was an Eskimo. I got to where I noticed that my mom couldn't speak the English language. And I knew that dad was fluent in speaking the Eskimo language. He had to learn it to be able to communicate with the Eskimo people he was mingling with up here. If he wanted to be understood he had to use the same language. But our mother, she never bothered to learn the English language, you know. She wanted us to go to school, she said, "So you'd be able to learn to speak the English language and be understood by your father. So you can speak to your dad in English." And at the same time we were learning that we couldn't use our Native language in school. When Harry and I were growing up we had the knowledge of both English and Eskimo, and I think when we went to school we stood out because of it. We couldn't express ourselves in Eskimo in school, but when we went home we could talk to our parents in it. We couldn't even learn or use the Native tongue within the school grounds, even outside playing.

꙳

Although Harry's formal school education stopped early on, his Iñupiaq education did not. Sadie explains how Harry acquired the skills that made him a good hunter as an adult:

He grew up mostly under a subsistence way of life, going with Mom and her hunting activity. He was quite good with his hunting and trapping. Dad never hunted; Mom was the hunter of our family. She was here and there when it came down to shooting ducks for feeding the lighterage personnel. We used to cook for the whole town when the ships came in, and feed them there at the Station [Cape Smythe]. When he was old enough, Harry was sent out duck hunting to get all the eider ducks that were needed for duck soup to feed the whole town.

Harry spent a lot of time with our uncles when he was growing up. With Alec Ahsoak and Carl Taalak, mainly. 'Cause Alec Ahsoak was about the only one that Mom would trust her boys with if they went out fishing or up the river. Those two are the main uncles that we knew that traveled quite a bit. Taalak was mainly in the east, but he moved his family here to Barrow in like '27, '28 after living a subsistence way of life, because they had to be in an area where they thought was good hunting to feed their families. Harry learned mainly from Ahsoak, I think, 'cause he probably went trapping with him.

It was a custom of our people that when a young person went out and hunted for the first time, these old people were brought in to tell the stories of what they should learn, of how you should treat the animals that you'd get, and where likely they would be found. So he was brought up this way. My mom wanted him to hear from his elders. And I think he listened to all that. Even though I was a girl I listened to all of it too when I was able to.

Our way of life is sort of two-fold: knowing the white man's way and then our traditional Eskimo ways were instilled in us. Dad always said—knowing from having lived with the Natives for so long—that if you're told a story, no matter how farfetched it may seem, don't ever shun the stories or the storytellers, you know. Because they were required to teach you through a story, to get the information out to us through a story form.

Typical of most large Iñupiaq families, Harry's older sisters looked after him while their mother was busy cutting up and preparing meat in the summer, helping with the reindeer herds during the November slaughter, or working with other women to prepare skins or food for holiday feasts. Sadie and her older sister, Maria, helped keep Harry and the other kids out of their mother's way.

Growing up we never had any problems with Harry. He was active all right, but not to where he was what we call rambunctious or mean. He was mischievous with the other kids, but I never saw Harry get in trouble growing up.

మ

As Harry got older he spent less time with his sisters and more time on his own and doing things for his father.

He was quiet, sort of. Dad had him hunting all the time with a packsack on. He roamed this northern area for specimens, like the northern birds, during the summer months. That's all I saw when I came back from school. He was quite a young man and doing all that part of Dad's work. Like even nesting time, he would go out and bring all those and then empty these eggs, then send 'em down to Smithsonian Institute or those museums in Arizona where they were asking for these northern specimens. Harry was involved with all that, because there was no local work, you know.

Harry got along with Dad good, only Dad was getting so old. He cared, but then he never really took Harry under his wing to care for the store or anything like the business for his trading post. It was mainly David and Tom and Robert.

మ

By the 1940s, Harry and Sadie were both adults with their own families to raise. Harry and Sadie's husband, Nate, worked together at the Naval Arctic Research Laboratory (NARL). As their own adult lives got fuller, Harry and Sadie saw less and less of each other. Harry was traveling around the North Slope to help scientists and build field research camps, and hunting and trapping foxes in his free time to support his family. Sadie was busy as a mother, teacher, welfare worker, and magistrate, but this did not keep her from noticing what her brother was up to.

Harry became a carpenter. He helped around with the Weather Bureau when needed and with our brother Bob [Robert]. He was a good carpenter. And from there then when the base [NARL] opened up in '47 he worked there. This town needed a research station sort of, and Max Brewer and John Schindler were sent up to open this Arctic Research Lab. For many years they ran it and that's where

Sadie Brower Neakok as a young girl carrying one of her siblings on her back, circa 1926. Presbytery of the Yukon Collection, Box 2, Album 3, Archives, University of Alaska Fairbanks.

Harry worked most of the time, because of his knowledge and hunting skills and doing carpenter work for that outfit.

Well, his work with the Arctic Research Lab really told the story, I think. Where he was entrusted with so much of the operation of that work there. And with his fellow workers, like old man Pete Sovalik and the ones that took care of the animals. And responsible for the whole lab area, their experimental thing. And I think that he was resourceful in getting some of their specimens.

Like Dr. Albert and some of the scientists that came up. Harry was forever working with them. They asked his expertise because even though he never was a fully trained person on all of it, his knowledge helped some of those scientists. It stood out.

Harry was known all over. I guess the people he worked and was in contact with spoke so highly of him that he got so he knew most everybody that came up. He was quite famous for his baleen boats and ivory work—his carving—that he did in his spare time. He built this little shop in his spare time, and when the tourists started coming up here he made a lot of money with all this. And sending out orders; he had so many orders he would fill for some of his work. In fact he even became quite rich with that.

Harry learned how to carve and make baleen boats on his own. And from his asking people who did this type of thing—scrimshaw and making baleen boats like Dad had made with some of Dad's patterns. He was always there when Dad was working on some of his basket making and his carvings on ivory, and making earrings and that type of stuff. I think that's where he adopted it, got his interest— some of his talent—in it. He was quite talented.

౨

I asked Sadie what was important to remember about Harry and his life. In a reflective tone, she replied:

Where he shared. He was always willing to show people things, and take in like homeless. He and Annie would have a house full, just like I guess we were taught from our parents. Well, our Eskimo way of life you know, we'd take care of the unfortunate. We share and that's the way we were raised. That's how Harry stood out. You hear Harry did this, Harry did that, for so and so. He never charged for any of his services needed. But he gave what he'd gotten to know and learned. Even some of his skills, too.

Sam P. Hopson

Sam Hopson knew Harry Brower, Sr. for almost fifty years. When Harry married Sam's sister, Annie, the two men became life-long hunting partners and close friends. Sam's wife, Mable, is also related to Harry. Her father was Harry's older brother, David.

Sam and his family moved to Fairbanks in the 1950s. He was an airplane cargo loader for Wien Airlines for more than twenty years. Even with full-time work and five children to support, Sam returned to Barrow regularly to hunt and whale. He and Harry whaled together for twenty years.

Sam passed away on March 3, 2004 at age 75. He had a full head of white hair, strong hands, and a squarish build. He chewed tobacco and periodically spat into a can as he talked. As a hobby, Sam made small decorative sleds out of caribou jawbones and baleen. As retirees, Sam and Mable spent most of the summer and fall traveling in their camper to hunt, fish, and pick berries along the road system of interior Alaska.

Sam and Harry hunted together when they were young. Although Sam was already a hunter in his own right, he mentioned a number of things he learned from Harry, like the best way to skin animals, how to hunt seals on top of the ice, and how to navigate on the tundra by using landmarks. "We got lost a couple of times, but we never said we were lost. We always just said we went the wrong way." Laughing, Sam tells one of his favorite Harry hunting stories:

When I got one of those movie cameras, I told Harry I'd like to go have a close up movie of a caribou. It was in the falltime and some of those bull caribou were just straggling when they were getting into the herds for mating season. We were camping, me and Kupaaq and George Ungarook. We had spotted a whole herd of caribou just moving toward us. One afternoon we were cutting up our caribou, getting it so it will freeze, and cleaning up, and there we spotted a bull caribou close to us.

At that time of the year when they see something moving ahead of 'em they go right up to it. So, Harry said, "Well, here's your chance, Sam. You gonna take your movie of your caribou close up? Just go out there, move around once in awhile; he'll see you and start coming at you."

I was just a little ways from our camp. I stood there and once in a while I moved around. That caribou started coming at me slowly. He didn't charge, but was getting closer and closer. I thought, "Gee that thing is getting close enough for me to take movies."

So, I took a movie—it was a silent movie—and it started coming and coming, getting closer and closer. It was about maybe twenty feet from me and I didn't realize I was backing up.

Harry yelled back at me, "Hey, I thought you wanted a close up. Don't move!"

I told him, I said, "Hey, he's getting too close for me! I got enough of it."

So I had to back out of there. The caribou never spooked from anything. George had a rifle ready just in case, I guess, so he said, "Well, I'll just shoot it here." We got that caribou right at the camp.

~

Because of the dangers inherent in whaling, the men must depend upon each other for their common safety and success. Kupaaq was appreciated for help he gave to other whaling crews. Sam relates one unfortunate incident in particular where Kupaaq's assistance proved invaluable to his fellow whalers:

I wasn't there, but I was getting ready to go down there. It was spring whaling. These people, they'd seen this whale come up but it was kind of choppy weather. It was good enough to go after it, I think. They didn't have much experience about getting to the whale, you know, so when they got to the whale they got on him on the wrong side. It was something like that. And when they struck the whale it came up with his flippers and tipped over the boat, and dumped all the crew in the water.

Kupaaq was one of the nearest crews that had been watching 'em, so they went down and rescued the crew, all but one. They couldn't get him; it was too late. Kupaaq probably drove his Ski-doo to the village for help, and they came down with the helicopter and took some of the crew. A couple of 'em were in pretty bad shape, you know, from the frozen water. So that's how it happened.

And all those young guys still remember Kupaaq for helping. He put them in his tent and used up all the available blankets and sleeping bags he had to wrap 'em up, to warm 'em up and keep 'em alive. So ever since, while Kupaaq was alive, every time they saw Kupaaq needed help or anything out at whaling camp—like if he was chasing a whale—they were out there with him, helping him. Or after he caught the whale, they'd haul some of the whale that he was saving for the feast and stuff to the safe place [landfast ice].

ᕐ

Sam visited Barrow each spring for whaling, geese hunting, and *Nalukataq*, and stayed at Harry's house. When they were together they talked about hunting a lot. They shared stories from the past and remembered trips together. But, much of their time was spent teasing each other and playing cribbage, their favorite game. They were boisterous and silly; they jokingly picked on each other. Amid this half-serious competition, I really saw their bond as friends, relatives, and hunting partners.

Me and Kupaaq, every time we went hunting we got to have a cribbage board. We played cribbage even at home. Every time we had a spare time or were doing nothing, that was the first thing we'd do—play cribbage. The best part of it we always teased each other, just like we were gonna go at it and have a big fight or something. It was just words back and forth.

We played just about around the clock when we were out geese hunting one spring. The weather was bad, there were no geese, so we just set up our tent, fixed up our gear, and went in the tent and started playing cribbage. Eugene was supposed to meet us up there in one of the geese hunting camps up on the Meade River. We played starting early in the morning and the only time we'd break was for coffee or something like that. We played, we played, we played. We must've played right through midnight. Finally we got sleepy. The wind was still bad—geese weren't flying—so we went to sleep.

First thing in the morning, or maybe in the afternoon—I don't remember the exact time—Kupaaq started to go out of the tent to see how everything was out there. He went out there, and he said, "Hey, Sam. Eugene is here."

"What?"

"Eugene is right there beside us."

We were playing so hard that time cribbage and got so tired that when we fell asleep we didn't even hear the snowmachine pull in. You know, you can hear a snowmachine miles and miles away. So we laughed. And Eugene laughed.

He said he looked in there and we both were like passed out, so he said to himself, "Well, I ain't gonna bother them." So he just fixed himself a little tent out of canvas and got into his sleeping bag. The weather was kinda warmish, windy, spring weather.

৵

One time we were playing with a regular cribbage board and we were arguing again. I told Kupaaq, "Hey, you're going the wrong way."

"No, I'm not."

"Yes. You was behind me and now you're ahead. You're going backwards."

We argued and argued. We finally settled down and he said, "Wait a minute, after we finish this I'm gonna show you something that don't cheat."

Before the next game he went back to his room and brought out a cribbage board that says twenty-nine. [It was in the shape of the number 29.] You can't go backwards. Once you start from the end you follow that around right to the other end. That's it.

So, he said, "That's what we'll use."

Anyway that's what we were starting to use 'cause after we started playing so long and argued, you know, sometime we didn't know if we moved or not. We just argued like we were going to fight. We called ourselves cheaters or stuff like that. I'd tell him, "Hey, you're so far behind, I can't even see you. I'm gonna have to slow down." Trying to out argue each other, you know, joking like that. I told him I skunked him so bad he stinks. We never were serious, but the words we gave each other were bad enough for people that were listening to make 'em believe that we were mad and it's all like that.

Then we got to where we couldn't remember who won them games more, so we started marking 'em down on a piece of paper. A lot of times he beat me; a lot of times I beat him. It was in between, you know, we were both winners far as ourselves were concerned. There was no loser between us. No matter how much you lose, you're still a winner. So that's the way we did it and that's where all the fun was.

෫

According to Sam it often seemed like Harry had an intuition of some sort for finding people in trouble. Sam did not try to explain it, but in a quiet tone offered a few examples:

He has saved two or three people. They could've been frozen if he hadn't done that for them. Once there were some guys that were broke down up out in the tundra in the wintertime and they ran out of gas. They were just about on their last stretch of their strength from walking. It was getting dark. And Kupaaq was camping out there—I think he's got a instinct or something that gets him to do something a lot of times—and he saw the little spark way out there in the dark. It was clearer than it is now. So he got on his snowmachine and headed out there and here these two guys were walking. One of 'em was just ready to fall down. That's when he got 'em just in time and took 'em to his tent and warmed 'em up, gave 'em some coffee, and then took 'em to the village.

Then he rescued one of the bush pilots. That was another good one. He was out in his trapline, checking his trapline for foxes. In them days when they first came up with the snowmachine, they had these small snowmachines with a one cylinder. They were good transportation. He was heading home on one of them and the next thing he knew right in the middle of the lake there was a airplane upside down. He thought somebody was already dead or something in that wreck. It was upside down. When he got there, there was a guy in the plane that was the pilot. Pete Merry was his name. He'd do a lot of wolf hunts and polar bear hunts when the polar bear hunt was legal. He'd take the polar bear hunters out of Barrow. So, he took him back. Pete was going to take some polar bear hunters out, and was taking his airplane to Barrow. Kupaaq got him back to the village. This other pilot was just ready to go out and search for him, but Kupaaq got him back.

Pete Merry was so happy, was so thankful, that one year he got a bunch of wolves—I don't know how many there were in the bag—and went over to Annie and Kupaaq's. He told 'em, "Hey, you folks want some wolf skins?"

"Sure, Annie always needs wolf skin."

So he brought the whole bag and he took 'em out from the bag onto the floor and told Annie to pick out the best one she could find there. He was still thinking about that rescue that Kupaaq did. He said he couldn't forget that. So they got one of the wolf skins.

Another guy that Kupaaq rescued was that Weather Bureau man, that black man. This is more like that instinct I was telling you about. Something in his mind that always bothers him. One day, it was evening, and he started worrying about his trapline. He said, "Gee, I better go check my trapline."

It was getting dark. He usually went early in the morning. But he just couldn't quit thinking about it. So, anyway, he just got on his little snowmachine and took off. He said, "I'll be right back."

It was only about twenty miles out, I guess. So he headed out. And way out there in the middle of nowhere there was some guy walking. And he was cold, you know. Here was this colored guy that worked for the Weather Bureau. He was out caribou hunting and got kind of lost and his Ski-doo wouldn't start.

Kupaaq always carried a little tent, so he set up the little tent and stove and warmed that guy up a little and then took him back that night. And Kupaaq said, "I don't know what he would've done. He could have froze to death. He was pretty, pretty, pretty slim."

That guy really appreciated it, so he told Kupaaq to come over and whatever he wanted from the Weather Bureau Commissary—from the groceries they had—he could have it, stuff they needed, like milk or sugar or coffee. Them days you don't have much of that; it was hard to get a lot of stuff. There was only one store and it was always running out of groceries. So Kupaaq said, "Well, I could use some flour or milk or something." And that black guy told him, "Yeah, come over. Whatever you need."

So Kupaaq went over there. Boy, he said he boxed him up some of the groceries that the kids wanted and everything. It was for appreciation, for thanking him for rescuing him.

And that guy's wife was so happy. And Kupaaq couldn't get over it when he walked in and here was this beautiful blonde woman. 'Cause, you know, in them days it was unusual to see a black with a white. So Kupaaq said, "Annie, she was so pretty. And married to this black man." He wasn't against anything, but he just couldn't believe himself. But he was the best friend he ever met, too. They were friends ever since.

3^

While Sam and I talked, his wife, Mable, sat across the room on the sofa, sewing small pieces of fur together into a doll-sized parka. She sells her handmade dolls, yo-yos and masks at local and statewide craft bazaars. When Sam was done talking, she added her own perspective on Kupaaq's instinct:

It's just that when he got that feeling, I think he followed up on it. If he thought there was something wrong, then he did something about it; go out, check things out. Also, there were times when he got some kind of food and he took it to some certain people and these people would say, "I've been thinking about some of this things and was hoping somebody would bring me some." This happened to him more than once.

3^

Like many long-married couples, Sam and Mable's thoughts intermingled to tell a single story or to make a point. Mable prompted Sam with a nudge about a particular story. Sam would pick up a story Mable had begun, or he added a story of his own related to one of Mable's points, as he did here:

Just like when he was out way up in the Brooks Range with some surveyors and they got these whistling squirrels. The big squirrels. Whistlers they call it, *siksrikpuk*.[5] This old guy, Okomailak—he was my favorite man 'cause I'd known him ever since I was a little boy—he used to hunt those in his young days up there. So when Kupaaq got some of them *siksrikpuk*, he saved the meat and took 'em home. He was thinking about Okomailak that always talked about how good eating they were. He'd never had 'em for many years, 'cause he was a really aged man. So Kupaaq took a couple of 'em over to his house. He just looked at him, and Kupaaq said his tears just came down, he was so happy to see those squirrels.

Okomailak's wife was telling Kupaaq, she said, her husband was talking just a few days before about those *siksrikpuk* and how good eating they were. He said he wished he could have had some.

Max Brewer

Max Brewer first went to Barrow in 1950 studying permafrost for the United States Geological Survey, and served as director of the Arctic Research Laboratory (later renamed the Naval Arctic Research Laboratory or NARL) in Barrow from 1956 to 1971. During those years, he established field camps and ice stations, and supported a record number of research projects that led to many important scientific discoveries. In 1971, he became Alaska's first commissioner of Environmental Conservation.

Max was seventy-four years old when I interviewed him, retired, and living in Anchorage. He has a commanding presence. He is tall, has a rectangular face with large round glasses, and a full head of white hair. He speaks slowly with an authoritative voice, interjected with frequent pauses as he draws on his pipe. Max has told the same stories about his adventures in Barrow over and over for many years, so he is well rehearsed.

Max hired Harry in 1957 as a carpenter. As they worked together Max grew to appreciate Harry's knowledge as an arctic naturalist, so he began to send Harry out to help scientists on field projects. Over the course of their fourteen years of working together, they also became friends.

It was as director that I first really got to know Harry Brower. In the spring of 1957 I wanted to hire some more Native people from the village and I hired one, Kenneth Toovak, to be the mechanical shop foreman and equipment operator. And I hired Harry Brower and Joe Ahgeak for a term of three months. The three months was beginning in the spring of 1957. They lasted through my tenure, until July 1971. Obviously it took Harry and Joe a lot longer to complete their work than I had originally planned! Harry was a quiet fellow with a sly sense of humor and an ability to bond very well with the scientists.

It was during the early period that Harry worked at the laboratory that as a going-away present for one of the maintenance people Harry took a lemming skin and made a lemming skin rug in the same way that you would make a polar bear skin rug. This lemming skin rug was a big hit. A lot of people needed them, so Harry was busy in the evenings making up these little lemming skin rugs. And he charged 5 dollars apiece. Well, this was fine. Until he got this order from someplace in Mexico for 5,000 lemming skin rugs. He threw in the towel at that point.

Harry was the last of the Brower boys to have been taught taxidermy by his father. And in the early years, his father had quite a lucrative trade going with museums in the South 48 where he would furnish bird's nests, particularly eider duck nests, with eggs and skins of one sort or another. Harry, of the boys, probably became the most expert in the taxidermy business.

You know, he was a carpenter, but I used him for many, many things. For instance, all the bird skins at the lab were prepared by Harry. Those eventually went to the university and probably if you went into the museum you'd find quite a number of them there.

I'm not sure as to how much schooling Harry actually had. I think it was seventh or eighth grade, but I'm not positive. And yet, in his taxidermy where he would record the various statistics about the bird or the animal he was more meticulous than most graduate students who had the chore of doing that. He'd picked up that people liked to have this sort of information. Very meticulous was his approach to carpentry, too. Harry did excellent work; he was a finish carpenter and had great pride in his work.

Harry would be doing taxidermy, because he was so doggone good at it. The scientific investigators were always down watching him, and they would be talking and he would be explaining things. He'd tell them about how things were and so on. They would pick up the subtle knowledge. Generally the ones that would be talking to him would be the graduate students. He enjoyed it immensely, and they enjoyed it.

It was this understanding that Harry had that enabled him to be so influential with the grad students that would come to the lab. He would never tell anybody of that group—and I sort of doubt it if even at home he'd tell 'em—what to do, but he used example and gentle persuasion. You see, lots of people can be in the position of being a teacher, but there're not all that many teachers. Harry wasn't in the teaching business, per se, he was just a teacher. Harry was always trying to teach the young fellows about things. And he'd throw in humor.

Harry was a trapper at heart. He dearly loved trapping foxes; for Harry that was a lot of fun. After they had power, Harry got Annie an automatic washer. That year he caught about 700 foxes. He was out every Sunday and sometimes he'd take an extra day off work. Harry could skin a fox without making any more holes in the skin than nature gave it. But to send fox skins out for tanning you had to clean 'em. And so he decided, well, automatic washer, that's the way to go. So he put twenty skins in. Put them through the deal and he ended up with twenty skins with no hair! The washer was pretty well haired up. He'd tell that story on himself and just laugh like a bandit.

ॐ

Even though Max Brewer and Harry Brower were only six months apart in age, Max considered Harry one of his arctic teachers. So I asked Max what he thought was most important about Harry and his life that others should remember and learn from.

In Harry's case it was his use of example and gentle persuasion. And what you may not recognize is that although Harry was the youngest boy of the Brower family, he ended up being the patriarch of the family. For instance, when there were family arguments—and I have reason to believe that some of them were pretty heated—it was Harry who would finally say, "It is this way." Now for the youngest boy in the family to command the respect of his siblings who knew all his weaknesses, it says quite a bit for the person's character and integrity. That's what his family saw in him: the depth of the man.

And, I think that his example as carried on and remembered by people—because they do remember—is probably his greatest legacy. I mean those who didn't know him won't have the benefit of his sly humor, or the grin, but he was a teacher. And that came through.

John Schindler

John Schindler first went to Barrow in 1960 as a botanist, became assistant director of the Arctic Research Laboratory the following year, and took over as director in 1971. He left Barrow in 1973, but continued to travel to the North Slope doing work related to the oil industry. He is now retired and lives in Anchorage.

With his dark hair, jovial laugh, and cheerful smile, John seemed much younger than his sixty-seven years. He has a casual and easygoing manner. He kicked off his shoes and put his feet up on the coffee table as we talked. One of his hobbies is painting. John tells stories in a relaxed, friendly style, laughing often about something funny he has just remembered. John cherishes his friendship with Harry and Annie Brower. He recalls how he first got to know Harry:

Harry was working at the lab when I first got there in 1960. He was what we called second carpenter in those days. Eddie Hopson was lead carpenter.

I first got really to know Harry that summer they were making what they called the ARLIS [Arctic Research Lab Ice Station] buildings and Harry was in charge of that, I think, even though Eddie was lead carpenter. It seems to me Eddie was doing something else and Harry was in charge of that. I was not on the lab staff, I was a scientist then, so about the only connection we would have is if I would go to the shop or they would come over for the coffee break and sit in the coffee room. And that's really when I got to know Harry.

In those days it was a totally different world. It's hard to explain but the lab, even though I think 80% of our staff was Native, we didn't really socialize except on certain occasions. You'd go to the school things with them, or you'd go to Christmas parties, but people really didn't stop at each other's houses. It was just not done. It was a different time. It really was.

I think the first house that I ever went into was Harry's and Annie's. And even then you could tell that the other people—not Harry—were uneasy. I think Harry really liked the lab, mainly because he got to meet so many people, to see so many different things.

When I think back now, you know, we, very selfishly in many ways, used the people in the village. And yet, because they had something to offer us and we had something to offer them, you know, it was really a great arrangement. I used to give the contractor on the other side of the street a hard time. "You don't know what you're missing," I'd say. They'd hire everybody off the streets in Fairbanks and bring 'em up; the support contractor [who ran NARL] or the DEW–line. The DEW–line especially seldom hired Natives. I think at one point there wasn't even a Native on the entire line. The DEW–line in Alaska was built in Barrow, right in that camp.

⁓

John had his favorite stories that showed the type of man Harry was.

He traveled his trapline so much; he was religious about it, you know. A lot of guys would put a trapline out and they'd leave it out a week, but Harry would run his trapline sometime in the middle of the night or early in the morning and then have to be at work at eight o'clock. He never, never missed it.

He got to the point where there was a polar bear denning out there—I think this was on the southwest side just down below Skull Cliff if I remember correctly—and she had cubs. As the season went on and he was still running the line, he started taking bits of seal meat with him and throwing them out for this polar bear. Well, in time he got so friendly with the sow and two cubs, if you can imagine this, she let the cubs crawl up in his lap on the Ski-doo.

You know when you think about this, this is unbelievable. But, that's the type of a person he was. He had tremendous patience, and he was so easygoing and so laid back he could do this sort of thing. Then we used to tease Annie about it, "Harry's got another girl. A white girl, too!" We'd give her the hardest time.

⁓

As John and I talked in his Anchorage living room on a sunny March afternoon he suddenly remembered a story that he said really represented who Harry was. In 1964, Alaska Senator Ernest Gruening was trying to change an outdated law that prohibited the government from selling resources from Naval Petroleum Reserves to the public.[6] Because of this law, NARL utilized the natural gas near Barrow in Petroleum Reserve No. 4, but they were unable to provide this same service to the people of Barrow, who relied upon fuel oil. Staff at NARL were asked to help the senator make his case that natural gas would be a cheaper way for the Iñupiat to heat their homes.

There's a story about Harry I never even thought of. We were helping Gruening. You know, good government employees, the senator asks for something and you do what you're supposed to do. Gruening was making the case that it was terribly expensive for the people to heat their homes with oil. Houses in the village were about as big as my living room, in those days, and they all lived in the one room, because they couldn't heat 'em. There was simply no way.

So I was trying to run up a study of costs of heating oil against the costs of the gas. So I went to Harry one day and I said, "Harry, how much oil do you burn?"

He said, "Drum a month."

I said, "OK. That's cold weather or warm weather? How much do you burn in January?"

"Drum a month."

"How much do you burn in April?"

"Drum a month."

"What do you do when it gets cold?"

"Drum a month. When you run out, you're out!"

'Cause they couldn't afford more than one drum a month. And he just sat there with that little smile on his face. "Drum a month," is all he would say, you know, until I finally got smart. Because that's the way Harry did everything, you know. He had that twinkle in his eye until you got the message, you know, that sort of thing.

To me Harry was a big teaser. But his teasing was always just a couple of words. It wasn't a big deal, you know. And that twinkle he'd get in his eye, you knew when he was teasing. He had that look! You couldn't miss it.

I was just perfectly at ease with Harry. He was that type of a person. I always enjoyed his company. He had tremendous patience, and he was so easygoing and so laid-back.

He was just not a demonstrative person at all. And yet, you felt he was just as strong as a rock, you know; just as solid as could be. Great, great character. He just had his own opinions, but he never pushed anything.

But he managed to teach you things about the Eskimo people and the Arctic Slope, you know, the natural bits of things. Like the way foxes could avoid a trap if you weren't careful. All these little tidbits of stories he used to tell. He could teach you things and you never felt like you were being lectured to.

Harry was one of these strong people that just are attractive because they are so self-confident. They're not cocky. They just are sure of themselves, their inner selves. And Harry was one of those solid people.

He had probably a thousand friends. Barrow used to be pretty torn up in rivalries, you know, but Harry was loved by everybody. 'Cause he never asked anything of anybody. And he had this way of telling you things with that little twinkle in his eye and teasing you about 'em as he did it.

And it's funny that I cannot remember specifics. I can just remember the way he looked, the way he handled himself.

Tom Albert

Tom Albert, who was chief scientist for the North Slope Borough's Department of Wildlife Management until 2001, first came to the Arctic Research Laboratory in 1975 from the University of Maryland to conduct research on the arctic marmot. Harry told Tom about marmot behavior, showed him where to collect some, and constructed observation boxes for the marmots to live in that were similar to their burrows.

In 1978, Tom Albert became one of the first scientists to study bowhead whales for the Alaska Eskimo Whaling Commission and the North Slope Borough. Tom consulted Harry on a regular basis about whales, whale behavior, and arctic wildlife in general. Tom and Harry became close friends and worked together for fifteen years.

Tom Albert is a tall, thin, man in his early sixties with pale complexion and graying black hair. His twenty years in the Arctic show in his dark eyes and wearied face. He speaks with a pointed tone, almost like giving a lecture.

The way I regard Harry is essentially as a very, very smart man who was very modest also. He had a tremendous amount of knowledge about the animals and the environment in his area, and he was able to explain it to somebody in a very clear way. He was very patient about answering questions. He wanted you to learn. And he was always available to help. If he was living in Pennsylvania and grew up there, he would probably be the head of a zoology department. He'd be a great scientist, or the dean of a college of science or something like that. He was a really gifted sort of guy.

I used to go down and talk to him. Since I had been in school for most of my life it seems like, I was used to going to talk to professors and teachers. And I was also used to going to the library. At that time there was no library in Barrow. So I would go and talk to Harry in the evenings about all sorts of things. And he always seemed interested in talking.

I mean I've had in my life so many teachers it seems like, but I can count the number of good teachers I've ever had on one hand. It would take many hands to count the number of less than good teachers. But he's one of the best teachers that I've ever had.

ॐ

Nowadays, measuring whales that are caught and taking biological samples from them is commonplace. Everyone is accustomed to seeing scientists crawling around the whale carcass in their yellow plastic rain suits, but it was not always this way. When Tom first began to do research on bowhead whales, the whalers did not want anything to interfere with their hunt and butchering, and they did not completely trust non-Natives and scientists. Tom explains how, thanks to Harry, these barriers slowly faded:

In the spring of '78 was the first time that any of us around here went out to collect specimens. The people that were doing this were Mike Philo and myself. We had gotten some money to get more information about the bowhead. And one of the things was how does this animal work.

Well, I was kind of emboldened, you might say, because I knew one of the critical people, Harry Brower. I knew Harry reasonably well. And he said that yes, he would help. And as luck would have it I got to meet Bill Kaleak [another Barrow whaling captain] earlier when our families were both on vacations. And he was very nice.

In the spring of '78, when it first came time to charge out there and try to get specimens, there was some hostility as to actually going out there. "Who are you, what are you doing out here?" This kind of stuff. I knew that was going to happen. But as luck would have it the very first whale that got caught in the spring of '78 was by Bill Kaleak. And when Mike Philo and I got out there Bill said, "What do you want? You can have anything you want." It was great. So, we got noticed by some people out there, other whaling captains and so on in a friendly atmosphere. Several other whales got caught and we more or less did all right.

And then a whale got caught by a young man who was not all that enthused about helping scientists, shall we say. Mike and I pulled up out there with our box of this and that, and I said, "Oh my gosh, how are we going to get these specimens?" And that captain was real cool to me about getting an eyeball and this kind of stuff. He didn't tell me to get lost or anything, but it was like kind of cool.

So, I went over to see Harry who was standing nearby with his brother, Arnold Brower, Sr. I said, "Harry, my gosh, we really need to get a couple of specimens out of this whale. Can you please help me get something?" He said, "Tom, you wait right here."

And I can see it as clear as I see you sitting there. He and Arnold walked away a little bit and they just motioned to that young captain. He walked over to these guys and Harry started shaking his finger to him and talking to him. And his head was going down.

A little while later, Harry motioned to me, said come here. I walked over to him and that captain. Harry said, "He has something to say to you." The captain said, "Tom, anything you want, you can have." And ever since then, he has been very, very helpful.

But, that was a real ice-breaking thing, right there. These two real senior guys, Arnold and Harry, talking to a young man who was probably not that interested in cooperating with scientists, and explaining to him that these people are only trying to help and let's cooperate with them. From that simple little exercise out there we've had excellent cooperation ever since. And it was one of these things that one of the most senior hunters, Harry Brower, was able to, in public you might say, right out there, give his blessing to these couple of young scientific guys. That was like sprinkling holy water on us!

Not everybody instantly became our friends, but there was very little problem in collecting specimens. And as the years went by, working for the Borough and so on, everybody understood. Well, most people have understood. That was one of the most significant events in the time that I've known Harry.

ᘔ

In 1981, Tom helped establish the North Slope Borough Department of Wildlife Management, whose main research focus was based upon what Harry told Tom about whale behavior. As a whaler, Harry had been observing bowheads over a long period, so Tom regularly turned to him for answers.

Harry said that these whales travel on a wide front when they come past Point Barrow. They're not confined to the lead. There's a lot of them out there under the broken ice. So this thing about them passing on a wide front was very important.

"Just let me give you an example," he said, "of how I know that they pass on a wide front and that they're underneath the ice." He said that "when we're out hunting in the spring, in the lead, in a boat and we get tired of paddling, if we're near the other side of the lead, namely where the floating ice is, sometimes we will just go over to the floating ice and hang on and take a break. Everybody rests." "But," he said, "when we're doing that, you can hear whales blowing out in this broken ice that is further off shore. We're on the edge of the broken ice and out there you can hear the whales blowing." So, he said, "I know they're out there. In fact, we all know they're out there. And you guys are the only ones who don't know that."

Research subsequently proved that there were more whales than originally believed and that subsistence hunting was not affecting the population. This led the International Whaling Commission to allow higher bowhead whale harvest quotas for Iñupiat whalers.

He has done a whole lot more for the Eskimo people than most of them realize. He was a fine man, good teacher and a whole lot more people owe things to him than realize. The good quota, the harvest quota, that people have nowadays is due as much to him as anyone, but very few people realize it. We said, OK let's design the study, year after year, to basically determine whether these things that Harry said are true. It wasn't quite that deliberate, but it's the way it worked out. And over the years, that's what we've done, to spend millions and millions over fifteen or more years documenting the movement of these animals. But the experimental design was set up to more or less determine what Harry was saying, whether it was true or not.

And now people have a very good harvest quota. And although lots of people from St. Lawrence Island to Barter Island benefit from all this, very few of them understand where the driving force, the little ideas, came from. Some of them think that the borough somehow magically did all this or that the federal government did it, or whatever. But on almost every occasion I get, I try to point the finger to where it belongs. If there's like an unsung hero so to speak in the resolving of this great controversy between IWC, federal government, AEWC and so on, I mean, Harry's the guy who was in behind the scenes who had the biggest impact of any single person. And in every speech that I've ever given on this subject I give him credit. And I think it's important that people try to give him the recognition that's due.

APPENDIX
Outside Looking In

L istening to Kupaaq on tape and revisiting his stories years after his death have brought back many memories for me. I wish I could once more be in the comfort of his living room, laughing with him, seeing his beaming smile, and being taken away from the stresses of my everyday life by his stories of distant places and simpler times.

While the stories Kupaaq told me from his life and that I have related in this book were entertaining and informative, they do not show the whole picture. They are excerpts, slices of life, things we happened to talk about, things he thought important, and things he was willing to include in a public record. There is much that he left out, and aspects of his life that I know nothing about because our time together as friends was so short. Kupaaq was not comfortable talking about private parts of his life. He did not share intimate concerns. He did not discuss painful or difficult times. He described events, but rarely told me how he felt about what happened. He reluctantly shared a few such moments when I asked specific questions, but spoke in a hushed tone and gave few details. He subtly moved on to other things, like what his kids were up to, how close to town the caribou were, or how the ice was moving.

There are many people who would be uncomfortable exchanging intimate feelings and emotions with someone they do not know very well or on tape as a public document. But in this case, the nature of public Iñupiaq storytelling also played a part. Kupaaq was used to sharing jokes, describing hunting escapades, and talking about the "old days" with a variety of audiences. To him, our sessions—at least at the beginning—were not much different, so he stuck to what he knew, what he was comfortable with, and what he believed was worth telling from his life.

I, too, stayed at a familiar level. I had not conducted oral history interviews before and was nervous. I did not want to pry, and lacked the interviewing skills to know how to ask about something very personal or controversial. I worried that I would offend. It is a fine line between garnering important details about the past and being so pushy that you just get an angry response. How do you ask someone in a community with a history of alcohol problems about his own drinking habits? How do you ask about his wife, what type of person she was, what their marriage was like, and how he misses her now that she is dead?

(Opposite) Harry Brower and Karen Brewster at Nalukataq, June 20, 1991.

How do you ask about how he raised his kids, what he taught them, important times they had together, or what kind of father he was, without getting into the private lives of his children?

Kupaaq and I talked like any two people getting to know each other over tea and cookies. He told me about his health problems: four months of radiation treatment for a spot on one lung, and nine intestinal surgeries in almost as many years—"They took out twelve feet one time." I watched him "smoke his pipe," an electronic, medicated inhaler that helped him breathe easier. He shared concerns about oil development. He showed disappointment that his grandchildren did not understand when he spoke to them in Iñupiaq. He was worried for the future of Iñupiaq, the language of his youth, the language of whaling and hunting camp, the sound of the landscape, the voice of the old ways. And he told me the stories of his past.

As I learned more about Kupaaq's life I saw there were parts I did not know, and I was ready to ask about them. What were the advantages and disadvantages of being the son of Charles Brower? How old was he when he first went out whaling? How did he feel about working with scientists? Unfortunately, he became too ill to continue taping and died before I had the chance to find out all I wanted to know.

A more comprehensive look at Kupaaq's life might be possible if he were still alive—if we could have done more taping, if I could have gone back and asked more questions to fill in gaps, and if he could have reviewed this manuscript. But I did not have this luxury. Throughout this project, my main goal has been to be true to Kupaaq. I hope he would be happy and proud of the result.

My friendship with Kupaaq involved more than just sitting at his dining room table listening to stories or talking about current events. He gave me the opportunity to experience Iñupiaq culture first-hand. He made me feel part of his community, his whaling crew, and his family. He fed me and entertained me. He teased me like a daughter. He gave me hand-carved gifts like a devoted grandfather would—an ivory and turquoise-bead necklace, a small *ulu* with a whale-shaped ivory handle, and a fossilized ivory bracelet. These are my souvenirs, my constant reminders of Kupaaq and our friendship. There was a way in which we each brightened up the other's somewhat lonely life. Times which gave me deeper glimpses inside Iñupiaq culture, made living in Barrow more fun and worthwhile for me, and which are now part of my own repertoire of stories and memories. I believe these shared moments with Kupaaq reveal yet another side to who he was, and add the final installment to the story of his life and our collaboration.

I had asked Kupaaq if I could help his crew if they caught a whale. I was eager to get involved and be useful. "Yeah, sure. I suppose so," he said. I showed up at his house early one May morning, the day after his crew landed a whale. Dolores and Molly stood outside and cut soft, pink *maktak* into three-inch-long and one-inch-thick pieces. Becca and Karen filled cardboard boxes and Rubbermaid tubs with pieces of meat and internal organs that had been cut up the night before. People delivered bag after bag of hot and greasy Eskimo donuts. I went inside and was immediately put to work. I helped ladle a runny, brownish-orange mixture of cooked dried fruit (*siiġñaq*) from big pots into Styrofoam cups for individual servings. We set up the 200-cup coffee percolator, cream, sugar, cups and stirrers on a low table against the wall of the main room. We put a narrow table across the entrance to the kitchen as a serving place; it looked like a McDonald's counter.

The food and the house were being made ready for feeding the community fresh whale. Charlotte, Eugene's wife, was in charge of the day's activities, even though Kupaaq sat in his usual spot at the head of the long, rectangular table in the dining/living room. He periodically piped in with comments on how things should be or answered questions when asked, but for the most part he just proudly sat by with his arms crossed around his chest and let the whirlwind encircle him.

I was given inside-cooking detail. I thought I was lucky, because I worried about staying warm while standing outside in twenty-degree weather cooking over a gas burner. Little did I know that an eight-by-sixteen galley-style kitchen can get as hot as a June day in the desert when there are two industrial-size pots of water on the stove boiling whale meat and *maktak*, and there is a constant stream of people trying to get to the sink, to the plates and cups, to the sugar, or to pour themselves a cup of fresh coffee. Rivulets of sweat trickled down my back. "Excuse me, coming through. Hot, hot!" Vera cried as she squeezed between me and the counter, carrying a large bowl of steaming *maktak*. "Karen, can you hand me an *ulu?*" Becca asked, since I was standing next to the dish rack where they were drying. Molly and I bumped into each other as we bent down at the same time between the two counters.

I was assigned to stir and watch the fist-size pieces of meat cooking. I was instructed to scoop the pieces out of the water when they were a bit under-cooked, when you could still see a hint of the reddish black color and blood of the raw meat. The meat's internal heat keeps it cooking after it comes out of the hot water. If left to cook too long, it ends up gray, tough and rubbery. "You don't want to serve food like that to people," Charlotte explained.

"Is it done yet?" I nervously asked as I nudged her arm.

"No, not yet. A little bit longer," Charlotte answered, keeping the same patient tone every time. She was used to teaching novices like me. Kupaaq's children, grandchildren, and the other crewmembers put up with me. He had said I could help and he was the captain. They tolerated my naiveté and calmly explained details of the process along the way.

"Don't mix *maktak* and meat in the same cooking water," Lollie said. "You want the *maktak* water to be clean. That scum floating in the meat water sticks to the *maktak*."

All morning, I steamed over boiling water, stirred many pounds of meat, scooped bowlfuls of cooked meat and *maktak* into garbage-bag lined boxes or three-foot-long stainless steel pans, and dumped new handfuls of freezing-cold, raw chunks of meat and *maktak* into the water. The work never stopped. Sweat oozed from every pore. My leg muscles ached from all the standing. A dull pain plagued my lower back from the bending. After four hours of cooking huge potfuls of whale meat, I finally got the hang of it. This time the meat was done when I asked Charlotte to check it.

Intermingled with the cooking, I helped fill paper plates with *maktak*, meat, heart, kidney, tongue, intestines, a donut, and a cup of stewed fruit for visitors. One piece of each was given per person. Most people took the plates to go, but some, especially elders, sat down and ate with Kupaaq, who happily presided over them all at the head of the table. He had barely slept the night before and did not eat any of what he served. I thought at the time that he was too excited and satiated with the joy of feeding the town. Years later, I heard Eugene tell the crew before *Nalukataq* that they should not eat from what they were serving. "It's for the people," he said in a scolding tone. The crew's turn would come after. I wondered if this was why Kupaaq had not eaten that day.

Captain's house feast at Harry Brower's house, May 1991. Photo by Karen Brewster.

We worked hard in the kitchen, but we also laughed and had fun. I pointed out that we had been talking mostly in numbers for the last few hours. The four others in the kitchen giggled, realizing it was true. People who got platefuls of food told one of our servers how many were in their family and so how many portions they needed. The server at the front called this number to the rest of us standing by the pans of cooked whale parts at the back of the kitchen.

"Two," Audrey, one of Kupaaq's teenage granddaughters, called out.

"Two," I repeated to Molly, a crew member's mother, as I put two pieces of hot *uunnaalik* (boiled *maktak*) and two pieces of meat from the pans in front of me into a gallon-size Ziploc bag. The code told Molly to put in two pieces each of heart, kidney, tongue, and intestines from the boxes nearest her.

"Two," I confirmed as I handed the full bag back to Audrey in front. She added two Eskimo donuts, handed the visitor two cups of sweet *siigñaq*, and thanked her for coming.

"Two," I called to Molly weeks later when I ran into her at the post office.

"Two," she laughed back. There was no need to say more.

The women took turns taking short breaks to sit down, to drink a cold soda, and to have a quick snack.

I felt guilty sitting too long at the table with the elders, so I was soon back in the kitchen helping serve or doing dishes. We started serving at noon and by 5 o'clock all the whale was distributed. The teenage girls in the family did the dishes, cleaned up, and mopped the floor. I collapsed into a chair next to Kupaaq. He giggled. He knew what hard work whaling was.

The men of the crew had been up all night butchering and hauling whale shares back to town. Kupaaq had taught them that you do not stop to rest until all the whale is butchered and put away. By mid-afternoon the guys were sound asleep on the living room floor. They still had their boots and grubby whaling gear on. Frederick sprawled length-wise on the couch, his feet hanging over the end. Eugene, Charlie, George, Jeff, and Price lay on the floor, one on his back, another curled up on his side, some used pillows from the couch, others wadded up jackets under their heads. Periodically, someone snored. Not even the constant bustle and loud talk from the people coming for food, the clang of metal pots in the kitchen, or the buzz of over twenty people in the house could wake them.

Although I was tired, it was, as they say, "a good tired." It was rewarding to see people so happy and thankful when you gave them a plate of food. And after two years in Barrow, it made me feel part of the community. As the only non-Iñupiaq woman in the kitchen that day, I was honored to participate. I felt a closer connection to Kupaaq, his family, and the other women of the crew. There is a camaraderie that comes from celebrating, and working to near exhaustion together. We now could always talk about that whale or our day together in Kupaaq's kitchen. There is also some sense of comfort that comes from being part of something, like the bonding between members of a winning sports team. This tangible experience of working with the whaling crew allowed me to feel and know about Kupaaq, his life, and aspects of Iñupiaq culture in a more direct way than listening to stories or reading about it could.

As I mustered the energy to stand up, put on my coat, and walk home, I could see Kupaaq was proud of me, too. He glanced out of the corner of his eyes and threw a sideways knowing look my way. The corners of his mouth turned up just a tad. Although he didn't seem to move, I thought for sure I saw a slight nod. I had seen this before, like when I finally understood his family's complicated genealogy, when I got the difference between a harpoon and a darting gun, and when I tried to say good-bye when he was dying. Kupaaq did not gush with emotion. He used words sparingly. But his looks told me all that I needed to know. I knew he understood that throwing myself full-scale into helping the crew was one way I tried to reciprocate for all he had given me.

My involvement with Kupaaq Crew did not end that day. There was a *Nalukataq* to host. Again I wanted to help. While a captain, his wife and their crew begin to prepare for *Nalukataq* starting the day after they catch a whale, I only came on the scene the day of the celebration. As the years went by, I helped with things in advance, like sewing parkas and skin boat covers before whaling started, organizing supplies at the captain's house before the celebrations, and preparing food like rolls and stewed fruit. But that first year, I just showed up at Kupaaq's house early on *Nalukataq* morning. The whole crew gathered around 9 A.M. They collected big aluminum teapots, a propane burner unit to boil water for tea and coffee, paper cups, cream and sugar, and rubber gloves. They retrieved the food prepared in advance. They stood in a circle, joined hands, and bowed their heads as Kupaaq acknowledged the special day with a prayer. It was a sunny, warm, windless day. The weather forecast predicted a high of 60 degrees. Perfect for being outside all day at the feast.

Just before noon, I hopped into the back of a blue pickup truck loaded full of pots of hot soup—goose, duck, or caribou—and off we went to the gravel-covered *Nalukataq* site by the beach. I ladled out bowls of soup from a big pot one of the male crew members carried alongside me. Other pairs of crew members did the same all around the circle of happy and hungry folks. Everyone sat on the ground encircled by a windbreak made from sheets of opaque plastic stretched over a wooden frame. Two other crews were co-hosting this day of *Nalukataq*, and all three joined together in making the windbreak, preparing and serving food, and celebrating.

After we served all the soup, bread, and tea and coffee, we piled the empty pots back into the truck, and took them home to be washed. At two o'clock we returned to serve *mikigaq*, fermented whale meat, blubber and blood that is an Iñupiaq delicacy. It tastes almost sweet when made to perfection. The

Karen Brewster and Charlie D. A. Brower serving at Nalukataq, circa 1994. Photo by Tom Lohman.

circle inside the windbreak was now packed full of people happily chattering amongst themselves. I was reminded of a penguin rookery with all the chicks anxiously waiting to be fed.

With my fingers tightly bound by plastic surgical gloves, I plunged my right hand into the black, slimy, mushy mass inside a five-gallon white bucket my serving partner had placed at my feet. I scooped out a handful of *maktak* and whale meat strips dripping with juice and blood, and quickly slopped it into someone's bowl, or into a Ziploc bag to be taken home and enjoyed later. When all of the *mikigaq* was gone, the crew once again clambered back into pickups and cars, took the empty buckets home to be washed, and prepared for the next round of food. By five o'clock, we were handing out pieces of frozen *maktak* and whale meat.

"How many?" I asked as a plastic bag was handed to me.

"Five," the middle-age woman replied. I quickly counted out five chunks of *maktak* into her bag from the heavy box my male partner held; one piece per family member whether they were there with her or not. It is common for people to collect shares for others, especially for elders who are not as mobile or able to be out as long in the cold air. As folks soaked up the sun, they cut slices off their shares, dipped them in salt, and popped them into their mouths. I could practically taste the ocean-like but not fishy flavor of the *maktak* and the richness of this burgundy-colored meat as I watched.

Then it was time for dessert. There were rectangular pineapple upside-down cakes and cupcakes with chocolate frosting covered in sprinkles. There was white cake, chocolate cake, yellow cake, carrot cake, and German chocolate cake. Dolores, one of our crew members, had spent days baking and decorating three large round cakes. These masterpieces were set in tiers on a table in the middle of the serving area. The largest cake sat in the center at the top of the tier and was decorated with Kupaaq Crew's red and green striped and white diamond flag design. The cake to the left had the orange peace-sign of Arnold Brower's flag on it. To the right were the red and blue stripes and diamond of George Ahmaogak's crew flag. The captains posed in front of their cakes for photos. Soon, there was nothing left but crumbs.

Kupaaq had come to the *Nalukataq* site in the early afternoon to briefly greet people and share in the joy of the day. He was weak and wheezed in fits and starts; he could not be out long. He slowly made his way around the circle. He visited with old friends, accepted thanks from happy eaters, and gained inner strength from seeing the community satisfied.

As the afternoon wore on, I worried about Kupaaq's health. He was hard to slow down, especially during whaling when he would get so excited. I kept asking if he was tired: "Do you want to go home and rest?"

"No. I'm fine," he curtly replied, a bit exasperated by all my worrying.

After a few hours, with extra encouragement from his sons, he did go home.

With the serving all done, the crew members went home for a quick rest and to put on their fancy mukluks and new parkas. I changed out of my grungy, patched jeans, Pac-boots, and black whaling crew jacket, all of which were covered in whale blubber and *mikigaq* juice, into my dressy *atikłuk* (snowshirt)—fire-engine red with gold trim—my red paisley parka with a wolverine ruff, and the shiny gray sealskin mukluks I had made from a skin Kupaaq gave me. By nine o'clock everyone gathered back at the *Nalukataq* site and blanket tossing was in full swing. A few days earlier, the skin cover of the *umiaq* had been removed and converted into a circular blanket with sturdy rope handles. It now was stretched between long ropes pulled across the cross arms of ten-foot-tall, wood stanchions set up twenty feet down the rope from the blanket. The blanket was raised seven feet off the ground. A large group of people surrounded the blanket, grabbed hold of a handle, and began to pull down and out in unison with all the strength they could muster. The blanket swayed up and down above their heads, and the person standing in the middle was pushed towards the sky as if bouncing on a trampoline. Screams rang out.

Flora Brower throwing candy while blanket tossing at Nalukataq. Photo by Karen Brewster.

Faces contorted into wild expressions of fear. Ripples of laughter spread through the crowd as participants and bystanders alike enjoyed the event.

I sat next to Kupaaq in the front seat of his beige Subaru station wagon. We were parked at the edge of the *Nalukataq* site. This spot offered a clear view of the blanket tossing without having to be outside in the foggy chill of the mid-summer evening. Kupaaq's grandson, Gregory, peered from the back between the front seats. However, he soon clambered out to run around with his friends and chase flying candy let loose by some of the jumpers. Being in the warmth of a car was a luxury for me. I only had a bicycle for transportation, which usually left me standing out in the cold and the wind when watching outdoor events, like the blanket toss or the spring games. Despite the gradual loss of feeling in my toes and fingers, I often would stay for hours not wanting to go home and miss anything. Being in the car also provided a chance to be seen in public with Kupaaq. I did not know if people knew we were friends. I periodically ran into him at Stuaqpak or the post office and stopped to chat, but most of our time together was at his house. Kupaaq was respected in the community, so I bubbled with pride to be seen with him, like an insecure adolescent who seeks popularity by association. I knew it offered me an entrée into an Iñupiaq world often kept hidden from outsiders.

My job as an oral historian and my ability to learn about Iñupiaq culture depended upon people's willingness to talk to me. And I did not like the separation that existed between Iñupiat, whites, and Filipinos in Barrow. I wanted to learn about people and lifeways different from my own, so I sought access into the Iñupiaq community. I took Iñupiaq language, dance, and skin-sewing classes. I attended predominantly Iñupiaq events, like Elders Conference, town potlucks, Eskimo Dances, and whale feasts; there were times when I was one of the few, if not the only, non-Native there. I visited elders, asked questions, and listened to their stories. My friendship with Kupaaq was key to my acceptance into these activities and the knowledge I gained about the community and culture.

I also had white friends. They were folks who had lived in Barrow a long time and considered it home. I had little patience for short-timers only interested in the high wages of the North Slope. I became part of a clique of professional, outdoorsy non-Natives who as long-term Barrowites fully participated in all the fun, adventure, and struggles that life there had to offer. Being part of a group assuaged the isolation of this remote place.

The long day of festivities and hard work serving food ended with an Eskimo dance at Piuraaġvik, Barrow's recreation center. It began at 11 P.M., after the blanket tossing was over. The round *ugruk* tarp used for the blanket toss was taken down from its perch at the *Nalukataq* site and laid out on the dance floor. The Barrow Dance Group, dressed in matching bright yellow snowshirts, black pants, and wolverine-tasseled mukluks, sat in two rows of chairs on the far side of the gym floor. Everyone else crammed into four rows of bleachers, sat on the floor around the perimeter, or stood along the back wall, the shyer ones purposely hiding in the shadows. There were eight drummers. The older, experienced ones, some close to eighty years old, sat in the middle, and the others, many of them teenagers who were still learning, sat on the ends. These men held their circular, white skin drums in front of their faces and hit the underside of the wooden rims with thin sticks. They flicked their wrists with strong steady strokes. A deep boom and rhythm echoed through the high-ceilinged room. I could feel it down to my bones and into my heart, like the way deep bass chords of an electric guitar resonate through every muscle in your body. The women of the dance group sat behind the men and accompanied the drum beat with high-pitched singing.

The successful whaling captains and crews danced on the blanket to celebrate the gift of the whale. The men stomped their feet, thrust their arms high into the air, and moved around the dance floor with intense energy. "Oo, oo," they called out in joy, sounding like a walrus grunt. The women danced in place, bounced up and down at the knees in time with the beat, and gracefully pushed their arms up and out to the sides, their gloved hands leading the flow. Each of the three crews hosting this day's *Nalukataq* danced two dances. I had heard it said that dances were supposed to be done in pairs; otherwise they would fall over because they were left standing on one leg. Then, one by one, other captains and their crews came down to dance. Everyone was dressed in their fanciest parkas and mukluks: bright new velveteen covers; lush wolf ruffs; furry polar bear boots. After that, it was a free-for-all; anyone and everyone from the audience was encouraged to dance and join in the fun. "Last song,"

Karen Brewster on a sled pulled by a snowmachine on a fall camping trip, circa 1990.

the dance group leader called, after more than an hour of singing and dancing. The whole crowd crammed onto the dance floor to enjoy one last round. Elbow to elbow, barely able to swing their arms without hitting someone, the mass of people swayed and bounced together like a single entity.

Although it was after midnight, it was still broad daylight when I left the building and slowly walked home. One of the Arctic's treats is there are no sunsets from May until August. The low sun shifted in and out of a thin veil of fog, giving the dusty town a soft glow and a deadening quietude. I was exhausted as I slowly dragged my feet along the dirt road, but what a magical day. I was reeling in the thrill of all I had done and wanted to believe that it was something few do. I could never quite believe that I, this former vegetarian, white girl from California, was butchering, preparing, cooking, and serving a whale. I would be in the middle of a task that an Iñupiaq woman might think mundane, and all of a sudden would be struck by the oddity of it in terms of my upbringing and previous experiences. Rinsing the inside and outside of two inch thick, four-foot long sections of whale intestines at the kitchen faucet. Being up to my elbows in a bowl of caribou fat as I whipped it into *akutuq* (Eskimo ice cream). Sitting on the floor among ten Iñupiaq women with five slimy *ugruk* skins weighing heavily across our outstretched legs as we sewed the special waterproof stitch for an *umiaq* cover. It was irrelevant that in actuality it is quite common now for non-Natives in Barrow to help with whaling, especially given the high rate of interracial marriage. To me, what mattered more was that I was involved in no small part because of Kupaaq.

Endnotes

Preface

1. Craig George, personal communication, October 3, 2000.
2. Iñupiaq, which literally translates as "real person," refers to the northern Alaska Eskimos. Iñupiaq is the name of the language spoken, is used as an adjective (such as Iñupiaq culture), and is the singular form of the noun for an individual Native of northern Alaska. Iñupiat is the plural form.
3. Finnegan (1992); Morrow and Schneider (1995).
4. Blackman (1989); Morrow and Schneider (1995); Nelson (1983).
5. Blackman ([1982] 1992); Blackman (1989).
6. Behar (1994: 273).
7. Albert (1995:Tape 1, Side A).
8. Bodfish (1991).
9. Blackman (1989).
10. Neakok (1996:Tape 1, Side A).

Chapter 1

1. There is discrepancy about Harry's birth date. He always thought it was October 11, but later discovered that his birth certificate read October 18. He figured it was the result of hard-to-read handwriting (Eugene Brower, personal communication, March 10, 1998).
2. *Muktuk* is the older misspelling by English speakers of *maktak* and is not in current use.
3. According to Harry's older sister, Sadie Neakok, their father outfitted multiple crews that his sons and local elders ran for him. In the early days of commercial whaling, these crews were sent out to obtain as much whale oil and baleen as possible, but by the time Harry was whaling in the late 1930s the demand had died down and the market had collapsed. Details are unclear, but apparently, Brower still put out more than one crew. He would have distributed the meat around the village, as he did when he pursued whales for their baleen and oil.
4. Eunice Brower Scheuring, personal communication, February 25, 1998.
5. Brower (1995:Side A).
6. Copies of the tapes are available at the North Slope Borough, Iñupiat History, Language and Culture Commission, P.O. Box 69, Barrow, AK 99723 and the Elmer E. Rasmuson Library, Alaska and Polar Regions Department, Oral History Archives, University of Alaska Fairbanks.

Chapter 2

1. *Nuvuk* means "tip or point" in Iñupiaq. Iñupiaq definitions throughout this work are from MacLean 1980. Spellings are also from MacLean (1980) where possible, but if the word was not listed, I consulted Larry Kaplan, Alaska Native Language Center, University of Alaska Fairbanks; and the Iñupiat History, Language and Culture Commission, Barrow, Alaska.
2. The settlement at Nuvuk was abandoned in the mid-1940s, when the last remaining families moved from their ancient, partially underground sod houses into Barrow to be closer to school, church, the hospital, and jobs. See Ford (1959) and Carter (1966)

for archaeological information about Nuvuk, and Bockstoce (1988) for an outsider's view of life at Nuvuk in the mid-1800s.

3. Ukpiaġvik is an alternate spelling. The name shifted to Utqiaġvik, either because it refers to potatoes (*utqich* in Iñupiaq) picked in the area, or over time people forgot the old word, turned it around, and mixed dialects, as happens in any language (Okakok 1981:120–121). The specific type of potato is not mentioned, however there is a plant known as "Eskimo potato," *Hedysarum alpinum* (*masu* in Iñupiaq) whose root the Iñupiat dig up and eat boiled.

4. According to the North Slope Borough Planning Department's most recent population figures Barrow is 53 percent Iñupiaq Eskimo (North Slope Borough 1999:BRW-1).

5. The other villages are: Anaktuvuk Pass, population 314; Atqasuk, population 224; Kaktovik, population 256; Nuiqsut, population 420; Point Hope, population 805; Point Lay, population 246; and Wainwright, population 649 (North Slope Borough 1999:NSB-4).

6. Each North Slope community has at least one dance group that performs locally and travels to Barrow or elsewhere for special events. In 1988, the North Slope Borough revived a mid-winter dance festival called *Kivgiq*, originally a trade and dance festival hosted by a successful hunter who invited those from a neighboring village to share in his success. It was last held around 1914 (Wooley and Okakok 1989). The modern *Kivgiq* brings all the North Slope dance groups together in Barrow for three days of dancing, celebration, and sharing. Dance groups also travel to the World Eskimo Indian Olympics in Fairbanks in July, the annual Alaska Federation of Natives convention in Anchorage in October, and other national and international events when invited. The Barrow Dancers participated in President Clinton's 1993 and 1997 inaugural parades in Washington, D.C.

7. See Hall (1989) for archaeological information on early houses at Utqiaġvik.

8. See Bockstoce (1986:40–41) for more information about these boats.

9. For more on the Iñupiat hunting ethos, see Bodenhorn (1988); Nelson (1982); Sonnenfeld (1956); Spencer (1959); and Worl (1979).

10. Issac Akootchook, interview with Joe Gross on August 13, 1982, page 2 of transcript in U.S. Department of the Interior 1983.

11. E.g., Bockstoce (1988); Murdoch ([1892] 1988); Spencer (1959).

12. "Although leads open more frequently and nearer to shore around the headlands, they also occur regularly off the entire coast. They are predictably farther offshore in protected areas, however" (Nelson 1982:12).

13. Plural of *umialik*.

14. For instance, Charles Brower observed: "Every superstition that these people had seemed to me to have some bearing on their whaling" (volume 1, part 1, page 72 of the unpublished diary of Charles D. Brower entitled *The Northernmost American: An Autobiography*, in three volumes. Stefansson Collection, Dartmouth College Library. Circulating copy available at Elmer E. Rasmuson Library, University of Alaska Fairbanks. Hereafter cited as Brower Diary n.d.).

15. Spencer (1959).

16. For further description of traditional whaling, see Brower Diary n.d.; Allen (1978); Spencer (1959); and Worl (1980).

17. However, whaling captains feel their years of comment and testimony have not been listened to or given much weight in the decisions made about offshore oil leases and development.

18. The season varies slightly every year depending upon the weather, ice conditions, and when the whales appear. The whales migrate from the south through the areas of open water that develop in the spring ice. Point Hope usually is the first North Slope village to land a spring whale, followed by Wainwright, and then Barrow.

19. Multi-year sea ice has been circulating in the pack ice for many years and its salt content has been leached out. This type of ice is identified amongst the jumble of ocean ice by its rounded, smoothed shape and deep blue color. Multi-year sea ice and fresh lake ice are preferred choices for drinking water over the chlorinated tap water, which the elder Iñupiat say tastes bad. Tap water is used for washing, cooking, and doing dishes.

20. E.g., Anderson (1980); Dumond (1987); Ford (1959); Giddings (1967); Larsen and Rainey (1948); Mason and Gerlach (1995).

21. Burch (1970, 1975b, 1980); Stefansson (1912, 1919).

22. This spelling of Smyth is from Beechey (1831).

23. Beechey (1831:414–426); Bockstoce (1988:3–4).

24. Murdoch ([1892] 1988); Simpson (1843); Simpson (1875).

25. Bockstoce (1988).

26. Bockstoce (1986:231–233).

27. Bockstoce (1986:233–244). John W. Kelly, one of Brower's competitors in Barrow's shore-based whaling industry, is also recognized for his innovations and success. He was the first to put up tents on the ice, to have men cook at whale camp, and to have women drive dog teams to bring his crews supplies. The Iñupiat were afraid these changes would keep the whales away. But, in 1891 he took twelve of the eighteen whales landed in Barrow by Native and non-Native crews (Bockstoce 1986:238).

28. Bockstoce (1986:233–234); Brower Diary n.d., volume 1, part 2, pages 117, 161.

29. Brower Diary n.d., volume 1, part 2, pages 117, 146.

30. Blackman (1989:11).

31. Pilot bread is a round, hardtack cracker introduced by whalers. They had them aboard ship because they lasted for a long time. These crackers became a popular snack food in Barrow. They are also known as "sailor boys," referring to the brand name of the original crackers.

32. Arundale and Schneider (1987); Bodfish (1991); Sonnenfeld (1959).

33. Jackson (1898); Stern et al. (1980:16–17).

34. Bockstoce (1986:290–323).

35. Stern et al. (1980:28).

36. Brower Diary n.d., volume 2, part 1 (1899–1911), page 56.

37. Sonnenfeld (1959:79).

38. Sonnenfeld (1959); Burch (1975a).

39. This was a period when adventurous young teachers and missionaries traveling to "exotic" and remote places were quite common among certain circles of Lower 48 society. They received a lot of attention when they returned home with stories of wild adventures, hardships endured, and so-called primitive cultures encountered.

40. The Iñupiaq wives of a number of Barrow's prominent white men do not appear in any of the photographs taken of parties during this period, e.g., Alfred Bailey Collection, Denver Museum of Natural History; Dr. Henry W. Greist Collection, IHLC; Terza Hopson Collection, IHLC; Liebes Collection, California Academy of Sciences; National Archives Collection; Yukon Presbytery Collection, Elmer E. Rasmuson Library, UAF.

41. Blackman (1989:36); Brower ([1942] 1994); Stefansson (1912, 1919).

42. Blackman (1989); Brower ([1942] 1994).

43. See D. Greist (2002); H.W. Greist (1961); and M. Greist (1968) for personal accounts of their lives and years in Barrow.

44. The Mother's Club went on to become a primary social service and political organization in Barrow by providing assistance to needy families and hosting community social events, like talent shows and Halloween costume contests.

45. Klerekoper (1937).

46. Chambers (1970).
47. Case (1984:203–204).
48. See Fortuine (1989) for information about disease and its effects in all parts of Alaska.
49. Burch (1970, 1975b, 1980).
50. Bockstoce (1986); Fortuine (1989).
51. Potter (1947).
52. Lindbergh ([1935] 1963).
53. See Naske (1996) about the history of the Meade River coal mine, and Libbey (1989) for more information about fuel usage in early Barrow.
54. The mine became too expensive to operate and people were buying less coal, so it was closed. Barrow changed from burning coal to buying oil subsidized by the navy, and now pipes in natural gas (Naske 1996).
55. Reed (1958). The area is now called the National Petroleum Reserve–Alaska and is managed by the Department of the Interior, Bureau of Land Management.
56. Reed (1958).
57. Roberts (1952).
58. Reed (1958:2); Roberts (1952).
59. Reed and Ronhovde (1971).
60. Norton (2001).
61. Brewster (1997, 2001).
62. Brewster (1997).
63. Initially, UIC just had caretaker authority for the NARL facility. The land title was finally transferred from the navy in 1989.
64. The 1924 Teapot Dome Scandal during President Harding's administration caused concern about the safety of the nation's petroleum supplies: Secretary of the Interior Fall secretly had leased the entire Teapot Dome area of Naval Petroleum Reserve No. 3 in Wyoming to a private oil company. In 1927, President Coolidge revoked the Department of the Interior's control of the reserves and returned them to the navy. The navy was directed to protect the resources in the ground for emergency need, instead of allowing them to be used up by private industry (Noggle 1965).
65. Naske (1996:11); Schindler (1996:Tape 1, Side B).
66. Sadie Neakok recalls, "Dad started baleen basket making here in Barrow. He was the first to teach the Eskimos to make baleen baskets.…Dad just gave his baleen baskets away to friends. Then he showed his brother-in-law, Taalak, how to make baleen baskets" (Blackman 1989:45). Brower may have developed the woven style of basket making, but the Iñupiat had been molding baleen into buckets, weaving it into fish nets, and using it for a variety of other things for generations. See Lee ([1983] 1998) for more about baleen baskets.
67. The Migratory Bird Treaty Act of 1916 states that waterfowl cannot be hunted between March 10 and September 1. Ducks and geese are only on the North Slope exactly when the law says it is not legal to hunt them (Case 1984:280–281). Nevertheless, the Iñupiat have continued to harvest this important food source and the United States Fish and Wildlife Service, which has enforcement authority, has chosen only to enforce protection of threatened or endangered species, like the spectacled eider. In 1997, the Migratory Bird Treaty was renegotiated between Canada and the United States. One result is that North Slope subsistence waterfowl hunting technically will no longer be illegal.
68. See Berger (1985) for a full discussion of ANCSA and its implications.
69. North Slope Borough (1999:NSB-4).
70. The NSB employs more than 40% of working residents on the Slope, and 50% if the North Slope Borough School District is included in the employment figures (North Slope Borough 1999:NSB-45).
71. See Huntington 1992:110. The Iñupiat first cited tribal authority as giving them

the right to whale, but the IWC was not friendly to this approach, so they turned
to the scientific angle (Ronald Brower, personal communication, March 29, 1998).

72. Albert (1992, 2001).

73. Brower (1995:Tape 1, Side A).

74. Some older whaling captains, including Kupaaq, have expressed concern about the
quota changing whaling practices. With a limit on how many whales can be caught,
they are afraid crews have become more anxious to get whales, that this has made
whalers less careful in where on the whale they place their initial strike, and that they
are more interested in pursuing their own whales instead of helping others land a
previously shot whale. But in general, captains agree that the quota has helped make
whaling practices more efficient and more humane.

75. The AEWC is comprised of a board with members from Barrow, Nuiqsut,
Kaktovik, Wainwright, Point Hope, Kivalina, Wales, Gambell, Savoonga, and
Diomede Island. Individual village practices are supervised by their own Whaling
Captains Association (in 1995 the Barrow Whaling Captains' Wives Association
was established as a way for the women to have more of a role), and crews are
required to register with AEWC each season they wish to participate in the hunt.
Only officially registered crews are eligible to earn shares. AEWC keeps track of
the numbers of whales taken or struck and lost. They supervise the transfer of extra
strikes between villages. They make sure crews abide by the whaling laws and rules.
And they lobby for the whalers in Washington, D.C. and before the International
Whaling Commission.

76. In November 1997, the AEWC received a five-year quota not to exceed 280 whales
(Craig George, North Slope Borough Department of Wildlife Management, personal
communication, March 1998). The AEWC Whaling Captains Convention met in
February 1998 in Barrow and divided this total into an annual quota of 67 landed whales
for the ten whaling communities in Alaska—Gambell, Savoonga, Diomede Island,
Wales, Kivalina, Point Hope, Wainwright, Barrow, Nuiqsut, and Kaktovik. Barrow
was allocated 22 landed whales for the 1998 spring and fall seasons (AEWC 1998).

77. Braund et al. (1988); Chance (1990:176–177).

Chapter 3

1. Brower n.d.:1.

2. Blackman (1989:33).

3. Brower Diary n.d., vol. 1, part 2, p. 103. Throughout his diary Brower spells her
name Toctoo, but current orthographic spelling is Taktuk.

4. Brower ([1942] 1994:234). Taktuk is reported to have saved Brower's life on at least
one occasion when he got lost while hunting (Brower [1942] 1994:17–19). Both
Sadie Neakok and Charles Brower refer to a rescue; however, the circumstances and
details of their stories differ (Blackman 1989:40–41, 256–257).

5. Groups of Iñupiat gathered at places like Niġliq and Sisaulik (Sheshalik) near
Kotzebue to exchange coastal and inland products (maktak, seal oil, caribou furs,
caribou meat, animal furs, as well as Western goods such as tobacco, iron, flour,
and tea) that they needed to survive. Groups traveled long distances over well-used
routes along the rivers, through the mountain passes of the Brooks Range and along
the coast. Some came to Niġliq from as far away as Canada or the Kotzebue Sound
region. These trade fairs were important for the exchange of goods, but also allowed
for social interchange—dancing, storytelling, and access to a wider spectrum of
people from which to choose a spouse. The establishment of trading posts did away
with this trade fair system (Burch 1970, 1975a and b, 1980; Libbey and Schneider
1987; Spencer 1959).

6. For Sadie Neakok's version of this story, see Blackman (1989:42).

7. Blackman (1989:43); Neakok (1996).

8. Hopson, who had been one of Brower's whaling partners, also married an Iñupiat

woman, Miriam (Aqsakaaq). They had a large family of their own, and their
children played with the Brower children.

9. According to Harry Brower's daughter Eunice Scheuring, Kate Brower went
to Eklutna School, Eklutna, Alaska, but it is not known when or for how long
(personal communication, February 25, 1998).

10. Blackman (1989:259).

11. It is unclear whether this was the highest grade offered locally, or if Harry
quit school for other reasons. There is discrepancy on the highest grade Harry
completed. Eunice Scheuring remembers her father saying he went through fifth
grade and that he joked with his wife Annie about her being smarter because she
finished the seventh grade (personal communication, February 25, 1998). Sadie
Neakok (Neakok 1995) and Max Brewer (Brewer 1996) both said Harry went
through the eighth grade.

12. Blackman (1989); Brower ([1942] 1994).

13. Only two Brower wives are mentioned in Blackman (1989) and Brower ([1942]
1994). However, at this point in the recording Harry said three. Sadie Neakok
mentions her father having a child with a woman at Nuvuk, but says they never
got married (Blackman 1989:256).

14. Ten children are indicated in Blackman (1989:75).

15. Rex Ahvakana has said that the Morris children "needed a translator to speak to
their parents," because they learned to speak Iñupiaq from the playmates they spent
so much time with. David Greist also became fluent in Iñupiaq, while his parents
did not (personal communication, 2002).

16. An Iñupiat game, called aqamak, is tug of war with the pinkie fingers of each player
hooked around the other.

17. Throughout this work, Harry uses Half Moon Three and Alaqtaq interchangeably
when he refers to the family's reindeer herding headquarters.

18. Blackman (1989:257).

19. Brower Diary n.d., vol. 2, part 2 (1920–1926), p. 3.

20. Blackman (1989:93–94).

21. Bodenhorn (1988); Chance (1990).

22. This was before the coal mine was developed on the Meade River.

23. The fuel problem in Barrow was exacerbated by an increasing population and
changes in housing. With the introduction of larger, wood-frame houses, people
needed more and more fuel, and fuel that could be burned in their cast iron stoves.
This prompted depletion of driftwood supplies, even going as far as destroying the
old qargiit (community houses) and sod house frames for the wood they offered.
(See also Steffanson 1919:8–9 and Libbey 1989.)

24. Aaqhaallich and ukpiich are the Iñupiaq plural forms for these words. "S" is not
used to make plurals in Iñupiaq, but this is how Harry said these words.

25. Some Point Hope people still collect the eggs from murre's nests by climbing
down the cliff face and dangling on a rope from the top. Boiled murre eggs are
now a delicacy because of the rarity and danger of their collection. I do not know
the specific kind of murre, but the thick-billed and common murre are the most
prevalent in the Cape Thompson area (Swartz 1966).

26. E.g., Colorado Museum of Natural History, Chicago Academy of Sciences, and
San Diego Museum of Natural History (Bailey et al. 1933).

27. Alfred M. Bailey from the Colorado Museum of Natural History did a lot of
fieldwork and bird collecting in the Arctic. He spent 1921–1922 in Wainwright
and Charles Brower made collections for him for many years after that. (See Bailey
et al. 1933 and Bailey 1948, 1971.)

28. There appears to be some discrepancy between what Harry is saying and what
historical documents indicate. As mentioned previously, reindeer were first brought
to Barrow in 1898 by the Jarvis Expedition to feed stranded whalers (Jackson
1898), and Brower got his reindeer from the government in exchange for taking

care of the herds Brower Diary n.d., vol. 2, part 1 1899–1911, pp. 55–56. There is no indication that Brower had reindeer before this or that Laplanders brought them. Laplanders did train Native Alaskans in the Seward Peninsula area to herd reindeer (Bodfish 1991). It is possible that I am misinterpreting what Harry meant by "before they started coming up." We had been talking about the increase in herd size, so he may have meant that his father bought reindeer before the herds started getting big, coming up in size, not before the herds came up to Barrow.

29. See Bodfish (1991) for another perspective on the North Slope reindeer herding experience.

30. See Arundale and Schneider (1987) and Brower (1983).

31. He was hired in 1939 by the Bureau of Indian Affairs as the unit manager for the Barrow herd. For an account of his activities in and around Barrow, see recording H89-2a/b at the Elmer E. Rasmuson Library, Alaska and Polar Regions Department, Oral History Archives, University of Alaska Fairbanks. Waldo Bodfish, Sr., also mentions Forshaug in his discussions of reindeer herding (Bodfish 1991:79). Administrative responsibility for reindeer was transferred to the Alaska Division of the Office of Indian Affairs in 1937, but the Reindeer Service continued to manage the program (Stern et al. 1980).

32. In his oral history interview, Forshaug mentions a conflict between the Barrow and Wainwright herders over the mixing of their herds that he worked on resolving (Forshaug 1989). I do not know if this is the trouble Harry is referring to, or if there were other troubles with the management of the Barrow herd.

33. Barrow did not receive long distance telephone service until the 1950s, and it was limited to a few businesses. Most private homes did not get phone service until after 1960, and even then not everyone could afford it.

34. The U.S. Coast Guard cutter *Northland* was built in 1927 as a replacement for the cutter *Bear* and did Bering Sea patrols in the 1930s. In 1934, "The cutter *Northland* commanded by Captain W. K. Scammel, completed a 14,000 mile cruise, which took her into the Arctic as far as Point Barrow during a seven month period, proceeding to San Francisco for the winter upon her return" (Newell 1966:429).

35. Berna Brower, originally from Wainwright, who was married to Robert Brower, remembers: "When he was a kid, Kupaaq had his tonsils taken out on the ship between Barrow and Wainwright. Got off at Wainwright and stayed at Jim Allen's store. I used to help his wife and was around the store. Kupaaq got an earache while he was in Wainwright. I got into his bed to help him feel better and sleep. He was just like a brother" (Brower 1993:Tape 1, Side A). Waldo Bodfish also remembers when tonsils were taken out (Bodfish 1991:128).

36. The first *Northstar* was built in Seattle in 1932 (Newell 1966:417). The *Northstar* was the primary supply ship serving Barrow from the 1930s to the 1960s.

37. The U.S. Army Signal Corps was established in Barrow in the 1920s to provide regular and reliable radio communications to the outside world. Sergeant Stanley Morgan was the signal corps operator in the 1930s who relayed the message out about the Rogers/Post airplane crash. Sgt. Morgan and his wife Beverly regularly attended Brower parties.

38. Brower ([1942] 1994:295).

39. Will Rogers and Wiley Post are both buried in their home state of Oklahoma. A monument to this event and the memory of these men was erected at the mouth of Walakpa Lagoon in 1937. Today, this area is commonly referred to as "Monument."

40. Wooley et al. (1992).

41. Dr. Greist is reported to have healed Marvin by soaking him for long periods in hot baths and slowly working his muscles and straightening his legs. Marvin still used crutches, but was more mobile than before (Rex Ahvakana, personal communication, n.d.).

42. It was too dangerous for Marvin to be out whaling, because if they had to evacuate camp from moving ice his crippled leg kept him from moving fast enough to escape. He still was able to get a share, because whaling captains distributed shares to everyone, especially to the elderly, the poor, and the houses without hunters. This widespread distribution was not necessarily done with other animals. Marvin had to participate directly in other types of hunting to earn shares and to provide for himself and his extended family of sisters.

Chapter 4

1. Naske and Slotnick ([1979] 1987:123–126).
2. Alaska's first National Guard battalions were formed in 1940 by Governor Ernest Gruening who was concerned about territorial defense with the threat of World War II. They shifted into regular military service once the United States became involved in the war. The Alaska National Guard was re-established by the Alaska legislature in 1949 (Marston 1969). For more information about the Native role in the ATG, see Hendricks (1985); and Wooley and Martz (1995a, 1995b).
3. It is unclear whether Kupaaq means Russians physically coming over to the United States or "came over" in the sense of joined our side of the fight. He may be referring to the Alaska-Siberia Lend-Lease Program. From 1942–1945, Russian pilots ferried American airplanes from Fairbanks through Nome to Siberia as part of the United States effort to bolster defense forces against Nazi Germany (Naske and Slotnick 1987:127).
4. Levi Greist fought in the Aleutians. Eddie Hopson was stationed in Nome, but returned to Barrow to train the ATG troops. See Hendricks (1985) and Wooley and Martz (1995a, 1995b) for more information about the ATG's role in training local leadership.
5. Lieutenant Commander William T. Foran was the geologist in charge of the navy's North Slope oil exploration program.
6. I remember Kupaaq mentioning Cliff Burglin another time in conjunction with fortunes made at Prudhoe Bay, so I think he may be this son-in-law. He was an independent oilman from Fairbanks who owned some of the original state leases in the Prudhoe Bay area, and made a lot of money by selling them after oil was discovered (John Schindler, personal communication, March 10, 1998). See Roderick (1997) for more information about the history of oil development in Alaska.
7. Wien Alaska Airlines, headquartered in Fairbanks, was the major commercial airline in Alaska from the 1950s to the 1980s. It was founded by bush pilot Noel Wien in 1930, and taken over by his brother Sig in 1949. Sig flew charters for the navy's oil exploration work in the 1940s, and it was the first commercial operation to provide regular flight service to Barrow (Potter 1947; Kennedy 1967). In 1954, Wien Airlines brought the first official tour group to Barrow. The airline went out of business in the mid–1980s.
8. "The site for Umiat Test Well 1, on a ridge between two branches of Seabee Creek, was picked on the basis of geologic and topographic reconnaissance mapping by a Navy party under Lt. W. T. Foran in 1944," (Collins 1958:75).
9. See Collins (1958) for information about Umiat test wells and the type of oil discovered there.
10. I did not ask Kupaaq what they did when it rained. They must have carried at least a tarp to protect them from the elements.
11. They were taking elevation measurements with a transit. The transit operator would stand in one spot and the rest of the crew would scatter out in various directions carrying stadia rods that provided information to the transit operator there. After he shot all his measurements, the transit operator would shoot a flare telling the men to regroup. They would return to where they started, though

the transit operator had already moved on to the next spot. By the time the farthest man caught up with the others, those who had been closer to the transit were rested and ready to go on.

12. To be fair, they rotated who got to be closest and farthest, so one man did not always have to do so much more walking than the rest.

13. For more about north Alaskan amber see Langenheim et al. (1960); Leffingwell (1919:179); and Wheeler (2000).

14. The U.S. Navy Seabees constructed their oil exploration camp in 1944.

15. See Cade (1960, 1967a, b); Kessel and Cade (1958); White and Cade (1971).

16. What Harry called Peter's Lake is identified as Lake Peters on USGS maps. For consistency, I will call it Peter's Lake as Harry did.

17. John Schindler provided this date of 1960 (Schindler 1996).

18. This may have been Colorado Oil and Gas Company (John Schindler, personal communication, March 10, 1998). See Mull (1982) and Roderick (1997) for more about this period in Alaska's oil exploration history.

19. Jack Lentfer was the Alaska Department of Fish and Game biologist studying polar bears at NARL at the time.

20. Polar bears in the wild are estimated to live between twenty-five and thirty years (DeMaster and Stirling 1981:3).

Chapter 5

1. Burch (1975a); Bodenhorn (1988).

2. See Schneider, Pedersen and Libbey (1980:170–178) for archaeological and historic information about the Iviksuk site. Ronald Brower believes they moved into Barrow in the early 1950s, when he was two or three. He remembers walking to town in the spring/summer, and being amazed at seeing wood-frame houses and windows for the first time (personal communication, March 29, 1998).

3. Schindler (1996:Tape 1, Side A).

4. Albert (1995:Tape 1, Side B).

5. According to IHLC records, Charles Brower's correspondence, and Sadie Neakok, Asianŋataq died on September 3, 1943. Sadie said her mother was in her sixties and died of a gallbladder infection (Blackman 1989:49–50).

6. Nowadays family members dig a grave in just one to three days. They often first use an augering machine to start the hole, and then enlarge it by hand with picks and shovels.

7. In an oral history interview, Dr. Earl C. Albrecht mentions the sacrifices Native Alaskans made by being sent away from home for TB treatment and the difference this made in the battle to stop the disease (O'Neill 1986). See Anonymous (n.d.); Fortuine (1989); and Vanhagen (1947) for more about tuberculosis in Alaska.

8. Harry may be referring to two things here. The weight of the load making the boat heavy and hard to pull, and the amount of freeboard left when the boat was loaded. If there is too little freeboard, it could easily swamp. Also a boat is harder to pull when it is so low in the water.

9. By 1952, Barrow residents were beginning to use fuel oil (Naske 1996:10).

Chapter 6

1. Brower (1995:Tape 1, Side A).

2. Polar bears were also hunted by non-Native sport hunters, until the Marine Mammal Protection Act (1972) and the Polar Bear Convention (1976) limited polar bear and other marine mammal hunting to Natives only (Case 1984).

3. The man was concerned that Kupaaq was hunting alone and did not have what he considered to be adequate weapons for polar bears. He scolded Kupaaq for not thinking about his safety and what he would have done if he had not killed the bear and it had come after him.

4. The Nunamiut of Anaktuvak Pass call the Big Dipper *Tuttugruk*. The bowl part is called *tupqich* (the tents), and the three stars of the handle are referred to as *tuvaat* (hunters going home) (Grant Spearman, Curator, Simon Paneak Memorial Museum, Anaktuvuk Pass, personal communication, February 20, 1998).

5. *Aagruuk* is a pair of stars that appears just after winter solstice in December signalling that daylight will return soon. The larger of these two stars is Venus and is referred to as the Morning Star in English (Larry Kaplan, Alaska Native Language Center, University of Alaska Fairbanks, personal communication, February 20, 1998, quoting from draft Iñupiaq dictionary in his possession).

6. It is unclear when Kupaaq says "the daylight coming up" or "just before the daybreak" if he is referring to the daylight coming back after solstice, as indicated above, or if he means when the daylight breaks in the morning. Before I knew about the Morning Star being associated with solstice, I assumed he meant the daylight coming back in the morning, because our conversation was about using this star to find your way home if lost. I remember him saying that you could wait until this star came up and then you'd know which way was east and that it would soon be light enough to travel.

7. According to Sam Hopson, this group of three stars is also called the three wise men, and shows up in December (personal communication, February 28, 1998). Based upon these descriptions, I believe this is the line of three stars known as "Orion's Belt."

8. The Iñupiaq story about the northern lights is that they are running around up in the sky playing traditional Iñupiaq soccer or football with a skull. Children are told to keep their hoods up when northern lights are out or the players will come down and take their heads for the game.

9. According to Ronald Brower, the trap under the Kleenex and snow looks like a lemming to the fox. And the tissue moves in the wind, which makes it look like a lemming moving. The fox will jump on the trap thinking he is pouncing on a lemming, his prey. Ronald remembers his father finding at least one fox who had both feet stuck in the trap, because he had leapt on it as if it were a lemming (personal communication, March 29, 1998).

10. Pieces of meat or bait are scattered all around the trap. The baitless trap lies under the snow in the middle. The fox will end up stepping on the trap when he tries to get the meat.

11. In the 1950s, the federal government instituted a bounty system on Alaska wolves to reduce what they believed was a population excess.

12. Point Lonely is about seventy-five miles east of Barrow. There is a U.S. Air Force DEW–line station and airstrip there.

13. Wooden parts of old tools were painted with this dye from the red ochre rock. Red dye for treating the backs of skins is obtained by soaking shavings of the outer bark of alder bushes in boiling water. The pieces of bark turn red when scraped from the branch. The plant/bark/dye is called *nunaŋiak* in Iñupiaq.

14. *Atiq* is an Iñupiaq relationship term for someone with the same name, your namesake.

15. Due to the ANCSA land claims settlement, ASRC owns subsurface rights to parcels of land within the refuge boundaries and so is bound to make money if oil is discovered. As a profit-making corporation, they have been strong promoters of oil development in the Refuge.

Chapter 7

1. For more information about Iñupiaq oral tradition, see Bergsland (1987); Bodenhorn (1988); Lowenstein et al. (1992); and Spencer (1959). For more about the performance aspects of storytelling refer to Finnegan (1992) and Morrow and Schneider (1995).

2. Brower (1995:Tape 1, Side A).
3. The man was a National Weather Service employee, and to show his appreciation for the rescue, he let Kupaaq have whatever groceries he wanted from the commissary. Sam Hopson also tells this story on pp. 187–188.
4. See Burch (1971) for more about the non-empirical world of the Iñupiat.
5. Hopson (1995:Tape 2, Side A).
6. E.g., Lowenstein et al. (1992); Murdoch ([1892] 1988); Spencer (1959).
7. Giving away the first kill establishes a special bond between a young Iñupiaq hunter and an elder (Bodfish 1991:43, 267). I do not know if this is what was going on here or if it was just the normal sharing with elders that he was taught.
8. When Harry started whaling, songs were no longer used. By then, missionary influences were very strong, and explosive darting and shoulder guns were used instead of stone-tipped harpoons that had required songs to help whales die more quickly.
9. Burch (1971).
10. James Ford from the American Museum of Natural History excavated house mounds at Piġniq in the 1930s. See Ford (1959) for discussion of his findings.
11. Harry's brother, Arnold, mentions this same couple in an oral history interview about the historic uses of the Chipp-Ikpikpuk River area (Arundale and Schneider 1987:10; Brower 1983).

Chapter 8

1. Barrow and Point Hope are the only North Slope villages that still use skin boats at all. Wainwright whalers carry aluminum boats on sleds to the lead. Nuiqsut and Kaktovik only whale in the fall when there is no ice and aluminum powerboats are the most efficient means for traveling the long distances necessary to find and pursue the whales in open water. The same is true for Barrow's fall whaling.
2. In keeping with the Iñupiat habit of adopting tools and practices that are most efficient and effective, a few years ago a handful of crews in Barrow began covering the standard wooden boat frame with fiberglass instead of *ugruk* skins. There is no consensus about how these newer boats compare to their skin counterparts. Some captains believe the fiberglass boats are faster than skin ones. Some captains say they are more durable and less expensive to make, because they do not have to hunt five or six seals and pay a group of ten or twelve women to sew new skins together every few years. Other captains believe that fiberglass boats are too heavy and are more easily damaged than skin boats, which flex, and that they make more noise, which scares the whales away. Skin boats are easier to repair in the field—only requiring a needle, thread and a scrap of skin for a patch.
3. Since 1986, Iñupiat whalers and the Alaska Eskimo Whaling Commission (AEWC) have been working with Norwegian weapons expert, Egil Ole Øen, to develop a more efficient and more humane explosive bomb. Prototypes of a new, penthrite bomb have been used and adjustments continue to be made (Øen 1995).
4. When stinkers resurface in open water they are easily retrieved and towed to the ice edge. When they come up under young slush ice or ice which is not too thick, the whalers will cut or blast the ice to get to the whale.
5. For more information about Iñupiat whale butchering and share division see George (1981).
6. For other descriptions of recent Iñupiat whaling see Foote (1992) and Nelson (1982).
7. Before the introduction and widespread use of reliable outboard engines, Barrow whalers used wooden hulled sailboats in the fall. These were the Yankee-style wooden dories with a single sail used by commercial whalers. According to Iñupiaq elder Rex Ahvakana, these boats were not often used in the spring, because they were hard to

transport by sled on the ice trails and because ice accumulated on the sides faster than on a skin boat, which made them heavier and harder to maneuver. In the fall, warmer temperatures made ice build-up less of a problem (personal communication, 1996).

8. To participate and earn a share during spring whaling a person must be on a crew officially registered with the AEWC. In the fall, crew membership is more flexible. Men can go in their own boat and catch a whale in the name of their captain's crew, or join someone else's crew for that season by going in their boat. Also, in the fall someone who is not part of a crew can earn a personal cutter's share just by helping butcher, and women can earn individual shares by helping cook and serve at a captain's house even if they are not part of that crew. While these also can be done in the spring, it is less common. Most of the women working belong to that captain's crew and get a portion of the crew's share.

9. Expertise and leadership qualities are still needed to be a whaling captain, but other factors may now motivate some people to put out crews who wouldn't have before. In the past, a man had to wait to inherit a crew. Now, you can declare yourself a captain by purchasing the gear, recruiting a crew of men, being approved by the whaling captain's association, registering with the AEWC, setting up camp on the ice, and putting out a boat. Money is more easily available to purchase the equipment and to pay the costs of running a crew than it used to be, and modern technology has reduced some of the dangers of traditional whaling that necessitated a lifetime of knowledge about the ice and the whales. One new crew was formed in Barrow because the old crew had too many people on it.

10. ICAS v. United States II, affidavit filed by Harry Brower, 1981 (9th Circuit Court of the US, Anchorage), Appendix G:3 as quoted in Bodenhorn (1988:215).

11. This feast, *Aŋiruq*, is no longer held in Barrow. Instead, candy is given out when the crew departs for the ice. In Point Hope, successful spring captains who have caught less than five whales in their careers host this tail section feast in the fall, when the young slush ice is just beginning to form. Successful captains with five or more whales in their careers host "the whale tail festival" in March, before the new whaling season begins (Foote 1992:16).

12. Charles Brower put out multiple crews in an effort to garner as much baleen as possible. Some of these crews were run by Iñupiat, some by white men who worked for Brower. The crewmembers were a combination of white men and Iñupiat who were unable to whale with their own people because of taboos or because they were from other regions. At some point, Kupaaq must have been in charge of one of these crews. By the time Kupaaq was a teenager in the 1930s the commercial whaling market had collapsed, but perhaps his father still put out multiple crews for other reasons. So some confusion remains about Kupaaq's early whaling experience.

13. The average butchering time today ranges from three to twelve hours, although it is quite variable depending upon the size of the whale, the number of people participating, and the ice and weather conditions.

14. Nowadays, the feast at the successful captain's house is only one day.

15. U.S. Weather Service data correlated with survivors' observations indicate that this ice event occurred in May 1957. Other survivors remembered it happening in the late 1950s or early 1960s, instead of the early 1950s as Kupaaq suggests. See George et al. in press, Huntington et al. (2001).

16. Before 1976, when Barrow got its high school, children were sent away to complete their education. Mt. Edgecumbe in Sitka, Alaska, was one of the places where students from all over Alaska went. Chimauwha Indian School in Oregon was another common destination. Many of the current generation of Alaska Native leaders in their forties and fifties went to these boarding schools. It was expensive to pay the airfare for children to travel between home and school, a problem exacerbated by large families and a lack of high-paying jobs in Barrow at the time.

17. Spencer (1959).

18. The rest of the crew stands on the ice and holds onto the rope and maneuvers the boat around so the harpooner is above the whale and then they pull the boat back to the ice after he throws the harpoon.

19. So that you do not get pulled in, and because a backwash of water from the sudden stopping can swamp the boat if you are not careful.

20. Bombs can also misfire if the black powder is not packed right, or the ignition cap is not fitted properly.

21. He would throw the darting gun, then turn around and grab the shoulder gun that was right there and fire it.

22. If the float comes off before a bomb has been put into the whale and the whalers believe the whale was not injured and swam away, then it does not count as a strike, or a lost whale.

23. The quota had been reached, the other crews had gone home, and he stayed out to whale anyway. When he got a whale there was nobody to help him kill it, tow it, or butcher it. He was unable to get the whale all by himself.

24. Now, with so many crews in Barrow that get whales, there is usually more than one day of *Nalukataq*. Each day is hosted by a different successful captain or captains.

25. They cover the floor of the tent with plywood sheets, caribou skins, or a polar bear hide for sleeping pads, and some crews even use thick pieces of blue foam insulation to keep out the cold from the ice below.

26. During *Nalukataq*, each successful crew raises its flag on a pole. In the few cases when a crew lands more than one whale they fly as many flags as whales they got. Multiple whales per crew were more common in earlier days, when there were fewer crews in Barrow. A crew's flag is passed on along with the equipment when a crew is transferred between generations or family members. It is not clear when the flag tradition began, but it is possible that the flags are related to triangular pennants or identifying flags flown on whaling and trading ships in the early 1900s, or to the flags flown by commercial whaling ships to signal to other boats that they had caught a whale.

27. Eugene has this book and continues to enter size and date information about the whales he catches (Eugene Brower, personal communication, March 10, 1998).

28. The first bomb in a whale indicates which captain the whale belongs to, but other crews help kill it by putting in more bombs and helping chase it down. The final killing shot may come from a crew that did not strike the whale first. The distribution of shares of meat and *maktak* can be effected by how much a crew helped and what their role was.

29. Hollywood is the name of a place on the coast eight to ten miles south of Barrow, where the Disney movie "Track of the Giant Snow Bear" was filmed in the 1960s.

30. A hit to a vertebra can disable the whale immediately. If the spine is severed, the whale is immobilized and it comes straight back up. The bones break apart, the fragments cause internal injury, and the whale dies quickly. Hitting a bone also stops the bomb from traveling farther. In comparison, a whale shot in the heart will also die, but will keep swimming for a while first, just like a caribou shot in the heart will keep running before it finally falls. The best spot to hit a whale is the back of the head, striking the brain (Sam Hopson, personal communication, February 28, 1998).

31. See Epilogue for other stories about this event.

32. Mike Philo was another veterinarian who had worked at NARL, was hired to help Tom Albert, and later worked for the North Slope Borough Department of Wildlife Management.

33. Personal communication, March 1996.

34. According to Eugene, Kupaaq meant that because this man's crew killed a mother

with a calf, which is not an acceptable whaling practice, Kupaaq got sick. He said that these actions affected Kupaaq directly, because he was so in tune with whales (personal communication, February 14, 1997).

35.   Kupaaq means that this man's crew acted like they were always supposed to get a whale when they go out, and as if it is their whale instead of the whole community's. Kupaaq chastised him for improperly whaling when he killed a mother with a calf and then did not even want to take care of the baby one. Kupaaq also criticized the other crew for not appreciating a whale as a gift.

Epilogue

1.   The following stories are excerpted from oral history interviews I conducted. The recordings are available at the North Slope Borough, Iñupiat History, Language and Culture Commission, P. O. Box 69, Barrow, Alaska 99723 and the Elmer E. Rasmuson Library, Alaska and Polar Regions Department, Oral History Archive, University of Alaska Fairbanks, Fairbanks, Alaska 99775. The tapes are listed in the references by the speaker's name.

2.   See Gallagher (1974:118) for another perspective on this visit and for more about the early history of the Iñupiat land claims efforts.

3.   Brower (1995:Tape 1, Side A).

4.   Ronald Brower, personal communication, March 29, 1998.

5.   Sam calls them squirrels in English, but according to MacLean (1980), *siksrikpuk* are hoary marmots (*Marmota caligata*).

6.   See Noggle (1965) for information about the Tea Pot Dome Scandal, which in 1924 established this limit on access to National Petroleum Reserves. Gallagher (1974) states that Senator Bartlett got the bill passed.

References

Alaska Eskimo Whaling Commission (AEWC)
1998   Personal communication with Karen Brewster (faxed response to author's February 17, 1998 email request for information), April 23, 1998.

Albert, Thomas F.
1992   Impacts by Science and Scientists on People of Alaska's North Slope. In *Arctic Uumaruq 1990—Arctic Alive*. David Norton, ed. Pp. 24–25. Barrow, AK: Arctic Sivunmun Iḷisaġvik College, North Slope Borough Board of Higher Education.
1995   Oral History Interview with Karen Brewster, November 16, 1995, Barrow, Alaska. (Tape H99-16-03, on file at the Oral History Archives, University of Alaska Fairbanks and North Slope Borough, Iñupiat History, Language and Culture Commission, Barrow, Alaska.)
2001   The Influence of Harry Brower, Sr., an Iñupiaq Eskimo Hunter, on the Bowhead Whale Research Program Conducted at the UIC-NARL Facility by the North Slope Borough. In *Fifty More Years Below Zero*. David W. Norton, ed. Pp. 265–278. Calgary: Arctic Institute of North America.

Allen, Arthur James
1978   *A Whaler and Trader in the Arctic—1895 to 1944—My Life with the Bowhead*. Anchorage, AK: Alaska Northwest Publishing Company.

Anderson, Douglas D.
1980   Continuity and Change in the Prehistoric Record from North Alaska. In *Alaska Native Culture and History*. Papers presented at the Second International Symposium, August 1978. Yoshinobu Kotani and William Workman, eds. Senri Ethnological Studies 4. Pp. 233–251. Osaka, Japan: National Museum of Ethnology.

Anonymous
n.d.   Tuberculosis in Alaska. Government Report with no cover or title page. Part I—Tuberculosis in Alaska. Part II—Hospital Needs in Alaska (non-military) and Congressional Legislation pertinent to Alaska Health Program; report submitted by C. Earl Albrecht.

Arundale, Wendy H., and William S. Schneider
1987   Quliaqtuat Iñupiat Nunaṇiññiñ—The Report of the Chipp-Ikpikpuk River and Upper Meade River Oral History Project. Barrow, AK: North Slope Borough Planning Department.

Bailey, Alfred M.
1948   *Birds of Arctic Alaska*. Popular Series, 8, April 1, 1948. Denver, CO: The Colorado Museum of Natural History.
1971   Fieldwork of a Museum Naturalist 1919–1922, Alaska: Southeast, Alaska: Far North. Museum Pictorial Number 22, December 3, 1971. Denver, CO: Denver Museum of Natural History.

Bailey, Alfred M., Charles D. Brower, and Louis B. Bishop
    1933   Birds of the Region of Point Barrow, Alaska. Program of Activities of the
            Chicago Academy of Sciences 4 (2), April 1933. Chicago, IL: Chicago Academy
            of Sciences.

Beechey, Frederick W.
    1831   *Narrative of a Voyage to the Pacific and Beering's Strait to Co-operate with the Polar*
            Expeditions: Performed in His Majesty's Ship "Blossom," Under the Command of
            Captain F. W. Beechey, R.N. in the Years 1825, 26, 27, 28. London: Henry
            Colburn and Richard Bentley.

Behar, Ruth
    1994   *Translated Woman: Crossing the Border with Esperanza's Story.* Boston, MA:
            Beacon Press.

Berger, Thomas R.
    1985   *Village Journey, The Report of the Alaska Native Review Commission.* New York:
            Hill and Wang.

Bergsland, Knut, ed.
    1987   *Nunamiut Unipkaaŋich—Nunamiut Stories.* Told in Iñupiaq Eskimo by Elijah
            Kakinya and Simon Paneak of Anaktuvuk Pass, Alaska. Collected 1949–1950
            by Helge Ingstad with the help of Homer Mekiana. Barrow, AK: North Slope
            Borough Commission on Iñupiat History, Language and Culture.

Blackman, Margaret B.
    1989   *Sadie Brower Neakok, An Iñupiaq Woman.* Seattle, WA: University of Washington
            Press.
 [1982] 1992 *During My Time: Florence Edenshaw Davidson, A Haida Woman.* Seattle, WA:
            University of Washington Press.

Bockstoce, John
    1986   *Whales, Ice and Men: The History of Whaling in the Western Arctic.* Seattle, WA:
            University of Washington Press.

Bockstoce, John, ed.
    1988   *The Journals of Rochfort Maguire, 1852–1854, Two Years at Point Barrow, Alaska*
            Aboard HMS Plover *in the Search for Sir John Franklin*, Volume I & II. London:
            Hakluyt Society.

Bodenhorn, Barbara
    1988   *Documenting Inupiat Family Relationships in Changing Times*, Volume I & II.
            Report prepared for the North Slope Borough Commission on Iñupiat History,
            Language and Culture, Barrow, Alaska and the Alaska Humanities Forum,
            Anchorage. (Manuscript on file at Iñupiat History, Language and Culture
            Office in Barrow, AK and Rasmuson Library, University of Alaska Fairbanks.)
    1989   *'The Animals Come to Me, They Know I Share'—Inupiaq Kinship, Changing*
            Economic Relations and Enduring World Views on Alaska's North Slope. Ph.D.
            dissertation, Department of Social Anthro-pology, University of Cambridge,
            England.

Bodfish, Waldo, Sr.
    1991   *Kusiq: An Eskimo Life History from the Arctic Coast of Alaska.* Fairbanks, AK:
            University of Alaska Press.

Braund, Stephen R., Sam W. Stoker, and John A. Kruse
  1988   *Quantification of Subsistence and Cultural Needs for Bowhead Whales by Alaska Eskimos.* Anchorage, AK: Stephen R. Braund and Associates.

Brewer, Max
  1996   Oral History Interview with Karen Brewster, March 16, 1996, Anchorage, Alaska. (Tape H99-16-01, parts 1-6, on file at the Oral History Archives, University of Alaska Fairbanks and North Slope Borough, Iñupiat History, Language and Culture Commission, Barrow, Alaska.)

Brewster, Karen
  1997   Native Contributions to Arctic Science at Barrow, Alaska. *Arctic* 50(3):277–284.
  2001   Historical Perspectives on Iñupiat Contributions to Arctic Science at NARL. In *Fifty More Years Below Zero: Tributes and Meditations for the Naval Arctic Research Laboratory's First Half Century at Barrow, Alaska.* David W. Norton, ed. Pp. 23–26. Calgary: The Arctic Institute of North America.

Briggs, Jean L.
  1970   *Never In Anger: Portrait of an Eskimo Family.* Cambridge, MA: Harvard University Press.

Brower, Arnold
  1983   Oral History Interview with William Schneider and Wendy Arundale for the Chipp-Ikpikpuk River and Upper Meade River Oral History Project, January 1983, Barrow, Alaska, Tape R38. (On file at the Elmer E. Rasmuson Library, Alaska and Polar Regions Department, Oral History Archives, University of Alaska Fairbanks.)

Brower, Berna
  1993   Oral History Interview with Karen Brewster, March 18, 1993, Barrow, Alaska. (On file at the North Slope Borough, Iñupiat History, Language and Culture Commission, Barrow, Alaska.)

Brower, Charles D.
  n.d.   *The Northernmost American: An Autobiography*, Volume 1–3. Unpublished diary, Stefansson Collection, Dartmouth College Library. (Circulating copy on file at Elmer E. Rasmuson Library, University of Alaska Fairbanks.)
  [1942] 1994 *Fifty Years Below Zero: A Lifetime of Adventure in the Far North.* Reprint with a preface by Terrence Cole. Fairbanks, AK: University of Alaska Press.

Brower, Eugene
  1995   Oral History Interview with Karen Brewster, November 15, 1995, Barrow, Alaska. (Tape H99-16-04, on file at the Oral History Archives, University of Alaska Fairbanks and North Slope Borough, Iñupiat History, Language and Culture Commission, Barrow, Alaska.)

Burch, Ernest S., Jr.
  1970   The Eskimo Trading Partnership in North Alaska. *Anthropological Papers of the University of Alaska* 15(1):49–80. Fairbanks, AK: University of Alaska.
  1971   The Nonempirical Environment of the Arctic Alaskan Eskimos. *Southwestern Journal of Anthropology* 27:148–165.
  1975a   *Eskimo Kinsmen: Changing Family Relationships in Northwest Alaska.* New York: West Publishing Company.

1975b   Inter-Regional Transportation in Traditional Northwest Alaska. *Anthropological Papers of the University of Alaska* 17(2):1–11. Fairbanks, AK: University of Alaska.

1980   Traditional Eskimo Societies in Northwest Alaska. In *Alaska Native Culture and History*. Papers Presented at the Second International Symposium, August 1978. Yoshinobu Kotani and William Workman, eds. Senri Ethnological Studies 4. Pp. 253–304. Osaka, Japan: National Museum of Ethnology.

Cade, Tom J.
1960   Ecology of the Peregrine and Gyrfalcon Populations in Alaska. *University of California Publications in Zoology* 63(3):151–289. Berkeley, CA: University of California Press.

1967a   *Ecology of Raptor Populations in Arctic Alaska* (ONR-391). Ithaca, NY: Laboratory of Ornithology and Division of Biological Sciences, Cornell University.

1967b   Ecological and Behavioral Aspects of Predation by the Northern Shrike. In *The Living Bird, Sixth Annual of the Cornell Laboratory of Ornithology*, Volume 6. Olin Sewall Pettingill, Jr. and Douglas A. Lancaster, eds. Pp. 43–85. Ithaca, NY: The Laboratory of Ornithology at Cornell University.

Carter, W. K.
1966   *Archeological Survey of Eskimo, Or Earlier, Material in the Vicinity of Point Barrow, Alaska*. Final Report to the Office of Naval Research and Arctic Institute of North America, Contract Number: ONR-110. (Manuscript on file at the University of Alaska Fairbanks.)

Case, David S.
1984   *Alaska Natives and American Laws*. Fairbanks, AK: University of Alaska Press.

Chambers, John R.
1970   *Arctic Bush Mission: The Experiences of a Missionary Bush Pilot in the Far North*. Seattle, WA: Superior Publishing Company.

Chance, Norman A.
1990   *The Inupiat and Arctic Alaska: An Ethnography of Development*. Chicago, IL: Holt, Rinehart and Winston.

Collins, Florence Rucker
1958   *Test Wells, Umiat Area, Alaska. Exploration of Naval Petroleum Reserve No. 4 and Adjacent Areas, Northern Alaska, 1944–53, Part 5, Subsurface Geology and Engineering Data*. U.S. Geological Survey Professional Paper 305-B. Prepared and published at the request of and in cooperation with the U.S. Department of the Navy, Office of Naval Petroleum and Oil Shale Reserves. Washington, D.C.: U.S. Government Printing Office.

DeMaster, Douglas P., and Ian Sterling
1981   *Ursus maritimus. Mammalian Species* 145:1–7.

Dumond, Don E.
1987   *The Eskimos and Aleuts*. London: Thames and Hudson.

Finnegan, Ruth
1992   *Oral Traditions and the Verbal Arts: A Guide to Research Practices*. London: Routledge.

Foote, Berit Arnestad
    1992   *The Tigara Eskimos and Their Environment*. Point Hope, AK: North Slope Borough Commission on Iñupiat History, Language and Culture.

Forshaug, Jens
    1989   Oral History Interview with William Schneider, Fairbanks, Alaska, January 4, 1989. Recording H89-2a/b. (On file at the Rasmuson Library, Alaska and Polar Regions Department, Oral History Archives, University of Alaska Fairbanks.)

Ford, James A.
    1959   Eskimo Prehistory in the Vicinity of Point Barrow, Alaska. *Anthropological Papers of the American Museum of Natural History* 47(1).

Fortuine, Robert
    1989   *Chills and Fever: Health and Disease in the Early History of Alaska*. Fairbanks, AK: University of Alaska Press.

Gallagher, Hugh G.
    1974   *Etok: A Story of Eskimo Power*. New York: G.P. Putnam.

George, John Craighead
    1981   Current Procedure for Allocating the Bowhead Whale, *Balaena mysticetus*, by the Eskimo Whalers of Barrow, Alaska. In *Tissue Structural Studies and Other Investigations on the Biology of Endangered Whales in the Beaufort Sea*, Volume II. Final Report for the Period April 1, 1980 through June 30, 1981. Contract No. AA851-CTO-22. Thomas F. Albert, ed. Pp. 789–803. Anchorage, AK: U.S. Department of the Interior, Bureau of Land Management, Alaska OCS Office.

George, John C., Henry P. Huntington, Karen Brewster, Hajo Eicken, David W. Norton, and Richard Glenn
    In press   Observations on Shorefast Ice Dynamics in Arctic Alaska and the Responses of the Iñupiat Hunting Community. *Arctic* 54(4).

Giddings, J. Louis
    1967   *Ancient Men of the Arctic*. New York: Alfred A. Knopf.

Greist, David
    2002   *My Playmates Were Eskimos*, Elizabeth Cook, ed. Louisville, KY: Chicago Spectrum Press.

Greist, Henry W.
    1961   *Seventeen Years with the Eskimo*. Manuscript, Dartmouth Library. (Copy on file at the Iñupiat History, Language and Culture Commission office in Barrow, AK and the Elmer E. Rasmuson Library, University of Alaska Fairbanks.)

Greist, Mollie
    1968   *Nursing Under the North Star*. Indiana: White County Historical Society.

Hall, Edwin S., Jr., ed.
    1989   *Report of the Utqiagvik Excavations, 1981–1983, Barrow, Alaska*. Barrow, AK: North Slope Borough.

Hendricks, Charles
    1985   The Eskimos and the Defense of Alaska. *Pacific Historical Review* 54, August 1985:271–295. Berkeley, CA: University of California Press.

Hopson, Sam and Mable
    1995   Oral History Interview with Karen Brewster, December 8, 1995, Fairbanks,
                Alaska. (Tape H99-16-02, parts 1 and 2, on file at the Oral History Archives,
                University of Alaska Fairbanks and North Slope Borough, Iñupiat History,
                Language and Culture Commission, Barrow, Alaska.)

Huntington, Henry P.
    1992   *Wildlife Management and Subsistence Hunting in Alaska.* London: Belhaven
                Press.

Huntington, Henry P., Harry Brower Jr., and David W. Norton
    2001   The Barrow Symposium on Sea Ice, 2000: Evaluation of One Means of
                Exchanging Information between Subsistence Whalers and Scientists. *Arctic*
                54(2):201–204.

Jackson, Sheldon
    1898   *Eighth Annual Report of the Introduction of Domestic Reindeer into Alaska.*
                Washington, D.C.: U.S. Government Printing Office.

Kennedy, Kay J.
    1967   *The Wien Brothers' Story.* Fairbanks, AK: Wien Air Alaska.

Kessel, Brina, and Tom J. Cade
    1958   Birds of the Colville River, Northern Alaska. *Biological Papers of the University
                of Alaska* 2. College, AK: University of Alaska.

Klerekoper, Fred G.
    1937   *Dogsled Trip from Barrow to Demarcation Point, April 1937.* Reprinted in 1977.
                Barrow, AK: North Slope Borough Iñupiat History, Language and Culture
                Commission.

Langenheim, Ralph L., Jr., Charles J. Smiley, and Jane Gray
    1960   Cretaceous Amber from the Arctic Coastal Plain of Alaska. *Bulletin of the
                Geological Society of America* 71(9):1345–1356.

Larsen, Helge and Froelich Rainey
    1948   Ipiutak and the Old Whaling Culture. *Anthropological Papers of the American
                Museum of Natural History* 42. New York.

Lee, Molly
    [1983] 1998 *Baleen Basketry of the North Alaskan Eskimo.* Seattle, WA: University of
                Washington Press.

Leffingwell, Ernest K.
    1919   The Canning River Region, Northern Alaska. *United States Geological Survey
                Professional Paper* 109. Washington D.C.: U.S. Government Printing Office.

Libbey, David
    1989   Utqiagvik Ethnohistory. In *Report of the Utqiagvik Excavations, 1981–1983,
                Barrow, Alaska*, Volume 1. Edwin S. Hall Jr., ed. Pp. 462–519. Barrow, AK:
                North Slope Borough.

Libbey, David, and William Schneider
    1987   Fur Trapping on Alaska's North Slope. In *Le Castor Fait Tout: Selected Papers of
                the Fifth North American Fur Trade Conference, 1985.* Bruce G. Trigger, Toby

Morantz, and Louise Dechene, eds. Pp. 335–358. Montreal: Lake St. Louis Historical Society.

Lindbergh, Anne Morrow
[1935] 1963   *North to the Orient.* New York: Harcourt, Brace and Company.

Lowenstein, Tom, Asatchaq, and Tukummiq
    1992   *The Things That Were Said of Them: Shaman Stories and Oral Histories of the Tikiġaq People.* Berkeley, CA: University of California Press.

MacLean, Edna Ahgeak
    1980   *Iñupiallu Tanŋiḷḷu Uqaluŋisa Iḷaŋich—Abridged Iñupiaq and English Dictionary.* Fairbanks: Alaska Native Language Center, University of Alaska.

Marston, Marvin R. "Muktuk"
    1969   *Men of the Tundra: Eskimos at War.* New York: October House.

Mason, Owen and S. Craig Gerlach
    1995   The Archeological Imagination, Zooarcheological Data, the Origins of Whaling in the Western Arctic, and "Old Whaling" and Choris Cultures. In *Hunting the Largest Animals: Native Whaling in the Western Arctic and Subarctic.* Allen P. McCartney, ed. Pp. 1–31. Studies in Whaling No. 3, Occasional Publication No. 36. Edmonton: Canadian Circumpolar Institute, University of Alberta.

Morrow, Phyllis, and William Schneider
    1995   *When Our Words Return: Writing, Hearing, and Remembering Oral Traditions of Alaska and the Yukon.* Logan, UT: Utah State University Press.

Mull, Gil
    1982   History of Arctic Slope Oil Exploration. In *Alaska's Oil/Gas and Minerals Industry.* In *Alaska Geographic* 9(4):188–198.

Murdoch, John
[1892] 1988   Ethnological Results of the Point Barrow Expedition. Washington, D.C.: Smithsonian Institution Press.

Naske, Claus-M.
    1996   Mining Coal on the Meade River, Alaska. *Pacific Northwest Quarterly* 88(1):3–12.

Naske, Claus-M. and Herman E. Slotnick
[1979] 1987   *Alaska: A History of the 49th State,* second edition. Norman, OK: University of Oklahoma Press.

Neakok, Sadie
    1996   Oral History Interview with Karen Brewster, January 10, 1996, Barrow, Alaska. (Tape H99-16-05, parts 1 and 2, on file at the Oral History Archives, University of Alaska Fairbanks and North Slope Borough, Iñupiat History, Language and Culture Commission, Barrow, Alaska.)

Nelson, Richard K.
    1982   *Harvest of the Sea: Coastal Subsistence in Modern Wainwright.* A Report for the North Slope Borough's Coastal Management Program, December 1981. Barrow, AK: North Slope Borough.
    1983   A Mirror on Their Lives: Capturing the Human Experience. In *Sharing Alaska's Oral History, Proceedings of the Conference Held at the Captain Cook Hotel,*

Anchorage, Alaska, October 26 & 27, 1982. Pp. 14–36. Compiled by William Schneider, Alaska and Polar Regions Department, Elmer E. Rasmuson Library, University of Alaska Fairbanks.

Newell, Gordon, ed.
1966   *The H.W. McCurdy Marine History of the Pacific Northwest.* Seattle, WA: The Superior Publishing Company.

Noggle, Burl
1965   *Teapot Dome: Oil and Politics in the 1920s.* New York: W.W. Norton and Company.

North Slope Borough
1999   *1998/99 Economic Profile and Census Report.* Barrow, AK: North Slope Borough, Department of Planning and Community Services.

Norton, David W., ed.
2001   *Fifty More Years Below Zero: Tributes and Meditations for the Naval Arctic Research Laboratory's First Half Century at Barrow, Alaska.* Calgary: The Arctic Institute of North America.

Øen, Egil Ole
1995   A New Penthrite Grenade Compared to the Traditional Black Powder Grenade: Effectiveness in the Alaskan Eskimos' Hunt for Bowhead Whales. *Arctic* 48(2):177–185.

Okakok, Leona
1981   *Puiguitkaat—The 1978 Elders Conference.* Barrow, AK: North Slope Borough, Commission on History and Culture.

O'Neill, Dan, ed.
1986   Recorded History: Science Series, "Thirteen Radio Scripts Based On Oral History Recordings of Alaskan Scientists." Alaska Historical Commission Studies in History, No. 212, June 1986. (Manuscript on file at the Elmer E. Rasmuson Library, University of Alaska Fairbanks.)

Potter, Jean
1947   *The Flying North.* New York: Macmillan Co.

Reed, John C.
1958   Exploration of Naval Petroleum Reserve No. 4 and Adjacent Areas, Northern Alaska, 1944–53, Part 1, History of the Exploration. *Geological Survey Professional Paper* 301. Washington, D.C.: U.S. Government Printing Office.

Reed, John C. and Andreas G. Ronhovde
1971   *Arctic Laboratory—A History (1947–1966) of the Naval Arctic Research Laboratory at Point Barrow, Alaska.* Washington, D.C.: Arctic Institute of North America.

Roberts, Palmer W.
1952   Employment of Eskimos by the Navy at Point Barrow, Alaska. In *Science in Alaska, 1952.* Proceedings of the Third Alaskan Science Conference, Mt. McKinley National Park, September 22–27, 1952. Pp. 40–43. Fairbanks, AK: American Association for the Advancement of Science, Alaska Division.

Roderick, Jack
    1997   *Crude Dreams: A Personal History of Oil and Politics in Alaska.* Fairbanks, AK:
              Epicenter Press.

Schindler, John
    1996   Oral History Interview with Karen Brewster, March 14, 1996, Anchorage,
              Alaska. (Tape H99-16-06, parts 1 and 2, on file at the Oral History Archives,
              University of Alaska Fairbanks and North Slope Borough, Iñupiat History,
              Language and Culture Commission, Barrow, Alaska.)

Schneider, William, Sverre Pedersen, and David Libbey
    1980   *Land Use Values Through Time in the Barrow-Atqasuk Area.* Fairbanks, AK:
              Anthropology and Historic Preservation, Cooperative Park Studies Unit,
              University of Alaska, and North Slope Borough.

Simpson, John
    [1875] 1988 Observations on the Western Esquimaux and the Country They Inhabit. In
              *Journals of Rochfort Macguire, 1852–1854, Two Years at Point Barrow, Alaska
              aboard HMS* Plover *in the search for Sir John Franklin*, Volume II. John
              Bockstoce, ed. Pp. 501–550. London: Hakluyt Society.

Simpson, Thomas
    1843   *Narrative of the Discoveries on the North Coast of America, Effected by the Officers of
              the Hudson's Bay Company During the Years 1836–1839.* London: Richard Bentley.

Sonnenfeld, Joseph
    1956   Changes in Subsistence Among Barrow Eskimo. Arctic Institute of North
              America, Project no. ONR-140.
    1959   An Arctic Reindeer Industry: Growth and Decline. *Geographical Review*
              XLIX(1):76–94. New York: American Geographical Society.

Southeast Alaska Empire
    1971   *Southeast Alaska Empire Newspaper* 65(173), September 7, 1971. Juneau, AK.

Spencer, Robert
    1959   *The North Alaskan Eskimo: A Study in Ecology and Society.* Bureau of American
              Ethnology Bulletin 171. Washington, D.C.: U.S. Government Printing Office.

Stefansson, Viljhalmur
    1912   *My Life With the Eskimo.* New York: Harper and Brothers.
    1919   The Stefansson-Anderson Arctic Expedition of the American Museum:
              Preliminary Ethnological Report. *Anthropological Papers of the American
              Museum of Natural History* 14(1). New York.

Stern, Richard O., Edward L. Arobio, Larry L. Naylor, and Wayne C. Thomas
    1980   *Eskimos, Reindeer and Land.* Fairbanks, AK: Agricultural Experiment Station,
              School of Agriculture and Land Resources Management, University of Alaska.

Swartz, L. G.
    1966   Sea-cliff Birds. In *Environment of the Cape Thompson Region, Alaska.* Norman J.
              Wilimovsky and John N. Wolfe, eds. Pp. 611–678. Washington, D.C.: United
              States Atomic Energy Commission, Division of Technical Information.

U.S. Department of the Interior
   1983   *A Description of the Socioeconomics of the North Slope Borough, Appendix: Transcripts of Selected Inupiat Interviews*. Technical Report Number 85A. Anchorage, AK: U.S. Department of the Interior, Minerals Management Service, Social and Economic Studies Program, Alaska Outer Continental Shelf Region.

VanHagen, George E.
   1947   T.B., Alaska's Time Bomb. Anchorage: Anchorage Times Publishing Company. (First appeared in the *Forty-Ninth Star*, August 10, 1947; this pamphlet is included in the bound volume *Tuberculosis in Alaska*, anonymous, n.d. On file at the Elmer E. Rasmuson Library, University of Alaska Fairbanks.)

Wheeler, Robert
   2000   Alaskan Amber: A Mysterious Non-Wood Forest Product. *Under the Canopy* (Forestry and Forest Products Newsletter of the Alaska Cooperative Extension, Fairbanks). February, issue no. 11.

White, Clayton M., and Tom J. Cade
   1971   *Cliff Nesting Raptors and Ravens Along the Colville River in Arctic Alaska*. Ithaca, NY: Laboratory of Ornithology, Cornell University.

Wooley, Chris, Karen Brewster, Jana Harcharek, Dorothy Edwardsen, and Mabel Panigeo
   1992   Marvin Peter's Inupiat Family Album. In *Alaska: The Great Land. Alaska Geographic* 19(2):64–67. Anchorage, AK: Alaska Geographic Society.

Wooley, Chris, and Mike Martz
   1995a   ATG: Alaska's Patriotic Militia. In *World War II in Alaska. Alaska Geographic* 22(4):66–71. Anchorage, AK: Alaska Geographic Society.
   1995b   *Uncle Sam's Men*. Video production, 26 minutes. Bethel, AK: KYUK-TV, Bethel Broadcasting, Inc.

Wooley, Chris, and Rex Okakok
   1989   Kivgiq: A Celebration of Who We Are. Paper presented at the 16th Annual Meeting of the Alaska Anthropological Association, Anchorage, Alaska, March 3, 1989.

Worl, Rosita
   1979   Values of Subsistence to North Slope Iñupiat Culture. In *Native Livelihood and Dependence: A Study of Land Use Values Through Time*. Prepared by North Slope Borough Contract Staff for National Petroleum Reserve in Alaska Work Group 1, Field Study 1, June 1979. Pp. 17–26. Anchorage, AK: U.S. Department of the Interior, National Petroleum Reserve in Alaska.
   1980   The North Slope Inupiat Whaling Complex. In *Alaska Native Culture and History*. Papers Presented at the Second International Symposium, August 1978. Yoshinobu Kotani and William Workman, eds. Pp. 305–320. Senri Ethnological Studies 4. Osaka, Japan: National Museum of Ethnology.

Index

Page numbers in italics refer to illustrations. HB refers to Harry Brower, Sr.

A

Aalaak Crew, 163
Aamodt, Patsy Nusunginya, 36
Adams, Mary, 45, *46*, *64*
Ahgeak, Fredrick Quniaq, *64*
Ahgeak, Joe, 97, 103, 182
Ahgeak, Joe, 104
Ahgeak, Maria (Brower), 45, *46*, 64, 97
Ahlaak (Aalaak), Lottie, 98, 107
Ahmaogak George, crew of, 198
Ahmaogak, Roy, 34
Ahngasuk, Ross, 76
Ahsoak, Alec, 4, 49, 58, 67, 103, 172
Ahsoak, Mark, Sr. (cousin of HB), 60
Ahvakana, Rex, 36, 48
Akootchook, Isaac, 120
akutuq (Eskimo ice cream), 202
Alaqtaq, 31, 48, 62
Alaqtaq River, 169
Alaska Eskimo Whaling Commission
    (AEWC), vii, 41, 74, 146, 187, 207n75,
    207n76
Alaska National Guard, 73
Alaska Native Claims Settlement Act
    (ANCSA), 16, 40, 214n15
Alaska Native Service, 37
Alaska Territorial Guard (ATG), 73, 74
Albert, Tom, x, 41, 103, 131, 153–154,
    157, 174, 187; describes HB, 187–190
alcohol, 100, 191; introduction of, 32, 37
Aluiqsi (father of Asiaŋŋataq), 46
amber, 81
American Museum of Natural History, 7, 60
Amundsen, Roald, 32
aŋatkut (shamans), 124, 125, 128
Animal Research Facility (ARF), 89–90
Aqargiuluk, Israel, 98
Apuġauti (feast), 148, 149
Arctic National Wildlife Refuge (ANWR):
    and oil drilling, 119–120
Arctic Research Laboratory (ARL), 39
Arctic Research Laboratory Ice Stations
    (ARLIS), 82, 184
Arctic Slope boundaries, 166
Arctic Slope Native Association, 40

Arctic Slope Regional Corporation (ASRC),
    vii, 16, 40, 119, 120
Arctic Village, 77
Asiaŋŋataq (mother of HB), 3, 45–46, 47,
    52, 97, 103, 104, 211n5
atiq (namesake), 12, 212n14
Atqasuk (Meade River), 38

B

baleen, 37, 40, 135, 139, 145, 168, *169*,
    174, 175, 205n3, 208n66, 216n12;
    basket making, 36, 68–69, 204n3;
    demand for, 29–30; use of, 29
banding birds, 86
Barrow, 9, *14*, 15–17, 19–20, 22, 33; as a
    "dry" community, 37–38; economic
    development of, 91–92; history of,
    28–30
Barrow, Sir John, 28
Barrow Whaling Captains Association, 96,
    155
Bartlett, Senator E. L. "Bob," 39
basket making, 36, 68–69, 204n3
bearded seals. *See* seal; *ugruk*
Beck, John, 84
Beechey, Frederick W., 28
Behar, Ruth, ix
beliefs: about the supernatural, 124,
    204n14, 213n4
berries: collection of, 27
Big Dipper (*Qayutaniqłuk*), 110, 111, 212n4
birds, 61, 86, 109, 208n25
Blackman, Margaret, ix
blanket toss, 148, *149*, 198, *199*, 200
bowhead whale (*Balaena mysticetus*, *aġviq*),
    22, 24, 27, 82, 133; populations of,
    41–42, 153, 190; research on, 7,
    188–189. *See also* whales; whaling
Brewer, Max, 84, 86, 173, 181–182;
    describes HB, 182–184
Brewster, Karen, *2*, *192*, *197*, *201*;
    experiences conducting interviews,
    191–194, 200
Brower, Annie (née Hopson), *92*, *94*,
    95–96, *99*, 109, *152*, 175, 183, 184;
    description of, 96; and tuberculosis,
    95, 98
Brower, Arnold, Sr., 45, 46, *46*, 54, 63, 166
Brower, Charles Dewitt, 3, 4, 45–46, *50*;
    early years in Barrow, 29, 45; visit to

California of, 55–56; use of coal, 38, 58; death of, 97–98; family life of, 48, 49, 50–51; scientific collections of, 60, 61, 208n27; trading operations of, 4, 29, 30–31, *47*; whaling operation of, 29–30

Brower, Charlie (son of HB), *94*, 95, *152, 164, 197*

Brower, Charlotte, 149, 193

Brower, David (brother of HB), 45, 46, *46*, 48, *53*, 62, 63

Brower, Dorothy (daughter of HB), *94*, 95

Brower, Eugene (Aalaak, son of HB), *94*, 95, 103, *152*, 161, *164*, 165; describes HB, 165–171

Brower, Eunice (daughter of HB), 95

Brower, Flora, *199*

Brower, Gregory (grandson of HB), 6, 11, *13*, 70, 200

Brower, Harry, Jr. (son of HB), *94*, 95, 119, *152*, 157, *164*

Brower, Harry Kraft, Sr. (HB), *2, 13, 44, 46, 64, 92, 94, 99, 102, 122*, 162, *164, 192*; army service of, 73–76; awards of, *vi, 72*; beliefs of, 123, 163; boyhood, 3–4, 8, 45, 48, 49, 57–58, 60; as a craftsman of baleen and ivory, 5, 8, 168, *169*, 174–175, 206n66; education of, 36, 69, 172, 208n11; death of, 163; early collection experience, 60–61, 173; description of, 5; use of dog teams, 55; family life of, 95–96, 98–99; health of, 10, 11, 192; home of, *4, 5, 7*; as a hunter, 103–109, 169–170; as a leader, vii, 136; name of, 12; and NARL, 82, 83–84, 86–91, 173–174; as a naturalist, 7, 182–183, 190; navigational skills of, 112; as a navy employee, 39; opinion of oil drilling, 120–121; experience reindeer herding, 62–65; relationship with Karen Brewster, vii–ix, 192, 195; rescue of others, 177, 179, 180; as a scientific consultant, 39, 41, 154; assisting scientists, 167, 174, 189; speech of, 6, 208n24; surveying the North Slope, 76–81; and trapping, 112–114, 116–118, 183; as an *umialik* (whaling captain), 12, *130*, 136, *152, 155*, 167. *See also* whales, stories about; whaling, stories about.

Brower, James (half-brother of HB), 75–76

Brower, Jennie (sister of HB), 45, 48

Brower, Mattie (cousin of HB), 54, 55

Brower, Price (son of HB), *94*, 95, 150, *152, 164*

Brower, Robert (brother of HB), 45, *46*, 48, *53*, 55, 59, 62; reindeer herding of, 63

Brower, Ronald (son of HB), *94*, 95, *152, 164*

Brower, Teresa (daughter of HB), *94*, 95

Brower, Thomas (brother of HB), 31, 45, 46, *46*, 48, 54–55, 63, 97, 173; reindeer herding of, 62, *62*

Brower, Vera (daughter of HB), *94*, 95

Browerville, 16, 54, 163, 165

Bureau of Indian Affairs (BIA), 35

C

Canada, 28

Cape Halkett, 63, 64

Cape Lisburne, 29, 77

Cape Simpson, 62, 121

Cape Smythe Whaling and Trading Company, 29, 30, 46, 62

Cape Smythe Whaling and Trading Post, *47*

captain. *See umialik*

Cat train, 83

Chambers, John, 34

Christianity, 32, 34–35, 124

Christmas, 51, 57, 149

cigarettes, 55

coal mining, 38, 206n54

Coast and Geodetic Survey, 76, 77

Cold War, 39

Colville River, 77, 78

Connery, Flossie, 36

contact: between Iñupiat and non-Natives, 28–29, 32

Corwin Bluffs, 45

cribbage, 177–178

Crosson, Joe, 67

culture. *See* Iñupiaq culture

D

dancing, 148, 200–202, 204n6

darting gun, 132–133, 144, 215n21

Davidson, Florence Edenshaw, ix

Diomede Islands, 74, 75

disease and medical care, 32, 37. *See also* tuberculosis

Distant Early Warning (DEW–line) radar stations, 39, 77, 83, 185

dog teams, *25*

driftwood: use of, 58–59, 208n23

drumming, 201

duck hunting, 26, 40, 103

Duck In, 40

E

economic development. *See* oil exploration and development

education, 32, 35–36, 58, 69, 140, 172, 214n16

Edwardsen, Charlie, 45, 54, 63

Edwardsen, Dora, 45

Edwardsen, Eddie, 45, 63

Edwardsen, Tony, 45

eggs: collection of, 60–61, 208n25

Eielson, Carl Ben (aviator), 38
Elson Lagoon, 11, 98
Elson, Thomas (British explorer), 28
Explorers Club, 46

F

Fairbanks, 67, 78, 79, 175
feasts, 146, 148, 149, 194, 214n11. *See also*
    Nalukataq.
Fifty Years Below Zero, 48
fishing, 26, 27. *See also* hunting; subsistence;
    whaling
food. *See* Iñupiaq food; *akutuq*; feasts; *mak-
    tak*; *mikigaq*; *uqsrukuaqtaq*; *uunaalik*
Foran, Bill, 78
Ford, James, 128
Forshaug, Jens, 65
fox, 113–116; fur, 30, 113, *115*
Franklin, Sir John, 29
fur trade, 30–31, 95, 112, 113–115, *115*,
    116

G

George, J. C. "Craig," vii, 157
Gordon, Tom, 29
Greist, David, 51, 208n15
Greist, Henry W. (doctor), 34, 67, 70,
    209n41
Greist, Levi, 76, 210n4
Greist, Mollie, 34, 70
Gruening, Ernest, 73, 185, 210n2

H

Half Moon Three reindeer station, 48,
    54–55, 63, 97, 113
harpoons and harpooning, 28, 141, 144,
    146, 213n8
heating fuel, 58, 168
herds and herding, 31, 62–65, *66*; Barrow
    herd, 63, 64, 65; use of dogs for, 63–64;
    Wainwright herd, 63, 64. *See also*
    reindeer
Herendeen, Edward Perry, 29
Herschel Island, 121
Hess, Bill, vii, 73
Hickel, Walter J., 120
honey bucket toilets, 16
Hopson, Al, 65
Hopson, Eben, Sr., 16, 41, 76
Hopson, Eddie, 76, 89, 184
Hopson, Edward, Sr., 73
Hopson, Eunice, 95
Hopson, Fred, 48, 51
Hopson, Mable, 124, 175, 181
Hopson, Sam P., 109, 150, 175; describes
    HB, 176–181
Hopson, Steve, 95
Hopson, Terza, 91
hospitals: in Barrow, 37

houses, *28*, 47, 204n7, 208n23; sod, 67
Hula Hula Pass, 77
hunting, 10, 21, 24, 27, 28, 204n9; birds,
    60–61, 206n67; caribou, 26, 27, 98;
    duck, 26, 40, 103; goose, 25, 109; polar
    bear, 105–108; seal, 25–26, 131; walrus,
    26; wolverine, 117; wolves, 117–118.
    See also whaling
Husky Oil Company, 118

I

ice, 14, 27, 82, 205n19; hunting on,
    105–106, 131, 133, *134*, 137–138, *140*
Immiññaurat (little people), 11
Indian country, 166
intermarriage, 32
International Whaling Commission (IWC),
    7–8, 41, 42, 133, 146, 153, 190
Inuit Circumpolar Conference, 9
Iñupiaq culture, 10, 19, 21, 27, 192; and
    white culture, 171–172, 200.
Iñupiaq food, 3, 4, 21, 36, 50, 96, 135, 148,
    193. *See also maktak*; *mikigaq*
Iñupiaq language, 19, 36, 171–172, 203n2;
    speaking in school, 36, 69
Iñupiat: history of, 27–32
Iñupiat History, Language and Culture
    Commission, 10, 68
Ipalook, Fred, 36
Ipalook, Percy, 34
Itta family, 63
Iviksuk, 95, 211n2

J

Jackson, Sheldon, 31
Jarvis Expedition, 31, 208n28
Jennie (aunt of HB), 55–56

K

Kaktovik, 81, 120
Kaleak, Bill, 188
Kaveolook, Harold, 76
kamiit (boots), 47
Kelly, John W., 205n27
King Island, 46
Klerekoper, Fred, 34
Kotzebue, 9, 28
Kupaaq. *See* Brower, Harry Kraft, Sr.
Kupaaq (mother of Asiaŋŋataq), 46–47

L

land claims. 166–167. *See also* Alaska Native
    Claims Settlement Act
language. *See* Iñupiaq language
Laplanders, 62, 63, 208n28
leads (*uiñiq*), 14, 22, 204n12
Leavitt family, 63
Leavitt, Jonah, 111

Leavitt, Mildred (Uiññiq), 58
Leavitt, Oliver, 166
lemming skins, 182
Lentfer, Jack, 90, 211n19
Lindbergh, Anne Morrow and Charles, 38

M

Mackenzie River, 121
MacLean, Edna Ahgeak, *64*
maktak (whale skin and blubber), 3, 4, 17,
    24, 133, 135, 139, 146, 148, 193, 194,
    197–200, 203n2
Marsh, H. Richmond, 34
Marston, Major Marvin ("Muktuk"), 73, 74
Meade River coal mine, 99, 206n53
Meade River (Atqasuk), 38
meat sharing, 135, 137, 146, 149, 195,
    210n42, 213n5
Merry, Pete, 179
mikigaq (fermented whale meat, *maktak*,
    and blood), 148, 196–199, *198*
missionaries: in Barrow, 34, 205n39
Morgan, Barrow, 51
Morgan, Beverly, 51
Morgan, Stanley, 51, 67, 74
Morris, Charmaigne, 51
Morris, Cleo, 51
Morris, Oliver, 51
mosquitoes, 79
Mt. Edgecumbe, 98

N

Nageak, John, *94*
Nageak, Vincent, Sr., 108, 113
Nalukataq, 24, 148, 149–150, 194, 196,
    198, 200, 201
names, 12
National Weather Service, 82
natural gas, 39, 185–186
Naval Arctic Research Laboratory (NARL),
    39, 82, *83*, 151, 173, 181; polar bears
    at, 90–91. *See also* Brower, Harry Kraft,
    Sr., and NARL
Naval Petroleum Reserve Number 4 (NPR4;
    later National Petroleum Reserve), 38,
    39, 185, 206n64
navigation, 109–110
Neakok, Arthur, 62, 89
Neakok, Billy, *64*
Neakok, Nate, *64*, 103, 173
Neakok, Sadie (née Brower), xi, 45, 46,
    46, 48, 51, 56, *64*, 171; describes HB,
    171–175; describes her mother, 47
nets: use of, 26, 27, 79
Niġliq trade fair, 46, 207n5
Noatak River, 77
Nome, 74
North Slope Borough, 16, 41, 96, 187,
    206n70; Department of Wildlife

Management, 41, 82; Fire Department,
    165; Iñupiat History, Language and
    Culture Commission, 10, 68; Planning
    Department, 9; School District, 36;
    School Board, 96
Northland, 65, 166, 209n34
Northwest Passage, 28
Nuiqsut, 160
Nuvuk (Point Barrow), 15, 34, 73, *127*,
    203n1–2

O

oil exploration and development, 17, 38–39,
    40, 76, 87, 118–121, 210n6
Okomailak, 181
Okpeaha, Clair, 67–68
oral history, ix, x, 6, 10, 191
oral tradition: Iñupiaq, 123, 212n1
over-hunting, 30, 37

P

Pacific Steam Whaling Company, 29, 45
paniqtaq (dried meat), *21*
permafrost, 16
PET4 oil exploration program, 38
Peter, Marvin (Saġvan), 36, 68–69, *69*,
    70–71, 209n41, 210n42
Peter's Lake [Lake Peters], 87, 211n16
Philo, Mike, 154, 188, 215n32
Piġniq (Shooting Station), 6, 26, 126
pilgaurat (*Cassiope tetragona*), 79
Plover, 29
Point Barrow, 15, 34, 73, *127*
Point Hope, 45, 125, 146
Point Lay, 83
polar bear (*nanuq*), 90–91, 211n20; cubs, 59;
    hunting of, 104–108, 211n2; skin values
    of, 108; stories about, 104–105, 105
politics. *See* International Whaling Commis-
    sion; land claims; North Slope Borough;
    subsistence rights
Post, Wiley, 32, 38, 67–68, 209n39
Presbyterian Church, 20, 34–35, *35*, 37,
    57, 163
Prudhoe Bay, 77, 87, 120–121, 208n28,
    209n29–32; oil discovery at, 16. *See also*
    oil exploration and development

Q

qanitchaq (enclosed entry), 3
Qiṇaqtaq (basket maker), 36, 70
Quliaqtuat (personal experience stories), 123
Quonset huts, 38, 39, 84
quotas. *See* whaling, quotas

R

Rasmussen, Knud, 32
reindeer, 26, 31, 62–65, 98; mixing with

caribou, 64–65. *See also* herds and herding
Rexford, Herman, 62
Riley, Harry, 57
Ritchfield Company, 118–119
Rogers, Will, 32, 38, 67–68, 209n39
Russians, 75, 210n3

S

Saali. *See* Brower, Charles Dewitt
Saġvaġniqtuuq [Sagavanirktok] River, 120
Sakeagak, Kate (née Brower), 45, *46*
Schindler, John (NARL director), 84, 96, 173, 184; describes HB, 184–187
scientific research, 60, 62, 82; on whaling, 7, 41–42, 154. *See also* Naval Arctic Research Laboratory (NARL)
seal, 25, 26, 131, 213n2; oil, 3
seasonal round, 25–27. *See also* subsistence; *ugruk*; whaling
shamans (*aŋatkut*), 124, 125, 128
sharing, of meat, 135, 137, 146, 149, 195, 210n42, 213n5
shoulder gun, 41, 132, 133, 140, 141, 144–145, 150, 215n21
Sigma Xi Scientific Research Society, vii, 7, 73
Siġvan, Steven, 110–112
siksrikpuk (squirrels), 181, 216n5
Sikvayugak, Joe, 58, 65
Simmonds, Abe, Sr., *64*
Simmonds, Samuel, 35
skin sewing, 131, *132*
Smyth, William (British explorer), 28
snowmachines (Ski-doo), 16, 117, 131
sobriety movement, 100. *See also* alcohol
Solomon, Bill, 68
Sovalik, Pete, 90, 174
squirrels (*siksrikpuk*), 181
stars and constellations, 110–112, 212n5–7
St. Lawrence Island, 74, 190
Stefansson, Vilhjalmur, 32
Stevenson, L. M., 34
stinker (*avataayyuniq*), 133, 213n4
stories, vii–viii, x, 123, 172; about shamans 128. *See also* whales, stories about; whaling, stories about
subsistence, 10, 21, 24, 167. *See also* fishing; hunting; seasonal round; whaling; subsistence rights, 7–8, 40, 41

T

Taalak, Carl (uncle of HB), 4, 57, 103, 172
taboos, 22, 28, 29, 142
Taktuk (first wife of Charles Brower), 45, 207n3, 207n4
tax base, 41
taxidermy, 183

tobacco, 50
Toovak, Kenneth, Sr., *72*, 182
trade, 27–28, 37, 207n5; fur, 30
trading posts, 30
trapping, 27, 30, 112–118, 185; fox, 27, 95, 113–114, 116, 212n9–10. *See also* fur trade
tuberculosis, 38, 98, 211n7
tundra, *20*
Tupaagruk, 83
Tupaagruk River, 113, 171

U

Ualiqpaa (Walakpa), 67, 68
uati (captain's share of whale meat), 149. *See also* meat sharing
Ugiaġnaq (brother of Asiaŋŋataq), 47
ugruk (bearded seal) 4, 19, 20, *21, 26*, 131, *132*, 148, 213n2;
uiñiq (leads in coastal sea ice), 14, 22, 204n12
Ukpeagvik Iñupiat Corporation (UIC), 39, 46, 96
Ukpiaġvik. *See* Barrow
umialgich (sing. *umialik*). *See* umialik
umialik (whaling captain), 12, 22, 24, 42, 136, 163, 214n9; behavior of, 22, 24, 153–154; share of whale (*uati*), 149; role in research, 24, 204n17
umiaq (skin-covered boat; pl. *umiat*), xiv, 4, 5, 25, 131, *133, 147*, 202
Umiat, 78
Ungarook, George, 176
Unipkaat (explanatory stories), 123
United States Bureau of Education, 31
United States Army Signal Corps, 65, 67, 209n37
United States Fish and Wildlife Service, 40, 88
United States Navy, 8, 38; Seabees, 38, 76, 211n14
University of Alaska, 89, 174
uqsrukuaqtaq (Eskimo donuts), 148
uunaalik (boiled *maktak*), 135, 197

W

wage labor, 40
Wainwright, 35, 66, 111
Walakpa (Ualiqpaa; Rogers-Post crash site), 68, 209n39
walrus. *See* hunting, walrus
wannigans, 39, *84*
Weber, Antonio, 123
Webster, Donald, 34
whalebone, *xiv, 28,* 29
whale oil, 30
whales: butchering, *23, 134,* 135, *138,* 139, 213n5, 214n13; behavior of, 141, 143; parts of, 135, 146, 197; research on, 41;

respect for, 22, 136; stories about, 126, 128, 136–139, 141, 143, 145–146, 150–153, 156–157. *See also* bowhead whales; whaling

whaling, 20, 22, *142*; accidents, 145–146, 177; alcohol and, 153–154; boats and, 131, 144, 213n1, 213n7; bombs, use in, 132–133, 141, 145–146, 151, 215n28; camp, *140*; challenges to, 7–8, 41–42; commercial, 29–30; gear and technology, 24, 41, 131, 139–141; preparations for, 131–132; quotas, 33, 41, 133, 145–146, 152, 155, 160, 190, 207n74, 207n76; research on, 7, 41–42, 154; and shares of meat, 135, *137*, 146, 196–200, 213n5; stories about, 141, 159–160, 161–162; women's role in, 131, 141–143. *See also* bowhead whales; darting gun; floats; International Whaling Commission (IWC); seasonal round; shoulder gun; *umialik*; whales

whitefish, 79

Wien Air Alaska, 77, 175, 210n7

Wilkins, George Hubert, 38

wolves, 31, 112, 117–118, 179–180